A History of TRANSPORTATION in WESTERN NORTH CAROLINA

Trails, Roads, Rails & Air

TERRY RUSCIN

Foreword by Robert Morgan

THE History PRESS

Published by The History Press
Charleston, SC
www.historypress.net

First published 2016

Back cover, top left: Chip Lamb. *Courtesy of Carroll Leroy "Chip" Lamb Jr.*

Manufactured in the United States

ISBN 978.1.46713.706.5

Library of Congress Control Number: 2016941437

Advance Praise for

A History of Transportation in Western North Carolina

Impressive.

—Robert Morgan, bestselling author, Cornell University, New York

Too many local histories are really folklore put into print. Not this one. Here we have tediously researched, accurate history recorded with pleasing prose and a sense of story. Those who have lived in western North Carolina for a long time know locations and snippets of our history. These are the dots. Ruscin connects them—just like transportation connects communities—and leaves us with a picture of the past. This is a must read.

—Stan Shelley, bibliophile and critic, Hendersonville

I grew up around the Meyer Flying Service airport, but Terry Ruscin has exposed information about western North Carolina's aviation history that even I did not know. A stickler for details, Ruscin shares facts about my family and North Carolina that I never imagined. In 1903, the Wright Brothers jumpstarted flight, but it lay dormant until around 1912, when Glenn Curtiss really started the ball rolling again. He trained my great-uncle Thornwell Andrews to fly, which in turn gave his nephew (my father), Oscar Meyer, an interest in aviation. Oscar became a western North Carolina aviation pioneer. Ruscin did an outstanding job in documenting facts and preserving the region's transportation heritage for all to enjoy now and forever!

—Jim Meyer, Raleigh

Transportation routes are arteries carrying the lifeblood of commerce to any community, and the shallow streams, mountainous terrain and rocky soils of western North Carolina have challenged man's skill and imagination for centuries. Through meticulous research, Terry Ruscin tells the stories of the men and women who paved the way for our contemporary way of life. This book puts into context the accomplishments of historical figures whose names are etched into area landmarks and whose exploits live on through regional lore.

—Diane Norman, executive editor, Times-News, *Hendersonville*

This journey, through the history of transportation in these mountains that I call home, stirs emotions important to our community: an overwhelming respect for the vision, hard work and tenacity of our forefathers to persevere and a calling for future generations to continue this drive.

—Steve L. Cannon, PE; district engineer, NCDOT, Division 14: District 1

This will enrich the lives and appreciation of all who read it. Bravo!

—Garland O. Goodwin, retired aerospace engineer; editor, Western North Carolina Air Museum newsletter; columnist, Tryon

As a child I spent many afternoons with my father at the Hendersonville Airport. I didn't realize then that I was surrounded by aviation legends. Thanks to Terry Ruscin, I now understand and fully appreciate those men and women with their flying machines.

—Chip Lamb, retired air force and commercial airline pilot, Southlake, Texas

Honoring western North Carolina transportation pioneers:
Solomon Jones, Oscar A. Meyer Jr., Sidney Vance Pickens, Valentine Ripley
and William Alexander Smith.

Contents

Foreword

The matter of conveyance in the mountains has always been a challenge. First there were rabbit trails that wandered in and out of thickets, briars and brush into the meadows where the bunnies browsed on grass and weeds and sometimes appeared to play games in twilight or on moonlit nights. And deer paths threaded through the forests, from yards hidden in deep coves to water and wild pea–vine glades. And often there were buffalo that moved seasonally from summer grazing in the highlands to winter pasturage in the foothills. Then came the Indians, who followed the ways of deer and buffalo through gaps and over mountains, along stream banks and by canebrakes, and created beaten routes of migration, warfare and trade. The most famous route in the mountains was the Warrior's Path, *Athiamiowee*, which came down the great Valley of Virginia to the Holston and Cherokee country, then west to Cumberland Gap and on into Kentucky and the Ohio Valley.

The first white explorers, traders, missionaries, trappers, coming into the mountains, followed the many trails of the natives. De Soto reached the Cherokees by 1540, and other Spaniards dug for silver and gold in the Blue Ridge Mountains. The English-speaking explorers came from the east in the seventeenth and eighteenth centuries, again following the Indian tracks along rivers and over mountains. With little navigable water, most travel was by footpath. The great French botanist André Michaux crossed the mountains in the 1790s, traveling from Kentucky to Charleston, South Carolina, and discovered many new species of plants along the way. Most of western North Carolina and eastern Tennessee was Cherokee territory, but hunters, such as Daniel Boone, had long poached furs and deer hides in its forests and along its streams. A deer hide was worth a Spanish dollar then, so a dollar came to be called a "buck."

Just before, and during, the American Revolution, white settlers began to invade and build cabins and clear land on territory the Cherokees had long claimed and fought to defend. There were treaties between the Cherokees and the colonial government, and then the state and federal governments, but no piece of paper could hold back the flood of settlers desperate for land of their own in the beautiful mountains. Even Indian attacks could only temporarily delay the stream of settlers. The westward expansion of the United States was less the work of governments and famous leaders than the acts of thousands of nameless, ordinary, but determined, people. After the Revolution, the stream became a tidal wave.

The first pathways into the mountains used by white settlers were called "traces." Usually following Indian trails and animal trails, the traces were just rough footpaths for people and livestock to follow single file. The most famous was Boone's Trace into Kentucky, cut in 1775, following the old Warrior's Path. But soon there were scores of others.

To bring in wagons, carts or coaches, the traces had to be widened and leveled, boulders and logs rolled away, bridges built over larger streams. Often, roads ran high along the mountainsides to avoid thickets, canebrakes, swamps and flooding streams. In winter, when the trees are bare, you can still see the lines of the old wagon roads on the sides of ridges.

The lack of good roads into the mountains kept the early settlers isolated and poor. Even if they grew a surplus of livestock or produce, there was no practical way to get it to market. Only corn distilled into whiskey, furs and ginseng were valuable enough by the pound to make hauling to towns in the foothills profitable. A distinct culture developed in the remote coves and hidden valleys, with its own music, folklore, cuisine and speech.

But there were enterprising souls who studied ways to build roads in the mountains, to bring the outside world into the hollows and let the mountain folk travel out. One of the first was Solomon Jones, who wanted to build a road from the foothills of South Carolina to Cedar Mountain in North Carolina. Having few, if any, surveying instruments, he reasoned that a pig will always find the best way to get where it wants to go. One day, he took his sow Sue down to Pumpkintown in South Carolina and let her loose. All day he followed Sue as she made her way home, blazing trees along the way to mark the route. The path Sue took passed through a gap that would become known as Jones Gap, where

Jones Gap State Park is now. With horses, oxen and strong men, Solomon Jones dug out one of the early roads into the mountains.

A more famous early road was the Buncombe Turnpike across the mountains from Tennessee into South Carolina. This pike served as a road for drovers driving cattle, hogs, horses, sheep and even turkeys across the mountains to markets in South Carolina. Local farmers along the way built taverns, called "stands," to serve the drovers, with many bedrooms and large pens and corncribs for the livestock. My ancestor Abraham Kuykendall operated one such stand in the Flat Rock area. It was Joel Roberts Poinsett, diplomat, politician and administrator, who provided for improvements to the road in upper South Carolina. Poinsett Bridge over a fork of the Saluda River is named for him. The first U.S. ambassador to Mexico, Poinsett brought back a plant with leaves that turn red around Christmastime, named poinsettia in his honor.

It was that road from South Carolina into the mountains that Lowcountry folk such as Judge Mitchell King followed to build summer mansions in Flat Rock, decades before the railroad ever reached the area. The railroad did not come to Hendersonville until 1879, long after the Civil War. But even in the early twentieth century, my grandpa, who farmed on Green River in southern Henderson County, would load his wagon every fall with produce, sourwood honey, beeswax, hams (pork, deer and bear), tallow cakes and sorghum and drive down to Greenville, South Carolina, to peddle his goods door to door. The route he took through Chestnut Springs and Travelers Rest became Old Highway 25.

When I was growing up in the Green River section of Henderson County in the 1940s and '50s, our roads were still gravel and dirt. Every month or so I was thrilled to watch the road-scraper roar into view, smoothing the potholes and washboard ripples of the roadbed. We did not have a car or truck, and one of my mother's greatest worries was about how to get to Hendersonville to pay bills, see a doctor or buy groceries. My dad had to ask others to drive his pole beans to market and bring fertilizer, seed and feed back. The struggle to find conveyance was a major issue in my early years. And then my dad got a used Chevrolet pickup truck in 1953, and it seemed the world opened up for us. We could go to Hendersonville when we needed to, to Asheville, and even to Pisgah National Forest and the Blue Ridge Parkway.

I will never forget seeing the new road to Brevard, built around 1956, for the first time, with its wide shoulders, sweeping contours and banked curves. I felt I was glimpsing the highways, the speed, the confident verve of the future.

In *A History of Transportation in Western North Carolina,* Terry Ruscin tells the epic story of travel in the mountains. His deeply researched, vivid account brings this history alive as no one else has. From Indian trails to stagecoach, steamboat, railroad and jet airplanes, this is an account of the southern Appalachian region as only he can tell it.

—Robert Morgan, North Carolina poet laureate and bestselling author of *Gap Creek*, *Boone*, *Lions of the West* and *Chasing the North Star*

From Hooves to Wings

Progress plodded languidly—until the outset of the Industrial Revolution, when cottage industries and agrarian traditions morphed swiftly to agricultural breakthroughs and traditions of manufacturing and mass transit and emergent urban centers. The "revolution" sprang from England between 1760 and 1820, reaching western Europe and America shortly thereafter. But its effects would not impact the mountains of North Carolina until several decades later.

The nature of western North Carolina's topography and inherent isolation impeded its industrial progress until the late nineteenth century, when the first Western North Carolina Railroad excursions of the Spartanburg–Asheville line reached Tryon in 1877, Saluda in 1878, Hendersonville in 1879 and Asheville in the 1880s.[1] Transportation schemes not only opened avenues for technological advancement but also boosted the average standard of living.

Nooks in the Blue Ridge had already earned ostensible fame as destination resorts, the outcome effecting land speculation, which burgeoned throughout the mountains. Suddenly, steam power and machinery began to replace the labor of man and beast, advancing agriculture at a rapid pace. Textile mills and logging operations dotted the valleys and slopes. And inns sprang up to lodge sojourners who were then equipped to reach the region more efficiently, given its improved inroads. Those vacationers, taken with the sheer majesty and setting of cities and towns such as Asheville, Brevard, Tryon and Hendersonville, snatched up vast parcels of acreage in the "Land of the Sky."

Visionaries swiftly swapped mule-drawn trolleys with electric adaptations to transport sightseers and speculators from passenger depots to towns and up slopes to observation towers with forever views. Before long, even more hotels, boardinghouses and tuberculosis sanitariums competed with the established ones for their shares of guests and health-seekers. Horseless carriages and flying machines were quick to follow.

Upon the French Broad floated primitive ferries before a network of bridges spanned its girth and the first church in these parts was organized proximate its banks.[2] Paddleboats met with failure as they attempted to ply this broad, yet shallow and ancient, river with low-slung bridges. Before long, rails would supply an efficient transportation mode for much-needed supplies and the business of trade. And as soon as humans took to the sky, an intrepid young man in Hendersonville established one of the region's earliest airfields.

This volume rakes back at transportation schemes from herding livestock by foot from Kentucky and Tennessee to stagecoaches and rails and airplanes and superhighways.

Fasten your seatbelt and enjoy the time travel.

The journey of a thousand miles begins with a single step.
—Lao-tzu

Acknowledgements

Works such as this come to be only with the collaboration of knowledgeable and amenable individuals. This particular work would have been bootless without the selfless and unfailing assistance of genealogist-extraordinaire Janet Goad Hill, NCDOT district engineer Steve L. Cannon, Oscar Meyer's son Jim and my esteemed friend and history colleague Gayle Hamilton Stepp. Janet and Steve tolerated my obsessive queries and pulled rabbits from hats; Jim opened his personal archives to share resources, memories, facts and photographs; and Gayle—who knows practically everyone—made connections with many of my subjects' descendants (including Jim Meyer). I am forever indebted to each of them.

Many thanks are also due to those who came forward with photographs and documents, clues, support and assistance, particularly the Apple Valley Model Railroad Club, the Baker-Barber Collection, Mary Louise Barber, Bill Barnwell, Richard Barnwell, Sally Berger, Carolyn Lamb Borman, L.C. "Cam" Boyd Jr., Alexandra Bradley, Mark Burdette, Lawrence Lee Burgin Jr., Sarah Brown Cannon, Buddy Chapman, Ethan Clapsaddle, the Community Foundation of Henderson County, Knox Crowell, Hillis A. Cunliffe, Jim Davenport, Stella Faye Lance Edney, John Fadok, Stephen Fosberg, Paul Freeman, Betty Girard, Garland O. Goodwin, the Greater Asheville Regional Airport Authority, Martha Connell Grose, P.H. Grose III, Sindy Drake Hamilton, A. Paul Hansen, Krista Hare, David H. Hauser, Daphne Hedden, the Henderson County Genealogical and Historical Society, the Henderson County Heritage Museum, the Henderson County

Public Library, Katherine Hunter, Helen Ingle, Leland Johnson, Carolyn Justus, Ruth Kidd, Jim Kilpatrick, Gary King, Tina Kinsey, Chip Lamb, John Lampley, John Laughter, Barbara Boone Kitchens Lewis, Garfield Long, Paula Coleman Machen, Sheila Mason, Don McCarson, Sam McGuirt, Mary Elizabeth McLeod, Theresa Mitchell, Robert Ray Morgan, Larry Morton, Diane Norman, Andrew T. Nottingham, Kenneth J. O'Brien, Charlene Pace, V. Leon and Jean Pace, Brian Parker, Margaret Payne, Arthur Pearsall, E. Hortence Potts, Colin Reeve/Ramsey Library/UNCA, Anne Ridings, Priscilla Burgin Rouse, Shane Shipman, Harley Stepp, Susan Flack Summerville, Ginny Thompson, Marcy Thompson, the Transylvania Public Library, R. Charles Waters, Chip Webster, Lu Ann Welter, A.B. Wexler/Mountain Farm & Home Museum, Kay Garrett Whitfield, Richard Wilson, Della Workman, Kaye Youngblood and William B. Zeeveld—and my editors Banks Smither and Abigail Fleming with The History Press.

What a team!

I
Afoot

North Carolina: A vale of humility between two mountains of conceit.
—Attributed to Mary Oates Spratt Van Landingham

Yesteryear's travel circumstances would seem downright brutal to modern commuters inured to the advantages of navigation apps, cruising leisurely on superhighways in air-conditioned or heated comfort. Yet in the brief interval of 150 years, conduits for travel evolved from animal migration routes, Indian paths and bridle trails to hard-surface roads crisscrossed with bridges. Not long thereafter, multilane interstates looped with interchanges—and boundless skyways overhead—abridged western Carolina itineraries by hours, days and even weeks.

According to 2014 North Carolina Department of Transportation statistics, in excess of fifty-two million tourists travel the state's roads annually, with more than fifteen million of them visiting the Blue Ridge Parkway. National transportation statistics rank North Carolina's state-maintained highway system as the largest in the nation.

As late as the turn of the twentieth century, a round-trip journey between Limestone (Fletcher) and Flat Rock—about fifteen miles—exhausted the better part of a day. Owing to this inconvenience, Fletcher's Calvary Church (1859) was born, after which north-county Episcopalians had no longer the need to trundle all the way to and from Flat Rock for Sunday services. In that era, an expedition from coastal South Carolina to Asheville, North Carolina, might log ten to fourteen days. On horseback, a traveler could cover up

Mountainside Park Road in Laurel Park, an unpaved track typical of western North Carolina's early twentieth-century roads. *C.H. Oak Collection; courtesy of the Henderson County Genealogical and Historical Society.*

to twenty miles a day and by wagon scarcely five miles on average. Presently a four-and-a-half-hour car ride separates the aforementioned destinations. Meanwhile, convoys of eighteen-wheelers clamber effortlessly through western North Carolina's passes, and hundreds of Harleys roar along its back roads, as scores of vapor trails garnish its atmosphere each day.

Hoofing It

One could say wild beasts and then hogs and cattle paved the way through the highlands of western North Carolina, opening the territory to agriculture, tourism and health resorts, boomtowns, textile mills and retirement communities.

Preceding the era when farmers drove inestimable cavalcades of livestock through the region, bison pursued logical contours of the topography in their quest to graze and breed. Other creatures, including deer, elk and bear—and prehistoric creatures before them—blazed the first passages through the Carolinas. In search of food and water and instinctively plotting the least-demanding itineraries and gentler grades, such animals followed grazing and migration corridors through the more navigable gaps, alongside waterways and directly through rivers and creeks, pacing the shallower depths later employed as fords and side fords by humans. Aping this more facile and plausible route, Native Americans traced the same paths, further beating their gathering and trading trails, which would one day map the way for carriageways and turnpikes. So, too, Indians exploited such paths for tracking game and for warfare.

THE RIGHT OF DISCOVERY

Well-trod trails opened the way for Euro-American pioneers and drovers and military troops. Visionaries widened these conduits for use as migratory wagon roads to accommodate settlers and miners. In turn, such pathways evolved into commercial arteries for trade and eventually transmuted into the paved roads and highways of today—many of which follow ancient passageways of animal herds and aboriginal peoples.

Within a span of two centuries, cast-iron and then steel rails and vulcanized rubber supplanted hooves and moccasins and wooden wheels. Settlers of European descent obliterated the entire population of American bison that once inhabited western North Carolina.[3] The same people, in the early nineteenth century, began to drive out the Indians en masse.

Trail of Tears. *Courtesy of the Museum of the Cherokee Indian.*

Young Deer. *Courtesy of the Museum of the Cherokee Indian.*

In colonial times, *discovery* many times implied *land title*—the *right of discovery*. This mindset led to displacement and dispossession of Native Americans with the goal of territorial expansion for Euro-American colonists, who introduced illnesses that decimated indigenous peoples. Smallpox proved a principal destroyer, with additional European contagions also contributing to depopulation of Indians—diseases such as measles, scarlet fever, typhoid, typhus, influenza, tuberculosis, cholera, diphtheria, chicken pox and venereal infections.

A number of Cherokees relocated voluntarily to the territory of Arkansas between 1775 and 1786. The government of Georgia removed them in 1829 to 1830 after gold was discovered there. In 1838–39, newcomers to the Southeast herded Cherokees in a mass relocation (nearly sixteen thousand) along the Unicoi Turnpike to a tribal jurisdiction area in the territory of Oklahoma held in trust by the federal government for the benefit of Indians. This expulsion, commencing in the spring of 1838, resumed in the summer, followed by a fall-to-winter migration into early 1839. During the eight-hundred-mile trek westward, at least four thousand Cherokees perished. Some, however, escaped the roundup and hid out in the mountains of western North Carolina. Many members of today's North Carolina Eastern Band of Cherokees descended from those fugitive rebels.[4] Today, more than fifty-six thousand acres encompass Cherokee tribal lands in five North Carolina counties.

The Oconaluftee people separated from the Cherokee Nation in 1819 and remained in the Great Smoky Mountains as North Carolina citizens. Some Cherokees hid from federal soldiers and avoided removal. Others lived on reserves in Georgia, Tennessee and Alabama, returning eventually to North Carolina to form the modern tribal communities. Today the Eastern Band has more than eight thousand members.

—*Indian Nations of North America,* National Geographic

Between tribes and with white settlers, Indians traded commodities such as mica, beads, shells, baskets, medicinal plants, including ginseng, and furs, hides, copper and pipestone for manufactured goods such as guns, bullets, flints, bells, tools, cloth and kettles. As noted by Cherokee author Barbara R. Duncan, gorgets (hand-carved marine shells) found in former Cherokee territory shine a light on evidence of trade with tribes as far away as the Atlantic coast and the Gulf of Mexico.

Their shoes, when they wear any, are made of an entire piece of buckskin; except when they sew a piece to the bottom, to thicken the sole. They are fastened on with running strings, the skin being drawn together like a purse on the top of the foot, and tied around the ankle. The Indian name for this kind of shoe is "moccasin."

In cold weather, the Chickasaw women wrap themselves in the softened skins of buffalo calves, with the wintry shagged wool inward.

– *James Adair*

We feel sure the Cherokee women were intelligent enough to do the same.

– *Garfield Long*

Cherokee mother and child, 1921. *Photo by Walter Matson Cline Sr.; author's collection.*

Explorers and Settlers

Primitive trails proved deficient, frequently steep, narrow and even dangerous, undulating as they did along natural clefts, gullies, precipices, crags and coves in western North Carolina's mountainous terrain. Rocks and boulders tumbled upon these rudimentary passageways and freshets scoured their surfaces, effecting potholes, washouts, landslides. Amid this roughness could be found venomous insects and serpents, beasts of prey and all manner of weather.

Spanish explorer Hernán De Soto (circa 1496–1542) and his expedition passed through the region in 1540–41 in search of gold. The explorers never discovered the mother lode and moved on, westward bound, where they traded with Cherokees and mined their lands. De Soto died at the Mississippi River from—according to some—a sudden and unknown illness. Luis Vásquez de Allyón (circa 1475–1526) preceded De Soto in 1526, and Juan Pardo explored the region in 1567.

In the Spaniards' wake came first a trickle and then a flood of other visitors seeking arable land at affordable prices, religious tolerance and new opportunities. In the early eighteenth century, coastal longhunters penetrated the mountains, and colonists from the north advanced into Indian country to scout for new homesites. Word spread about vast supplies of lumber, plentiful game, rich water sources and trade with hospitable Indians.

The Great Indian Warpath (also known as the Great Indian War and Trading Path, Great Warrior's Path or Seneca Trail) cut through the valley paralleling the western extreme of the Appalachian Mountains from Pennsylvania through West Virginia, Virginia, eastern Tennessee and Georgia. Tribes including Chickasaws, Creeks, Choctaws and Cherokees further blazed this north–south trail as they hunted and camped. This route, determined by watersheds and river crossings, would later become a major stage road.

In the 1760s and 1770s, settlers of western Virginia and North Carolina wrangled with their state governments over taxation, and squatters pushed over the mountains and claimed Indian lands as their own for settlement. Indians rented land to settlers for fees of goods such as guns, whiskey, fabric and jewelry. In the early days, few hostilities occurred between European pioneers and native peoples. The groups traded with each other and went their own ways. By the beginning of the Revolutionary War, however, the Cherokees, concerned with the encroachment of a slew of non-Indian settlers, aspired to dislodge squatters and reclaim their lands. But the white settlers had fled their native countries and then abandoned the northern colonies for the most part due to government intervention and were by then unwilling to give up their newly claimed land.

Revolutionary War veterans received land as payment for military service. They and others also purchased property for as little as five cents per acre, positioning the territory for settlement and growth. Within seven months, four million acres were sold to settlers who flocked to the eastern Tennessee territory, which at the time fell under the claim of North Carolina.

In this region, the rivers Clinch, Nolichucky and French Broad provided modes of transportation for early settlers as an alternative to walking or riding horseback. Some settlers traveled on flatboats with their belongings in search of land to purchase and upon which to establish their homesteads.

In 1772, frontier settlers in upper-east Tennessee, led by John Sevier (1745–1815), resolved to form their own semiautonomous government, the Republic of Watauga (also known as the Watauga Association), to organize and protect themselves from Indians and to escape the hold of North Carolina. The North Carolina legislature surrendered the state's western lands to the Continental Congress, and in early 1784, a convention of delegates from the counties of Washington, Sullivan and Greene in the northeast corner of the Tennessee territory met at Jonesborough and chose John Sevier as president of the delegation. Their objective: to form a new state. The delegation planned to include portions of western Virginia and northern Georgia in the new state. Cherokees and Creeks occupied much of this territory.

A second convention in December 1784 adopted a provisional constitution for the "State of Franklin," which would be independent of North Carolina. The land from Bristol to Fort Loudoun would become the State of Franklin, organized with John Sevier as governor. The site of Greeneville (Tennessee) would be the capital. With little money and no banking system, taxes could be paid in such commodities as animal pelts, beeswax, whiskey and tobacco. But a provision in Article IV of the Constitution prohibited the formation of a state within the jurisdiction of another state without consent from the latter.

Because the U.S. government did not recognize Franklin as a state and North Carolina refused to give up its holdings or grant settlers their independence, Sevier and his Overmountain Men launched an uprising to force North Carolina's hand but were unsuccessful in rallying a majority of the people. The settlers' lack of support for Sevier and North Carolina's eventual renouncement of this western territory brought an end to the State of Franklin by 1790, when it was dissolved. The U.S. government claimed this land, naming it the Southwest Territory (all lands south of the Ohio River). The settlement of Knoxville was chosen as capital and William Blount (1749–1800)—superintendent of Indian affairs for the southern district of the United States—was selected as governor of the territory.[5] John Sevier was given command of the eastern militia over the area of eastern Tennessee, which remained a part of North Carolina until 1796.

Inroads to Carolina

The Great Philadelphia Wagon Road

Originally a branch of the Great Indian Warpath, the Great Philadelphia Wagon Road (GPWR) cut an improved trail through the Great Appalachian Valley, stretching 455 miles from Pennsylvania to the Piedmont of the Carolinas and from points east of the Appalachians to

Map courtesy of Knox Crowell.

Augusta, Georgia. This primitive thoroughfare opened a corridor in the early eighteenth century (beginning circa 1720) for settlement of the southern United States, conveying German Palatines, Scots-Irish and other immigrants to the South. By the mid-1700s, milestones had been erected along the flanks of the heavily trafficked GPWR. Following an old Indian path that grew wider with prolonged use, the route passed westerly and southwesterly from Philadelphia through the Pennsylvania towns of Downing Mill, Lancaster, York, Gettysburg, Chambersburg and Greencastle; Hagerstown, Maryland; the interior backcountry of Martinsburg, West Virginia (part of Virginia at the time); Winchester via the Shenandoah Valley through New Market, Harrisonburg, Staunton, Lexington, Fincastle and Big Lick (Roanoke), Virginia; an artery from Big Lick through North Carolina to Tennessee; Wachau-die-Aue (Salem), Salisbury and Charlotte, North Carolina; Rock Hill, Chester and Newberry with an artery to Camden, South Carolina; and Augusta, Georgia.[6]

From Frederick County, Virginia, another course to the south became known as the Carolina Road or High Road, passing through Virginia and crossing the Potomac River via Noland's Ferry at the Point of Rocks. From Clarksville, Virginia, the road entered North Carolina approximately fifteen miles west of the Fall Line Road (currently U.S. Highway 1) and eighty miles east of the GPWR. South of Big Lick—later renamed Roanoke—the

A vintage postcard depicting bowed wagons in North Carolina. *Author's collection.*

GPWR was called the Carolina Road because, by the 1740s and 1750s, it continued through North Carolina. From this point, travelers continued to Hillsborough, Greensboro, Salem and Salisbury and then connected with the GPWR. Winston-Salem began as Wachau-die-Aue, or Wachovia, settled in 1753 by Moravians (German-speaking Protestants) who slogged the road from Philadelphia as a means of reaching North Carolina's Piedmont—an odyssey that could last up to six weeks. Today's Interstate 81 through Virginia and U.S. Highway 220 in North Carolina approximates the path of the GPWR through those states.

In the period between the French and Indian and Revolutionary Wars, the Great Wagon Road was said to have been the most heavily traveled route in colonial America. The eventual decline of this principal circuit can be traced to the construction of railroads in the second half of the nineteenth century.

The Wilderness Road

After 1770, a surge of more than 400,000 Scots-Irish immigrants had arrived in the colonies to escape the poor harvest, high tariffs and religious intolerance of Ulster. Since the colonies' prime lands had been taken, these immigrants pressed onward to the frontier of the western Carolina foothills.

In 1774, with a number of other prominent North Carolinians, Judge Richard Henderson (1735–1785) organized a land-speculation entity named the Louisa Company (renamed Transylvania Company in 1775). The partners planned to purchase land from the Cherokees on the Kentucky side of the Appalachian Mountains and establish a British proprietary colony. Henderson commissioned Daniel Boone (1734–1820), a skilled longhunter and scout from Pennsylvania who had explored Kentucky, to blaze a trail through the region of Fort Chiswell and the Cumberland Gap into central Kentucky. Boone commenced the task in 1775. Others would later lengthen the trail—following Native American passageways—to reach Louisville, Ohio.

Over the Appalachian Mountains—a formidable barrier to east–west travel from Pennsylvania to Georgia—settlers from Pennsylvania tended to migrate south along the GPWR through the Great Appalachian and Shenandoah Valleys.

Beginning on March 10, 1775, Boone and thirty-five axemen cut a trail from Long Island in Kingsport (Tennessee) through the forested mountains to Kentucky. Initially, this proved a rough and muddy trail, little more than a trench. The Transylvania Company had obtained title to Kentuckian territory from the Cherokees, Iroquois and Shawnees, but some of the Indians viewed Boone and other settlers as intruders. On March 24, 1775, Boone and his party stopped about fifteen miles distant from their ultimate destination of the Kentucky River and camped for the night. Before sunup, a group of Shawnees attacked the sleeping men, killing some in Boone's party and wounding others, but most managed to escape. Boone regrouped his men and drove off the attackers. In 1776, Shawnees joined the Chickamauga Cherokees in the Cherokee-American wars against the pioneers. The battle persisted until 1794.

The circuit of the Wilderness Road traced a protracted loop from the Great Philadelphia Wagon Road, near Big Lick, Virginia, southwesterly to Tennessee and then northward to Kentucky. From the Long Island of the Holston River (modern Kingsport, Tennessee) the road passed north through Moccasin Gap of Clinch Mountain and crossed the river to Devils Raceway and the North Fork Clinch River. It then crossed Powell Mountain at Kane Gap, Virginia. From the Kane Gap it ran southwest through the valley of the Powell River to the Cumberland Gap. After crossing over the Cumberland Gap, the road forked, the southern prong passing over the Cumberland Plateau to Nashville via the Cumberland River and the northern prong splitting into two parts—the eastern spur into the Bluegrass Region of Kentucky to Boonesborough on the Kentucky River and the western spur to the Falls of the Ohio (Louisville). As settlements spread southward, the road stretched all the way to Knoxville by 1792.

The Wilderness Road served as an important path of commerce for early settlers in Kentucky and Tennessee, where horses, cattle, sheep and hogs found an eager market in the Carolinas, Georgia, Maryland and Virginia. Drovers (managers) and their drivers (shepherds) herded hogs in drifts of five hundred or more down the un-graveled trails to their slaughter.

In 1792, the new Kentucky legislature provided funds to upgrade the road. As early as 1795, Governor Arnoldus Vanderhorst (1748–1815) of South Carolina had proposed a joint action in improving a road from Greene County, Tennessee, to Warm Springs, North Carolina, and along the French Broad River to Buncombe County. In 1796, an improved all-weather road opened for wagon and carriage travel. Voyagers abandoned the old Wilderness Road around 1840, although modern highways would follow much of its route.

Drovers' Roads

Situated between prosperous South Carolina and Virginia, North Carolina has been described as a "vale of humility between two mountains of conceit." Moreover, due to its isolation, western North Carolina was known as the "Land Beyond." Before railroad service and with no rivers navigable by ships, goods and livestock found their way to and through the Old North State via foot or on wagons or oxcarts. Contrasting with other southern states during the antebellum era, North Carolina bore the most substandard transportation system of any state—before the late nineteenth century brought the train. In sharp contrast, North Carolina would later become one of the South's leading states in terms of transportation.

The most direct and passable route between northeastern Tennessee and Kentucky to South Carolina and Georgia crossed through the counties of Buncombe and what would become Madison, Rutherford, Henderson and Polk. With open ranges of rich grazing lands and an increasing interest in livestock breeding, stock raisers of northeast Tennessee and Kentucky's southeastern and central foothills required markets for their swine, fowl, equines, sheep and cattle. For transporting most goods to market, rivers proved the most gainful method, but this was not the case with livestock. By the turn of the nineteenth century, chief markets of Tennessee and Kentucky meat included the Carolinas and Georgia, and the most prudent way to transport cattle and swine to those consumers was to drive animals, by hoof, two hundred to three hundred miles from producer to consumer over the mountainous terrain.

Meat in the East had become a primary source of income for farmers. Much of the livestock—mainly hogs—was driven mostly from Kentucky and Tennessee (the "Hog & Hominy State") to Spartanburg to be slaughtered and cured and the meat shipped to points beyond. Driving stock created an interlocking economy: the price of hogs had to do with the price of cotton, with hogs going for half the price of cotton per pound. On average, hogs sold for seven to ten cents per pound.

What became known as the Drovers Road, or "Old Stock Road," comprised a wagon trail from Tennessee rising up over the Blue Ridge at Hickory Nut Gap and down through the Fairview Valley into Asheville and points southward. Buncombe County lawyer, historian, bibliophile and author Forster Alexander Sondley (1857–1931) wrote that large-scale droving efforts from Tennessee passed through western North Carolina to South Carolina and Georgia markets as early as the late 1700s. The most

Map courtesy of Knox Crowell.

onerous leg of the journey included the rugged terrain dividing Tennessee and Asheville. Before laborers constructed the Buncombe Turnpike, drovers ventured along the banks of the French Broad River on their southbound journeys, as this course proved the route of least resistance. From the north, turnpikes led to the Old Drovers Road—the southern "turnpike"—essentially a footpath and provisional wagon road. "Rivers of hogs" and their drovers and drivers flowed almost nonstop from mid-October through mid-December from stockyards in Tennessee (Greeneville, Rogersville, Dandridge and Knoxville) through Warm Springs, Marshall, Woodfin, Asheville, Flat Rock and Pace's Gap (Saluda), North Carolina, and funneled through Travelers Rest, South Carolina, and into the market delta of Greenville and Spartanburg, where livestock was slaughtered, butchered, rendered and smoked and much of it hence conveyed on to Augusta and the seaports of Savannah and Charleston.

The journey south could eat up the better part of a month, with a quicker return without livestock in tow—on average within the span of one week. Drovers and drivers, eager to press home with goods and pocketfuls of money, considered the possibility of robbery along the way. Without their herds, the men could take shortcuts, completing the return journey in three to four days on horseback or a day or so longer on foot. Old accounts mention guard stations posted at points along the road as a measure of discouraging highwaymen from robbing the drovers.

Drovers sold northern farmers' livestock to buyers along the route but mostly to owners of cotton plantations based on the animals' weight. The river route made for easier travel, and livestock would lose less mass when driven through more level land. Along the pathway, when bluffs hindered routable traffic, the journey at times entailed crossing water. Some local men provided ferryboat service, levying a toll of, for instance, fifteen cents for passage of a horse and its rider, five cents for a single pedestrian, one cent per hog or sheep, two cents per head of cattle and one-half cent each for fowl.

Inestimable sounders of swine, flocks of turkeys and herds of cattle were driven by at least two men—one ahead and the others leading up the rear. Drovers typically relied on young boys as drivers to assist in this plan, some of them mastering the arts of hog calling and whip cracking to deter livestock from lagging or straying—whips many times fashioned from blacksnakes and brandishing a pennant of red flannel at their tips. Drivers earned ten to twelve dollars per trip plus room and board for moving livestock to South Carolina and Georgia.

In spite of skilled herding, the occasional hog, bovine or turkey would straggle into the woods. Local residents snatched pro bono livestock by rounding up such strays. Hog ranchers and drovers by and large marked their hogs not by branding but by mutilating an ear or both ears with "smooth-crop," "half-crop," "swallowfork," "underbit" or "overbit" incisions or a split or hole and combinations thereof.

A steady stream of drivers and their herds created the need for "stands" along the way to serve as stopping points for rest and sustenance. Because of their short legs, swine could travel only six to ten miles each day. Accordingly, stock stands or taverns grew up along the Drovers Road to service hogs and other livestock as well as their drivers. Stands, located at intervals of every five to ten miles, provided not only meals and lodging for drovers but also pens, fenced-in lots and fodder for the livestock.

During the droving season, convoys of mostly hogs crossed the state lines of Tennessee and North Carolina and directly through Morristown—a market town even before its incorporation in 1797 as the city of Asheville.

Tollgate records suggest that from 150,000 to 200,000 hogs traveled on the turnpike each year in droves of from 300 to 3,000 head each. David Vance (1792–1844) of the Vance Inn claimed to have fed 110,000 hogs during one

Bronze hogs and turkeys—an installation called *Crossroads* by Margery Torre-Godwin at Asheville's Pack Square—gracing a position of the city's Urban Trail project. *Photo by the author.*

especially busy month. Innkeeper Hezekiah Alexander Carr Barnard (circa 1780–1882) made a similar claim.

Lodgers shared quarters with several to a room, generally sleeping on floors overlaid with blankets or on pallets in spaces heated with log-heap fires. Before bedtime, an average table would be laden with sliced meat and boiled root vegetables or a whole roasted ox and platters of spare ribs and sausages with sides such as boiled cabbage or sauerkraut, baked beans, sweet potatoes, biscuits, cornbread, cracklin' bread and cornpone. Beverages included buttermilk, sweet milk and coffee. Innkeepers included the price of repast in the lodging fee—one dollar—or charged on average from twenty to twenty-five cents per meal. Certain innkeepers sold whiskey or brandy or applejack for an additional fee. While all of that might sound appetizing, travelers at times complained about filthy conditions, rude service and unpalatable food, including "chicken swimming in black grease served with lumps of soggy dough." Sleeping arrangements proved crowded with privacy nil. In some cases, the livestock likely ate better than their drivers.

Said not to travel well on full stomachs, the animals were fed only once daily, in the evening during the overnight stays, with livestock being slopped in order of their arrival. Innkeepers bought corn at approximately fifty cents per bushel and sold it for seventy-five to eighty cents per bushel. Local farmers and Indians provided fodder. Eight bushels of corn were stipulated for every one hundred hogs. Drovers many times purchased this feed on

The Allen Inn ("Allen's Old Stand"), Wolf Creek, Cocke County, Tennessee. *Author's collection.*

credit and reimbursed innkeepers on return junkets after having sold their livestock. At times, an innkeeper would take payment in lame animals.

Four-legged creatures slept in stockades, and turkeys roosted in the trees. Old accounts noted that it was with great difficulty each morning for drivers to coax the fowl down from their roosts.

The numbers of droves along this route peaked between 1830 and 1840. The state added gravel surfacing by the 1920s, and the federal government paved it in 1931. Eventually, railroads would provide more expeditious and cost-effective means of transporting livestock, with rail systems expanding briskly after the Civil War. By the late 1800s, most stock stands fell into disrepair or reverted to farmhouses or tourist inns. Others were torn down or left to rot.

The Estatoe Path

Further rudimentary roads in western North Carolina included the Estatoe Path out of South Carolina. A marker at Rosman, Transylvania County, North Carolina, describes it: "[A] trading route between mountain settlements of the Cherokee and their town Estatoe in what is now South Carolina." Under orders in 1792, Sergeant Lambert Clayton (1755–1828) and his militia built a road from the Catawba Trail, near what is now Flat Rock, through the Little River and Crab Creek settlements to the Davidson River. This conduit, partly known as the Crab Creek Path, coursed through the Blue Ridge Mountains to the Cherokee village of Estatoe in South Carolina—one of the first routes to unlock the rugged, densely forested terrain to travel and settlement. Clayton, born in Kent County, Delaware, relocated to Rowan County, North Carolina, before acquiring considerable tracts of land in what became Transylvania County. The region's settlement of Little River was once called "Hogtown" because of its importance as a stopover point for drovers and their livestock along the "Hogtown Turnpike" to the Buncombe Turnpike and on to points north and south. The Estatoe Path joined with today's U.S. Highway 64 West and the Old Turnpike Road/Boylston Highways 280 and 191.

Accommodations

Stock stands, stagecoach inns and taverns between Cocke County, Tennessee, and Anderson County, South Carolina, included:[7]

- Sawyer's Stand, owned by Arthur Sawyer (1828–circa 1900) at Rock Creek, Cocke County, Tennessee.
- Burnett's Stand, owned by William Claudius Burnett (1802–1880) at Wolf Creek, Cocke County.
- Huff's Stand, owned by John Huff (1758–1843), Mary Corder Huff (1766–1842) and Stephen Huff (1796–1870)—a log blockhouse converted into a thirteen-room inn on Long Creek at Del Rio, Cocke County.
- Jones's Stand, owned by Americus Jones (1815–1896), Big Creek (Del Rio), Cocke County.
- Allen's Old Stand, owned by George Washington "Wash" Allen (1812–1876), Wolf Creek, Cocke County.
- Farnsworth's Inn, a group of cabins about four miles above Warm Springs, North Carolina, at the mouth of Big Laurel Creek, owned by Washington Farnsworth, "negro." This was previously the property of David Farnsworth (1785–1860), "white."
- Stackhouse's Place, owned by Amos Stackhouse (1819–1909). Amos, originally from Philadelphia, owned a stock stand, sawmill and barite mine in his namesake village of Stackhouse, Madison County.
- The Willows, owned by Heinrich "Henry" Ottinger (1817–1891), four miles shy of Warm Springs, North Carolina. The inn later hosted boarders from Warm Springs' Dorland-Bell Institute,[8] a Presbyterian finishing school that later became part of Warren Wilson College. Ottinger also operated a ferry on the French Broad. With Amos Stackhouse and James Henry Rumbough (1832–1924), Ottinger formed the Warm Springs Toll Bridge Company.
- Warm Springs Hotel, owned by James Washington Patton (1803–1861) at Warm Springs. James Henry Rumbough (1832–1924) later owned this 350-room hotel (burned in 1884).
- White House, owned by John Erwin Patton (1805–1889) at Warm Springs; famous for its brandy.
- Garrett's Stand, owned by John Garrett (1790–1855) and Charles Thomas Garrett (1845–1924) on the north side of the French Broad River, opposite Warm Springs.
- Candler's Stand, owned by Zachariah Moorman Candler (1772–1844) at Sandy Bottom.
- Barnett's Station, owned by William Barnett (1792–1861) at Barnard.
- Lawson's Stand, owned by Francis Marion "Frank" Lawson (1823–1897) at Shut-in Creek. Lawson also operated a post office called Tennelina at this location.

- WIDOW MCDOWELL'S STAND, Madison County.
- WIDOW FRISBEE'S STAND, renowned for its sauerkraut. Research on the "Widow Frisbee" points to the widow of John Thomas Frisbee (1825–1865), a Confederate veteran. Mary Ann "Polly" Gilbert Frisbee was born about 1822 in South Carolina and, as stated in the census, lived at Spring Creek, Madison County, in 1880.
- NEILSON HOTEL, first owned by Philip Hale Neilson (1806–1891) and his wife, Sarah Baddily Howorth Neilson (1812–1864). A deaf-mute from birth, Neilson served as postmaster at Holly Grove. The Neilsons had thirteen children and later moved to Texas.
- CHUNN'S INN, owned by Samuel Chunn (1772–1855), four miles north of Lapland (Marshall) at Pine Creek.
- VANCE INN, owned by David Vance, father of Governor Zebulon Baird Vance (1830–1894), at Lapland.
- RICE'S STAND, owned by Joseph Marion Rice (1761–1850) below Lapland.
- RAMSEY'S INN, owned by William Ramsey (1857–1901) at Hays Run Creek.
- BROWN'S STAND, owned by Caney H. Brown (1872–1933) at Little Pine Creek.
- BARNARD'S INN, owned by Hezekiah Alexander Carr Barnard and Hester Anne Gahagan Barnard (1795–1881) at Barnardsville (Big Ivy), Buncombe County.
- ROLLINS' STAND, owned by Major William Washington Rollins (1830–1909) of the Western North Carolina Railroad, near Avery's Creek.
- BECKY POSTON'S TAVERN, owned by Rebecca Baldridge Poston (1764–1851), widow of John Poston Jr. (1764–1819), at Upper Hominy, west of Swannanoa.
- ALEXANDER'S INN, owned by James Mitchell "Jimpsey" Alexander (1793–1858) and Nancy Foster Alexander (1797–1862) on the east bank of the French Broad River about ten miles north of Morristown/Asheville at Alexander Station (present-day Alexander, Swannanoa). Acclaimed far and wide as supplying "superior accommodations," the inn, built in the early 1820s, included a general store, grist- and sawmills, the services of a cordwainer and wainwright, slave quarters, a river ferry operation and later a bridge. Robert Brank Vance (1828–1899) bought the enterprise from the Alexanders' son Alfred M. Alexander (1819–1889) and son-in-law Jackson Smith Burnett (1801–1893), who in turn sold to James Marion Vance (1823–1892), who operated the establishment for a short time. James Mitchell Alexander built the home that would become known as Hilliard Hall at Asheville's Public Square and owned the Alexander Hotel, Asheville's first (1814).

- Buck Hotel (1825), owned by James "I Dod" McConnell Smith (1787–1856) at Asheville.
- Reed's Stand, owned by Joseph (1797–1846) and James Eldad Reed (1799–1866) about 1.5 miles below Asheville (near the future site of Biltmore).
- Sulphur Springs Hotel, built by Robert Henry (1765–1863) and his son-in-law Colonel Reuben Deaver (1807–1852) in 1831 (burned in 1862). The hotel stood about five miles southwest of downtown Asheville.
- Vance Hall, owned by Robert Brank Vance, five miles out of Asheville.
- Foster's Inn, owned by Captain Thomas Foster (1774–1858), built circa 1796 on Sweeten Creek and the Swannanoa River near what is now Biltmore.
- Patton's Inn, owned by Preston Fidellia "Press" Patton (1841–1897) at the location of present-day Skyland.
- Case's Stand, owned by John MacAnally "Mack" Case (1838–1915) at Limestone, Henderson County.
- Fletcher's Tavern, owned by Dr. George Washington Fletcher (1829–1901) in Limestone (later Murrayville, then Fletcher).
- Murray's Inn, otherwise known as Rock Hall, Blake House and the Meadows, owned by William Murray (1783–1867) on Cane Creek at Murrayville/Fletcher.

The Meadows/Blake House. *Photo by the author.*

- RICHARDSON'S INN, owned by Benjamin Richardson (1796–1862) at Naples.
- McDOWELL HOTEL, owned briefly by Charles Gordon McDowell (1817–1907) at Naples.
- A drovers' stop at the home of Asa Edney (1772–1842) at Edneyville.
- A stand kept by John W. Jones (1831–1901) at Edneyville.
- Henry Ellis Lane (1809–1883) took in drovers and their livestock and stagecoach passengers at his expansive home in Rugby.
- RIPLEY HOUSE, owned by "Colonel" James M. "Valentine" Ripley (1807–1879) on Main Street at the corner of Aspen Street (today's Second Avenue West), Hendersonville.
- TABOR'S TAVERN, owned by Allen "Doc" Tabor (1801–1882). The operation included a butchery, shoe shop and general store near the present site of Flat Rock's village hall.
- KUYKENDALL'S TAVERN, owned by Abraham Kuykendall (circa 1719–1812) on the Saluda Path/today's Rutledge Drive, near Mud Creek Baptist Church at Flat Rock. Kuykendall sold the operation to his son-in-law Edmund Samuel McGuffey (1774–1827).
- BLUE RIDGE HOUSE, owned by George W. Summey (1810–1859) at Flat Rock.
- BRITTAIN'S INN, owned by William Brittain (1798–1867) at Flat Rock.
- FLAT ROCK INN, owned by William Hamilton Young (1775–1835) and George W. Summey.

Farmer's Hotel, known also as the Woodfield Inn. *Photo by the author.*

P.J. Hart's Splendor, May 5, 1913. *Photo by Herbert W. Pelton; courtesy of Octavia Freeman Beddingfield.*

- Farmer's Hotel (earlier called Flat Rock Inn and later called Woodfield Inn), operated by Henry Tudor Farmer (1817–1882) at Flat Rock.
- Splendor, the home, store, post office and stage stop of Philip Jackson Hart (1845–1917), near present-day Tuxedo, Green River Township.
- Posey's Stand, owned by John Posey (1855–1944), later operated by his widow.
- Guice's Inn, owned by Peter Guice (1788–1873) and his family above the Green River Gorge. The operation included a gristmill and blacksmith shop.
- Oakland, owned by "Colonel" John Davis (1780–1859) and Serepta Merritt Davis (1802–1889) above the Winding Stairs at the North Carolina/South Carolina line.
- Hightower's, owned by William Kinsey Hightower (1822–1871) and John William "Bose" Hightower (1851–1929) at Bayson Springs, Greenville County, South Carolina, at the head of the Winding Stairs. The property included a mill and a government distillery.
- Mountain Inn, owned by John Jackson Hodge (1802–1880) at Grindal Shoals on the Pacolet River on the Union/Cherokee County line.
- Fuller's, South Carolina.
- Murray's Inn, owned by Robert Murray, thirty-two miles from Greenville.
- Greenville Hotel, downtown Greenville.
- Pool's Stand, owned by John Pool (1797–1868), Greenville County.

Mimosa Inn. *Photo by the author.*

- A stand owned by John Roseman between Greenville and Anderson.
- Williams' Stand, owned by Captain Micajah Berry "Cager" Williams (1812–1897), Anderson County.
- Catlett's Stand, owned by John Catlett (1828–1902) in Anderson.

Judge Mitchell King (1783–1862) of Charleston, who owned a summer mansion named Argyle at Flat Rock, noted in his journal that wayfarers along the turnpike (present-day Greenville Highway) frequently mistook Argyle for an inn.

East of the turnpike stood Smathers' Inn, owned by John Charles Smathers (1826–1918), and to the west, Sherrill's Tavern (in continuous use from 1834 to 1909)[9]—the latter owned by William Bedford Sherrill (1810–1878) and Elizabeth Pamela Harris Sherrill (1819–1903) at Fairview. The Sherrills operated a stagecoach named the *Flying Cloud* that conveyed mail and passengers between Asheville and Rutherfordton.

Polk County inns included Ransom Woodruff Pace's (1835–1920) drovers' stop at Pace's Gap (Saluda), Dr. Columbus Mills' (later Dr. Leland Reid McAboy's) accommodations at Lynn (now the Mimosa Inn) and the Tryon City Hotel (later called Oak Hall) at Tryon.

II
A-Wheel

Do not go where the path may lead, go instead where there is no path and leave a trail.
—*Ralph Waldo Emerson*

Early road-builders—mostly hardscrabble farmers and hunters—lacked civil engineering skills, and with a paucity of costly black powder and a deficiency of suitable tools, the forging of the mountains' seminal roadbeds proved a sobering task. Because timber tended to be generally lightly scattered on ridge crests, such positions offered the least resistance to construction of roadbeds through this particular physiography. Down in the valleys, level stretches flanking waterways proposed additional positions where roads could be blazed with less effort and labor.

For the most part, bypasses "went to the woods," meandering away from obstacles such as rock cliffs. In situations proposing no other choices, builders—for lack of explosive powder and precious if they had it (about fifty cents per pound)—heaped logs atop rock ledges, set them ablaze and allowed the kindling to burn until the rock became blisteringly hot, at which point they removed the logs and doused the rock faces with water, effecting quarriable schisms. Some road builders jammed drenched rods of wood into crevices. As the wood swelled, the rock would many times shear away in layers. Another method involved driving cylindrical holes into rock obtrusions by hammering in steel-tipped bars to a depth of about two feet. Into these openings were thrust hollow reeds charged with gunpowder and the remaining spaces packed with earth. Natural fissures were similarly packed. A fire would be set to the opposing end of a "fuse" made up of woodland debris stretching several yards from the powder plugs, ultimately effecting a series of detonations after which sections of rock could be cleaved from the intended passageway.

The first road in Buncombe County ran from Old Fort to the Swannanoa River and Bee Tree Creek to the Davidson River in what is now Transylvania County, crossing the French Broad River at Avery's Creek. The route crossed the French Broad River below the mouth of Avery's Creek, passing through Mills River via "Boydsteen's" (present-day Boylston—at one time spelled "Boilston") Creek. According to Forster Alexander Sondley, the second road stretched from "the wagon ford on Rims [Reems] Creek to the road from Turkey Cove, Catawba and to Robert Henton's on the Cane River, after passing through Asheville."

Charles Lenoir Ray (*Postmarks*) wrote:

> *The Buncombe County Court ordered that William Fletcher, John Bradly Sr., Elijah Williamson, Harmon Reed, Nicholas W. Woodfin (1810–1876), David McCarson, Samuel Forgy* [alternatively spelled Forgie and Forgee], *John Newport, William Boyd, Abraham Kuykendall, John Craig, Abraham Reed, Benjamin Yardley and John Bradly Jr. be a jury to vies, mark and lay off a road, the nearest and best way from the ford of Cane Creek, to the flat rock near the blue ridge leading along the ridge that strikes mud creek a small distance above William Fletcher's and report to the April session, 1794. Basically this was to become U.S.* [Highway] *25 in our day, but it wound about a great deal due to the necessity of avoiding the swamp areas and lowlands subject to flooding. It was this route into which John Earle* [1737–1815] *connected when he completed his road through Saluda Gap from Landrum to Flat Rock in 1792 and over this road brothers Zebulon* [1764–1824] *and Bedent Baird* [1767–1839] *brought the first wagon from the South to Asheville.*

The Buncombe Turnpike

Completed in 1827 from Saluda Gap to Buncombe County courthouse and along the French Broad River by way of Barnard's and Warm Springs to the Tennessee line. Served as the major trade route through mountains of western North Carolina until 1882.

—Buncombe Turnpike historic marker on Main Street, fronting the Madison County Courthouse, Marshall, North Carolina

With no such mode as the Great Wagon Road or navigable water to reach the landlocked Blue Ridge Mountains between Greeneville, Tennessee, and Greenville, South Carolina, in 1824 the General Assembly of the State of North Carolina incorporated the Buncombe Turnpike—the first major thoroughfare linking the Tennessee line to South Carolina, passing through Paint Rock (two branches), Warm Springs (now Hot Springs), down the French Broad River gorge to Asheville, Hendersonville and Flat Rock and south through the Saluda Gap to Poinsett Bridge and points south. What is now Henderson County would serve as the "southern gateway" to western North Carolina via this turnpike.

Increasing numbers of drovers, traders and settlers spurred such a thoroughfare to provide a safer, more convenient conduit through the mountains. Before 1824, Buncombe County legislator David Lowry Swain (1801–1868) proposed a bill for the purpose of an artery from the Saluda Gap to the Tennessee line. The Buncombe Turnpike Company formed when Buncombe County commissioners Samuel Chunn (1772–1855), James Patton Sr. (1756–1845) and George Swain (1763–1829); Burke County

Historic markers at Marshall, county seat of Madison. *Photo by the author.*

commissioners Isaac Thomas Avery (1785–1864), John Caldwell (1779–1857) and William Willoughby Erwin (1764–1837) of Belvidere Plantation; and Rutherford County commissioners Joseph McDowell Carson (1779–1860), John Paxton (1779–1856) and George Walton (1773–1835) were appointed to oversee the project. The North Carolina legislature directed the commissioners to receive subscriptions "for the purpose of laying out a turnpike from Salude [Saluda] Gap [where old U.S. Highway 25 crosses into South Carolina], in the County of Buncombe, by way of Smith's, Murrayville [Fletcher], Asheville, Warm Springs [Hot Springs] to the Tennessee line," where it would continue on the Tennessee Road, which linked the region to Kentucky. James Mitchell Alexander served as contractor for the project. The road would be twelve feet wide—a first-class toll road with a dirt and gravel surface. Commissioners were authorized to sell $50,000 of stock in the company, and collection of tolls would further finance the construction and maintenance of the thoroughfare.

The turnpike followed the French Broad River through western North Carolina's mountains to what is now the state line of Tennessee. Built along the "old Drovers' road," it included Henderson County's Saluda Gap and Howard's Gap roads. It connected with the nineteenth-century resort town of Warm Springs, North Carolina; Knoxville, Tennessee; and eastern Piedmont communities. A bridge was built across the French Broad River at Warm Springs by 1832. The 420-foot-long span was rebuilt in 1842. The pike stretched from the Tennessee line to Paint Rock, Laurel Creek, Walnut Creek, Ivy Creek, Reems Creek and Beaverdam Creek and down Asheville's present-day Broadway Street to the French Broad River then across the town's center, Public Square (present-day Pack Square), down what is today's Biltmore Avenue and southeasterly, across the Swannanoa River, to Shufordsville (Arden). The road continued through Murrayville (Fletcher), Hendersonville and Flat Rock to the Saluda Gap and continued across the South Carolina line and joined with the old State Road.

Completed by 1827,[10] and with the introduction of its first tollgate, the seventy-five-mile-long stretch of the Buncombe Turnpike opened a channel that enhanced trade and settlement. Male inhabitants, required by local laws and by public conscription, spent specified numbers of days each year contributing to the clearing, grading, building and maintenance of the route. Such roadwork was considered "labor tax." The Buncombe Turnpike, deemed North Carolina's finest road, would become the most traveled passageway in the western part of the state. Many continued to refer to this pike as the "drovers' road" because communities within miles

Ox-drawn bowed wagon on the plank road in Henderson County. *Baker photo (Jody Barber P065); courtesy of D.H. Ramsey Library Special Collections, UNC Asheville.*

of it benefitted economically, particularly during the months of October through December—the peak season for livestock droving.

The turnpike included a few divergences for short distances in order to avoid obstructions such as cliffs and waterways. A tributary of the turnpike called the New Stock Road left the pike near present-day Burnsville Road and continued to Warm Springs, Jupiter and Ivy up to Greeneville, Tennessee.

In 1851, the legislature of the state of North Carolina incorporated the Asheville & Greenville Plank Road Company. Workers overlaid sections of the turnpike with thick oaken or heart-pine boards set on wooden sills stretching from south of Asheville through Henderson County. This concept—as well as "corduroy roads"—proved financially impractical and was short-lived (about eight years) due to the wear and tear on the wood. The stretch was deconstructed in the mid-1860s even though it had provided a mud-free journey on it. Plank roads employed hewed or planed boards placed side by side. Corduroy roads were built with logs placed side by side and chinked with earth. The scheme involved steam engines plying the planks, but wagon drivers found the surface rough and uncomfortable.

This type of "all-weather" road had proven effective on flatter surfaces but failed in the mountains. Remnants of the old plank road could be found in south Hendersonville as late as the mid-1900s, as witnessed by author Frank Lockwood FitzSimons Sr. (1897–1980). This section crossed Mud Creek at the intersection of U.S. Highway 25 South and U.S. Highway 176. The planking never reached Asheville or South Carolina.

Resources and transportation dwindled during the Civil War years, when drovers and other travelers were reduced to a trickle. General George Stoneman's (1822–1894) raiders gained entry to Asheville via the Drovers Road at Hickory Nut Gap in April 1863. The turnpike never regained its prewar status. In 1869, the Buncombe Turnpike Company turned over the route along the French Broad River to the Western North Carolina Railroad Company for stock in the corporation. The incursion of the railroad replaced the route as a method of transporting livestock. The building of the Piedmont Air-Line brought rail traffic as near as Greenville, South Carolina;[11] the Western North Carolina Railroad had brought trains to Hendersonville by 1879, and the Spartanburg & Asheville Railroad reached Asheville in the 1880s. Traffic on the turnpike diminished with each successive stage of the railroad. The extension of counties' public roads had a like effect.

Freight wagon train at Sapphire, North Carolina. *Courtesy of the Henderson County Genealogical and Historical Society.*

As traffic tolls dropped below the cost of upkeep, road stocks became worthless, and the turnpike companies had no other choice than to turn over their roads to the public roads system. Gradually, each county took over sections of roads running within its boundaries and abolished the tollgates. After the turnpike alongside the French Broad had been relinquished to the Western North Carolina Railroad Company for stock in that enterprise, all that was left to be surrendered was the road from the Henderson County line to Asheville, passing through Limestone (Fletcher) township. On September 5, 1881, the Buncombe Turnpike Company turned over this last section under its control to the Asheville and Buncombe County Board of Commissioners. By 1885, few farmers were transporting cattle by foot. Nevertheless, for more than sixty years, drovers trekked the Buncombe Turnpike, which approximated today's U.S. Highway 25 in Henderson, Buncombe and Greenville Counties in the Carolinas. And on it traveled bow-frame wagons, oxcarts, sleds ("stone boats"), pack mules, rolling hogsheads (horse- or steer-drawn tobacco casks) and stagecoaches—and later, tourists, health seekers, speculators agog with the land boom, new residents and campers.

Gaps

Old Indian trails and ox traces proffered passable approaches for explorers and settlers through the mountain gaps to the plateaus of Asheville and Hendersonville and beyond.

Some have suggested that when the first settlers set out to build a new road, they drove a hog or a "cow-brute" (steer) to the lowest gap in sight and then prodded the beast along the side where the road was to be located, the hoof tracks to be followed and staked and the road located exactly on them.

Coopers Gap approximates Coopers Gap Road in Polk County.

Deep Gap (today's Big Hungry Road and Deep Gap Road) skirts the Big Hungry River between Howard's Gap, Henderson County, into Polk County to Brights Creek.

Hickory Nut Gap (originally called Sherrill's Gap and then Hickorynut Gap) is today's U.S. Highway 64/74A alongside the Rocky Broad/Hickory Nut Gorge running through northeast Henderson County between Buncombe and Rutherford Counties. This route followed the Broad River into the piedmont of North Carolina. A branch to it ran

Miller David Justice (1886–1966), Bat Cave. *Courtesy of V. Leon Pace.*

from Edneyville through Reedy Patch into the Hickory Nut Gap north of Chimney Rock.

In 1829, the North Carolina General Assembly appropriated $12,000 to complete a toll road through Hickory Nut Gap to Asheville. In 1841, the assembly enacted a bill to extend the Hickory Nut Turnpike through Paris Gap to connect Rutherfordton with Asheville and the Buncombe Turnpike.

HOWARD'S GAP (partly today's Howard Gap Road with U.S. Highway 176 having replaced a section of it) follows an Indian trading path. Predating the Buncombe Turnpike, this gap furnished a primary artery used by settlers and traders entering western North Carolina. Captain Thomas Howard (1745–1822) and his mounted rangers pursued this trail—a primitive wagon road—to the Battle of Round Mountain (1776), which breached Cherokee dominance in the region. The route runs southeasterly through the Buncombe/Henderson County line, then east to Polk County, through Warrior Mountain and the Saluda Gap, bypassing Green River and Flat Rock and running up to Fletcher. In days of old, wayfarers' inns adjacent this route included the home of Dr. Columbus John Mills (1808–1882) and Dr. Leland Reid McAboy and Mrs. Mary A. Christy McAboy (1818–1883) at the present Polk County village of Lynn. Francis Asbury Thompson (1829–1913) also maintained a stage stop at the fork of the Howard's

Gap and Holbert Cove. The Howard Gap Road runs for about sixty-five miles—thirty in North Carolina. Near Union, South Carolina, it joined with supplementary routes leading to markets in Charleston.

Howard's Gap provided a course for nineteenth-century livestock drovers. A branch of it left the road at Fletcher's on Cane Creek toward the Saluda Gap to the southeast, by way of what is now Lynn (Polk County) and on to Spartanburg, South Carolina. U.S. Highway 176, completed in 1927, redirected much traffic from the old road. Most of its original route can be retraced, the major exception being the steep portion at the Green River Gorge that was obliterated with the construction of the Peter Guice Memorial Bridge on Interstate 26. The Howard's Gap historic marker reads:

> *Route used by Indians & settlers in crossing the Blue Ridge. Named for Captain Thomas Howard, 1776 militia leader.*

JONES GAP TURNPIKE was forged by Solomon Jones, using family labor, from about 1840 to 1847 with improvements made as time wore on. Jones

Left: Caesar's Head. *C.H. Oak Collection; courtesy of the Henderson County Genealogical and Historical Society.*

Above: Solomon Jones. *Courtesy of Daphne Hedden.*

laid off the road from River Falls at the fork of the Middle Saluda River and Oil Camp Creek in Greenville County, South Carolina, up the mountain to Transylvania County (Henderson at the time), North Carolina, to more than a mile above Caesar's Head at Cedar Mountain—ending at what became U.S. Highway 276 ("Caesar's Head Highway"). Jones's descendants continued to charge tolls on this corridor until 1910. A tollgate stood in South Carolina near River Falls. The four-mile route came up through the middle fork of the Saluda River from River Falls, South Carolina, through what is now Transylvania County, and included a serpentine loop called the "Winds." Jones referenced this road, "Middle Saluda Turnpike Road," in his will. The old roadbed now proffers a hiking trail in the protected Caesar's Head State Park. Jones sold the toll road to his family about 1875 and bought Mount Hebron in Henderson County, where he carved another road known as the "Jones Pleasure Drive."

Said to have surveyed and built roads without the aid of instruments, Jones is also credited for the Green River and Flat Rock turnpikes, Cashiers Valley Road and sections of present-day U.S. Highways 64 and 25. Legends suggest that pathfinder Jones's "instruments" included his keen eye, wisdom, judgment—and a sow named Sue.

Five years before his death, Jones commissioned James Joshua Blythe (1831–1912) to chisel an epithet into a monument that stands above his grave on Mount Hebron:

> *Here lies Solomon Jones, The Road Maker. A True Patriot. He labored fifty years to leave the world a better place than he found it. Born 7 March 1802. Died 23 April 1899.*

Judes Gap approximates the modern Judes Gap Road in north Henderson County (Edneyville, near World's Edge). The gap ran east from Mills Gap through Sugarloaf Mountain and Rutherford County and on to Harm Creek, Polk County.

Mills Gap ran northwest–southeast and east–west between Buncombe and Polk Counties. The trail left the road near the present town of Busbee (south of Biltmore) and ran by way of Hoopers Creek via Terrys Gap and then Clear Creek and Point Lookout, to Mill Spring and Green River and on to Spartanburg.

Saluda Gap Road was an old trail from Columbia that passed through the Newberry and Greenville districts to the Blue Ridge Mountains at the Saluda Gap. This track was an extension of the State Road from the Catawba Trail

Left: Hebron Tower. *Courtesy of the Henderson County Genealogical and Historical Society.*

Below: Tourists visiting Indian Cave, Mount Hebron, 1917. *C.H. Oak Collection; courtesy of the Henderson County Genealogical and Historical Society.*

in Upstate South Carolina to North Carolina's "Buncombe Road" and later the Buncombe Turnpike. Completed in 1820, the route proffered one of the earliest corridors from the south to the Blue Ridge Mountains and represented the southernmost section of the Buncombe Turnpike in present-day Henderson County as it crosses into South Carolina. The first "formal" road over the gap was constructed between 1794 and 1797, with petitions drafted to improve the road in 1807. In the mid- to late 1820s, completion of the State Road between the Carolinas and Tennessee included the Saluda Gap.

In 1792, John Earle accepted $4,000 to have a road carved from Landrum through the Saluda Gap to Flat Rock. Known as the "Saluda Path," this route cut through the South Carolina and North Carolina line and then zigzagged up the grade to Zirconia, Mine Hole Gap and Flat Rock by 1799. The path followed approximately the present-day pattern of U.S. Highway 176, then west along the Green River and up through Zirconia into Flat Rock and included today's Rutledge Drive south of Mud Creek. The latter was part of the old "High Road." An extension of the South Carolina State Road, this course provided one of the earliest routes from the south to the mountains of western North Carolina. The State Road connected the colonial port of Charleston through Columbia

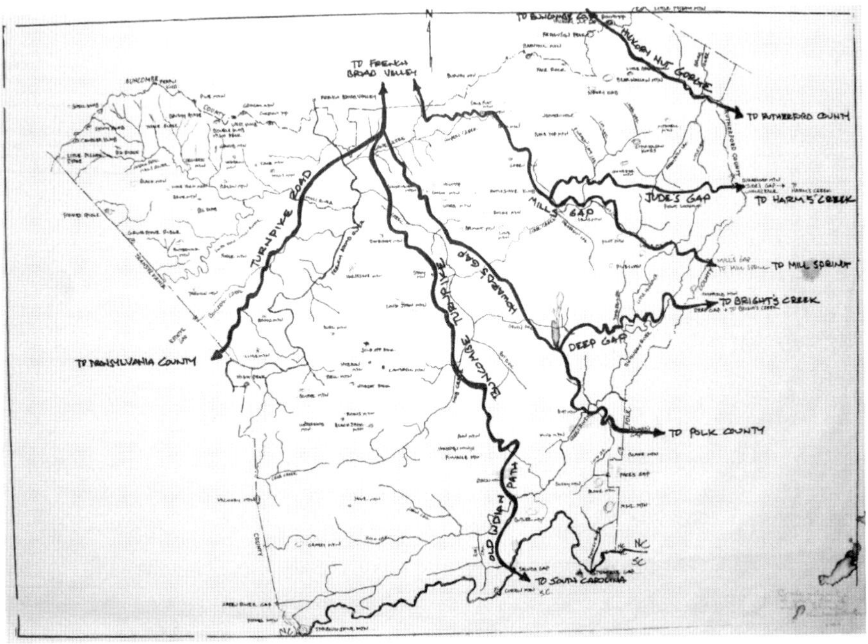

Gaps. *Map by Stuart Stepp; courtesy of the Henderson County Genealogical and Historical Society.*

to Spartanburg (about 180 miles) and later to Greenville and points northward, including Landrum.

Swannanoa Gap, couched within the Buncombe-McDowell County line near the head of the Catawba River, proffered a primary pass through which early settlers and Indians traveled to reach the Asheville plateau. The historic marker reads:

> *Used by Indians and pioneers in crossing the Blue Ridge. General Rutherford's expedition against Cherokee passed here, September 1776.*

In 1880, the Western North Carolina Railroad passed through this gap and then up and over Old Fort Mountain, completing the railway.

Terrys Gap begins at the head of Kyles Creek, running northwest–southeast through Hoopers Creek Township between North and South Mills Gap Roads. It was named for William Terry (1774–1837).

Further regional gaps included Beaverdam, Bent Creek, Cutthroat, Estatoe, Glady Fork, Green River, Sassafras, Stroupe, Trammel, Turkey Pen and Young.

The Old Turnpikes

The main roads were no more than well-trampled, one-way cart-ways in the backwoods sections where rapid transit was limited to horseback. Stagecoaches and carriages were few in number and to pull a loaded coach or a freighted cargo required a team of four or six.

Settlement and development of the upper French Broad River and its tributaries and of the valleys of Toxaway, Horsepasture, Whitewater, Little Tennessee and others farther west witnessed a growing demand for travel and, to meet this demand, in the early nineteenth century the Western Turnpike Road was constructed from Asheville through what are now Buncombe, Henderson, Transylvania, Jackson and Macon Counties. It followed approximately the Old Asheville Road as far as Brevard and the Cashiers Valley Road farther west, and closely followed the old Estatoe Path.

Tollgates were positioned every few miles—generally ten to fifteen miles apart—with many of the gatekeepers keeping facilities to care for travelers and their animals. The fare would include lodging and feeding anything from a single wayfarer to a house of militia—a meat supply that would vary from a snack to a whole roasted ox. With a small crowd, there was an abundance of room for all. With a large crowd, sometimes every nook and cranny of the building, the outhouses and barn lofts would be occupied. Stables and sheds were available and a number of pens could hold droves of cattle, sheep and hogs. The livestock for market traveled on their own shank mares versus iced refrigerators. The stand host never knew in advance whether he would have to feed one or a hundred men or animals.

To meet the needs of drovers and other travelers, the Little River Turnpike was constructed, connecting with the Western Turnpike in the Mills River section, crossing the ridge into the French Broad Valley near Etowah, crossing the French Broad at Shuford's Bridge (now Penrose), up Little River to Laurel Creek, then by Buck Forest and Cedar Mountain, connecting with the South Carolina road at Jones Gap.

With the standards of road building required at that time teams rarely traveled more than a few stages a day. Arduous travel required long rests and enterprising stand keepers accommodated the need. With ordinary travel, twenty to thirty miles per day was considered average. Rarely a greater distance was made except in the cases where relay teams were used.

There were enough men and boys with the drove to chase stragglers and keep them on the road. The drivers were paid their wages when the destination was reached and stock sold, being paid for the number of days actually taken to make the trip, including half that time estimated for their return home. The mode of operation was much the same for sheep and hogs.

Tolls for travel and the tavern and feed bills were ample to pay the innkeepers, maintain the roads and bridges, and pay good dividends to the stockholders. For a long time, a well-to-do farmer or planter or businessman considered his certificate of turnpike as one of his most conservative and best income-producing possessions.

—Brevard News, *January 11, 1929*

COACHING DAYS

With turnpikes having opened conduits for travel, wagon trains moved freely between farmlands in the north and consumers in the south. Journeys sometimes persisted for weeks, during which the itinerant farmers also sold their products at points along the way. Southern markets clamored for tobacco, corn, hams, lard, fatback, cabbages and apples from the

Coaching days. *Author's collection.*

north. Northern farmers returned home with products such as textiles and ammunition, indigo, salt, sugar, pepper, coffee and tea.

Bowed wagons and stagecoaches frequented the turnpike, laden with traders and produce and passengers from all directions and with summer visitors from the south. Roads had improved, but conveyances proved relatively fragile. Fractured wheels and axles were common, as were spooked or injured equines. Mountainous terrain loomed perilous at best, and descents could be treacherous. The first brakes for carriages and wagons were fashioned from hickory saplings, the branches twined around the front axle and bent around the hind wheels. Locking chains came later, and these would be attached to the carriage and passed between the wheel spokes to impede a vehicle's descent along steep grades. Saplings and branches dragged onto roadbeds further slowed the descents.

As a rule, stagecoaches assigned seating on a first-come, first-served basis, with three to a seat. Regularly scheduled coaches between Greenville, South Carolina, and Greeneville, Tennessee, included stops at John Davis's Oakland above the Winding Stairs then on to Hendersonville, Shufordsville (Arden) and Asheville. Seating choices included those inside or up top alongside the driver or at the rear of the deck. Because passengers inside the coach at times suffered from motion sickness, some of them preferred—weather permitting—to ride *en plein air* on the roof of the transport. During colder weather, ladies would employ heated stones wrapped in rugs or blankets to warm their feet.

Five dollars would buy a one-way fare between Asheville, North Carolina, and Greenville, South Carolina. Stage fares averaged about four pence per mile or seven dollars for first-class passage for an entire route. Second-class passengers were obliged to walk at difficult turns in the road, as were third-class passengers, with the added task of the latter having to push the coach on slopes as necessary.

Bumpy, Dusty Excursions

With a crack of a whip, the coach would be off, bucking and swaying, toggling and pitching its way across a pockmarked and rocky trail, dashing and hurtling passengers into one another—many of whom were sore or even bruised at journey's end. Added to the bone-rattling voyage, passengers and coachmen shouldered delays, weather issues, great clouds of dust and even overturns. Livestock many times barricaded stagecoaches during the October-to-December droving season.

Coaches could be stifling in summertime and frigid in winter. Narrow roads clung to up-thrust cliffs that pressed uncomfortably close to the passersby. Drivers many times needed to scale such vertical slopes and negotiate gaps and fords. Moreover, hazards included cracked braces, snapped axles or becoming mired in mud. On such occasions, passengers assisted in repairing their transports. At other times, commuters would be required to disembark and walk part of the journey as their coach navigated particularly steep elevations.

Adversity and danger were not unknown along the wilderness trails and included the possibility of Indian attacks and highway bandits. Fallen

A stagecoach jostling along a mountain pass. *Author's collection.*

timber and rocks strewn across the rude paths and violent shocks further removed any sense of enjoyment from an execrable journey. On the upside, passengers shared a sense of camaraderie and commiseration and enjoyed remarkable backcountry scenery.

Etiquette for commuters ran the gamut from helping to push the coach as may be necessary to not smoking or spitting on the leeward side of the transport. Alcohol was permissible, but imbibers were expected to share. Passengers were advised to not sleep on others' shoulders. Neither should they use pomade in their hair, lest the dust adhere to it. When a driver asked passengers to disembark and walk, they were not to grumble about it. (This generally did not apply to first-class passage.) Swearing was forbidden. And if a team of horses should suddenly bolt and run, it was advised to remain seated inside, as jumping from the coach could and usually did result in injury.

Concord coaches, suspended on leather braces mounted on frames, accommodated up to twelve passengers with space atop the equipage for additional fares and luggage. According to John Preston Arthur in his 1914 *History of Western North Carolina*, coach drivers were autocrats who carried long, English-style tin trumpets, which they bugled upon approach to stops, alerting innkeepers of incoming fares—each toot representing a lodger. Travelers supped and slept at wayside stops with a notice that they would be called at the unholy hour of three or four o'clock the next morning to resume the onerous journey.

The Concord Coach

References to stagecoaches in the Carolinas point specifically to models known as the Concord. Weighing more than two thousand pounds, the first Concords were built over the winter of 1827–28, with models priced from $1,200 to $2,500. (In the early twenty-first century, restored Concords have sold at auction for $250,000 or more.)

Lewis Downing (1792–1873), a wheelwright of New Hampshire, hired Joseph Stephens Abbot (1804–1871), a chaise builder from Salem, Massachusetts, as an apprentice. The two soon formed a partnership. Their manufacturing facility affixed twin, three-inch-wide rawhide, lengthwise thorough-braces (straps) under their coaches, which effected a swinging motion rather than the up-and-down jolting of spring suspension. Mark Twain once stated that a Concord was "like a cradle on wheels."

Due to disagreements, Downing and Abbot dissociated in 1847. Their separate companies—Downing Company and J.S. and E.A. Abbot & Company—remained fierce competitors until Downing retired in 1865, and the men, with their sons, revived the original enterprise under the name of Abbot, Downing and Company, which operated under that title until 1873, when it was incorporated as the Abbot-Downing Company. The partners included Downing's son Alfred Lewis Downing (1820–1901) and Abbot's sons Joseph Henry Abbot (1837–1896) and Edward Augustus Abbot (1830–circa 1910).

Abbot-Downing manufactured over forty different types of carriages and wagons—including the Celerity model, mud wagons and heavy drays—at its factory in Concord, New Hampshire. The company continued to build coaches, wagons, carriages and trucks until 1919 and employed as many as three hundred people. All were men, with the exception of Maria Foster Putnam (1830–1923) who, from 1865 to 1895, stitched leather seats and trim for every coach that rolled out of the factory, including those purchased by Wells Fargo & Company. For the entire thirty years, Putnam was the company's only female employee.

Each coach, characteristically painted red or green and trimmed with yellow, was assigned a number. Concord coaches earned the reputation for being sturdy, roomy and comfortable, with claims that they did not break, they simply wore out. Frames were crafted from oak and wheels from ash. Leather boots for baggage, mail and other valuables were affixed to the rear of each vehicle. The remainder of the luggage would be placed on the roof. Stagecoach models offered interior capacity for six, nine or twelve passengers and measured on average four feet of interior height with an overall height of eight feet, six inches. Space on the decks of the larger models furnished seating for up to nine additional passengers. Windows featured roll-down curtains of leather or canvas. Two or three leather- or plush-upholstered seats offered precious little legroom, allowing most travelers about fifteen inches of space if the coach were fully booked. With no back support passengers clung to leather straps suspended from the ceiling. Rear wheels measured five feet, one inch and front wheels, three feet, ten inches. Teams of two, four or six horses drew the coaches. The average speed clocked about eight miles per hour.

Abbot-Downing produced vehicles to traverse a variety of terrains, including the Overland Wagon, Mountain Wagon and Hose Wagon. Eastern models sported a rigid anterior boot box and an open rear luggage rack, a single front bunter and folding step, a rear axle mounted beneath the reaches with a kingpin in front of the axle, a splinter bar and standard castor. The Abbot and Downing interests produced approximately two thousand stagecoaches between 1826 and 1899.

In North Carolina, the establishment of stagecoach lines was contingent on individual proprietors or companies of investors. Other states licensed their early stage lines, but North Carolina exercised no oversight at either the state or local level.

Stagecoach lines supported considerable livelihoods: transport owners, drivers and ticket agents; coach manufacturers and blacksmiths; tavern owners and stable hands; and farmers who bred the horses and grew the fodder that kept the stages running.

Turnpikes rendered stage service faster and more reliable. The establishment of multiple local post offices and the expansion of postal service throughout the new nation between 1792 and 1828 facilitated the spread of stagecoach travel. The emergence of pikes, postal routes and stagecoach service created the nation's first communications network, over which the latest in news and commerce arrived with the weekly stages to nearly every community decades before the invention and widespread use of the telegraph. The conveyance took its name from the stages or distances it traveled between designated stopping places on a route.

In the early to mid-1800s, Asheville, North Carolina, became the hub of one of the most extensive stagecoach routes east of the Rocky Mountains. With partners Philip Spencer Rutledge (1816–1894) and Robert Coleman Poole (1802–1882), James M. "Valentine" Ripley (1807–1879) operated a stagecoach line for commuters and mail service between 1840 and 1865. The lines branched from Asheville through the Cumberland Gap to stations at Mount Sterling, Kentucky (245 miles); to Greeneville, Tennessee, via Warm Springs (57 miles from Asheville); to Greenville, South Carolina (61 miles from Asheville), via Hendersonville, Flat Rock and the Saluda Gap; to Salisbury (140 miles from Asheville) and points beyond. The company also ran a route through Hickory Nut Gap to Charlotte—including stops at Asheville, Rutherfordton, Shelby and Lincolnton. Rutledge, Poole and Ripley owned between fifty and sixty coaches—and employed more than one hundred men with up to four hundred horses, depending on the season. Each coach required hitches of four horses although a team of six was at times employed for steeper grades. Runs between stops many times necessitated transfers—the changing of horses. In western North Carolina's mountainous terrain, those relays were compulsory every eight to ten miles. Distances of fifty to sixty miles could be achieved on a good day.

In accordance with executive documents from the First Session of the Thirty-Sixth Congress (1859–1860) of the North Carolina House of Representatives, Rutledge, Poole and Ripley's stagecoaches departed Greenville, South Carolina, at 4:00 a.m., and arrived at Asheville, North Carolina, by 9:00 p.m., on Mondays, Wednesdays and Fridays.

Dr. Thomas Alexander Allen (1824–1914), Hendersonville's first mayor, wrote:

> *The old stage line back in 1840 was operated by the Stocktons of Maryland from Augusta, Georgia, via Greenville, South Carolina; Asheville, North*

Carolina; the Warm Springs and across Paint Mountain to Greeneville, Tennessee. Valentine Ripley bought the line that ran between Greenville, South Carolina, and Greeneville, Tennessee, in 1845 and settled in Hendersonville.

Ripley and partners sold most of their lines to John T. Poole (1810–1880) of Greenville, South Carolina, around 1855. When the railroad reached Greenville in 1855, Ripley ran daily hacks—with the exception of Sundays—between South Carolina and Greeneville, Tennessee, until 1865, when Terrell Wilkie Taylor (1826–1904) bought Poole's and Ripley's interests and continued running the stages until the Spartanburg & Asheville Railroad reached Tryon in 1877. Taylor served two terms as sheriff of Henderson County and was also a North Carolina senator.

As railroads approached nearer to Asheville, staging interests dwindled year by year. After Ripley retired, Blair & Hankins operated the lines from Greeneville to Greenville via Asheville to Morganton, to Warm Springs and to additional points for several more years. Edwin Theodore Clemmons (1826–1896) bought the line in 1871. An 1870 census lists Edwin Clemmons as a

The *Hattie Butner*, Clemmons Village Hall. *Courtesy of Clemmons Historical Society.*

stage and mail contractor, owning stage lines based in Salem and running to destinations including the towns of Clemmons, Edenton, High Point, Raleigh and Asheville, North Carolina, and Wytheville, Virginia. Edwin's great-grandfather Peter Clemmons (1749–1815), a Revolutionary War veteran, purportedly built the first bridge across the Yadkin River.

Edwin Clemmons moved to Buncombe County in the early 1870s and operated his stage line from Old Fort to Asheville. His stagecoach business continued to grow, as evidenced by his purchase orders for new coaches from the Abbot-Downing Company. He purchased his last and largest coach—a nine-passenger Concord—from Abbot-Downing in 1872. He christened this coach the *Hattie Butner* after his wife, Harriet Rebecca "Hattie" Butner Clemmons (1829–1910).[12] Clemmons sold the line to Weddin & Bradley, which continued running all the stages until 1883, when the railroad linked Asheville to Tennessee. Behind six white horses, John "Jack" Pence (circa 1832–1919) drove the *Hattie Butner* between Old Fort, Henry's Station, Ridgecrest and Asheville from 1872 to 1896. Weddin & Bradley gave up the line shortly after the Asheville & Spartanburg Railroad linked Hendersonville and Asheville.

The Ripleys

Hendersonville entrepreneur James M. "Valentine" Ripley of Rockbridge, Virginia, operated a wayfarers' inn in Hendersonville and a stagecoach line based in Asheville. From Virginia, Ripley removed to Asheville, North Carolina, in the 1830s and then to Hendersonville because of his interest in the mail route. In 1835, the business of mail contracts extending from Florida (when the state was a territory) to the upper part of South Carolina was almost entirely in Ripley's control and remained so until 1855. Ripley owned thousands of acres in the new county of Henderson, and the 1860 census recorded his having owned fifty-two slaves. He also served as justice of the peace. His prominence affected Hendersonville's early commercial development.

Ripley first married Ruth Williams Smith (1819–1858) of Asheville (daughter of James McConnell Smith) and second, Mary Ann McMahan Ewart (1828–1909) of Ireland and Columbia, South Carolina. Ripley had several children, including the public-spirited Lila Ripley Barnwell

Lila Ripley Barnwell. *Portrait by Clara Lawton Smith Childs; courtesy of Hendersonville Presbyterian Church, Sarah Brown Cannon and Gayle Hamilton Stepp.*

(1863–1961), an outspoken supporter of the suffrage movement and the protection of wildlife, a short-story writer, newspaper columnist, lecturer and poet laureate of North Carolina. She was the first president of the United Daughters of the Confederacy and a member of the DAR and the Board of Public Charities and described herself as "a Presbyterian and a

Republican." Her mother, Mary Ewart Ripley, was also a prolific writer and a contributor to leading magazines and periodicals.

Deeper research revealed another of Valentine Ripley's children, fostered out of wedlock with a slave. This was John Calhoun Markley (1848–1921), a renowned Flat Rock blacksmith. Descendants of this union claim that Ripley taught his son John the trade of blacksmithing. John married Sally (alternatively spelled Sallie) Samantha Dairty (1859–1959)—also spelled Dougherty and Doritis. Sally, a midwife, was a daughter of Soge, a Cherokee, and an African American mother, adopted by Alfred and Phyllis (also spelled Filis) Rhodes. The Markleys had fourteen children.

John Mills (1800–1842) built for Valentine Ripley the Ripley House—Hendersonville's first hotel—at the corner of Main Street and Aspen Street (today's Second Avenue West). Originally a stagecoach stop and an inn for drovers and circuit-riding attorneys to hang their hats, the building was later expanded and known by various names, including the Globe Hotel, New Globe, Imperial, Gates and the St. John. Ripley built several of the town's early commercial structures, including the Ripley/Huggins building (circa 1847) and the Ripley-Shepherd building (known variously as the "Major" Noe building/M.M. Shepherd building, circa 1847), each of the latter two standing today.

The Ripleys were among those who organized Hendersonville's First Presbyterian Church. Following the Civil War, Ripley, a secessionist and Confederate, formed a partnership with Captain Marion Columbus Toms (1843–1917) in a mercantile business. Ripley advocated for the railroad to Hendersonville, a dream he realized three months before his death.

The Ripley/Huggins building, constructed of granite, stands to this day at 101–5 South Main Street—the southwest corner of Main Street and First Avenue West in downtown Hendersonville. The two-story, coursed ashlar commercial structure is believed to be the oldest surviving building on Main Street—although it was likely completed just months before the city's second-oldest building, which was also Ripley's. The former building features a hipped roof with broad eaves. Writers of old stated that slaves hand cut the blocks for this building from Ripley's nearby granite quarry. The south lawn of the Ripley building featured a tennis court. An advertisement from 1917 lists Hendersonville Hardware Company as a tenant in the "Rock Building,"

The granite Ripley/Huggins building (*right*), downtown Hendersonville. *Photo by the author.*

with Raymond L. Edwards (1881–1944) and George Frederick Chaple (1874–1947),[13] proprietors.

Valentine Ripley had built what is noted in the National Register of Historic Places as the "Ripley-Shepherd Building" of parged brick with a hipped roof and bracketed eaves. This building stands at 218 North Main Street. Originally known as the "Ripley brick store house," it is believed to have served as a Confederate commissary under the direction of "Major" Joseph A. Noe (1798–1869). The building at one time housed a general store and post office under the tenure of James Waldrop (1876–1883). The building is remembered as Flavius Goodson Hart Sr.'s (1852–1940) Furniture & Undertaking business and the M.M. Shepherd Store.[14] Carolina Alliance Bank currently occupies the historic structure.

John Preston Arthur (1851–1916) stated in his book *Western North Carolina: A History from 1730 to 1913*, additional stage contractors included James Cornelius Hankins (1855–1922) of Greeneville, Tennessee, who operated a line from Greeneville to Warm Springs. Hankins halted this line when the railroad reached Wolf Creek in 1868. William Patterson Blair (1820–

1898) of Jonesboro, Tennessee, and Asheville, North Carolina, ran a stage line called the *French Broad* from Asheville to Greeneville, Tennessee, at the beginning of the Civil War, until Colonel George Washington Kirk (1837–1905) captured his stock and coaches. In July 1866, Colonel James Henry Rumbough of Warm Springs ran a stage line from Greeneville, Tennessee, to Greenville, South Carolina.

> *The "stands," as the stopping places were called, were breakfast at Warm Springs, dinner at Marshall, supper at Asheville.*
>
> —*John Preston Arthur*

Colonel Rumbough ran the line for about a year and a half, when Alexander Hamilton Jones (1822–1901), a Republican congressman and newspaperman, acquired the contract but failed to carry it out, and Rumbough took possession of it again.

The stage line from Morganton to the head of the railroad ran for several years before the Civil War. In 1834, William Bedford Sherrill (1810–1878) secured a four-year contract to haul the mail from Salisbury via Lincolnton and Michael Schenk's (1771–1849) cotton mill at McDaniel Springs and on to Rutherfordton and Asheville. Sherrill moved shortly afterward to Fairview. Ben Seney of Tennessee succeeded Sherrill as mail carrier on this route but did not complete his contract, having given it up before the expiration of the four-year agreement.

> *A stage and mail route from Salem to Greenville, South Carolina, passing through Morganton and Rutherfordton, allowed for four-horse coaches making two trips per week. In fact, in 1831 Rutherfordton could boast of being on six stage routes and of having a three-times-a-week mail service.*
>
> —*Ora Blackmun,* Western North Carolina: Its Mountains and Its People to 1880

Pinckney Clement Rollins (1835–1889) operated a weekly hack line, which carried the mail from Asheville to Murphy from about 1870 and shortly afterward expanded to a daily line. Rollins lost money in the deal. The stopping places were, in 1871:

> *Turnpike for dinner, Waynesville for supper, where a stop was made until the next day. Then to Webster for dinner at Josh Frank's, two miles east of Franklin, for supper and lodging. The third day took the mail through*

Franklin to Aquone for dinner at Stepp's at the bridge and to Mrs. Walker's at Old Valley Town for supper. Next day the trip progressed to Murphy for dinner and returned that night to Old Valley Town. As the railroad progressed toward Waynesville hacks ran from the various termini to that town.

—*John Preston Arthur*

From about 1840, stages and hacks ran from Salem via Wilkesboro, Jefferson, Creston through Ambrose Gap, to Taylorsville and Jonesboro, Tennessee; but these routes were withdrawn at least ten years before the Civil War, after which Captain Samuel E. Northington (1820–1884) ran a line of hacks from Jefferson to Taylorsville (now Mountain City), Tennessee. Stages ran from Lenoir via Blowing Rock, Shulls Mill and Zionville from 1852 to 1861.

The last use of stagecoaches occurred between 1890 and about 1918. Some have noted that the railroad affected the collapse of stage coaching, but it was more likely the motorbus that doomed horse-drawn transports. After the main railroad lines were established, it was frequently considered impractical to travel to loftier elevations by rail should the distances be short. By 1918, stagecoaches operated only in a few mountain resorts or through western national parks as part of the Wild West romance for tourists.

All Aboard!

Faintly…from a distance…a whistle…undulating…echoing mournfully.

Drawing closer, the pitch of it swelled, resounding off hillsides until all at once a resonance of pistons and huffing and panting and the belching of smoke ushered in an iron horse drawing a queue of Pullmans. As the clacking slackened and the beastly conveyance ground to a halt, "there'd be cinders spewing all over the place and the stench of smoke was stifling," Saluda native Tommy Thompson recalled, "and cinders in your eyes!"[15]

Silent rails above the Saluda Grade. *Photo by the author.*

By Rail

Railroads expanded rapidly in the eastern United States after 1830, when the country's first scheduled passenger service pulled out of Charleston on the nine-mile South Carolina Canal & Rail Road Company's tracks. The *Best Friend of Charleston*, a wood-burning steam locomotive, provided the motive power. As early as 1832, visionaries contemplated a rail line stretching between Spartanburg, South Carolina, and Asheville, North Carolina, along the old wilderness trail. But construction of the Spartanburg & Asheville Railroad—later known as the Asheville & Spartanburg—would not commence until many years later. (The Southern Railway Company absorbed this line on November 11, 1895.) With the sudden influx of railway traffic, farmers were obligated by law to fence their livestock to keep them off the tracks. The railroad abolished the isolation of western North Carolina, linking the region to markets and seaports, enhancing its own trade with markets beyond. Moreover, the railroad gave parentage to towns and cities and industry and tourism, which flourished alongside the ribbons of rails.

By 1835, a railroad from Cincinnati was projected to connect South Carolina seaports with the resources of North Carolina, Tennessee and the Ohio Valley. Cincinnati sent a delegation in 1836 to the Great Southwestern

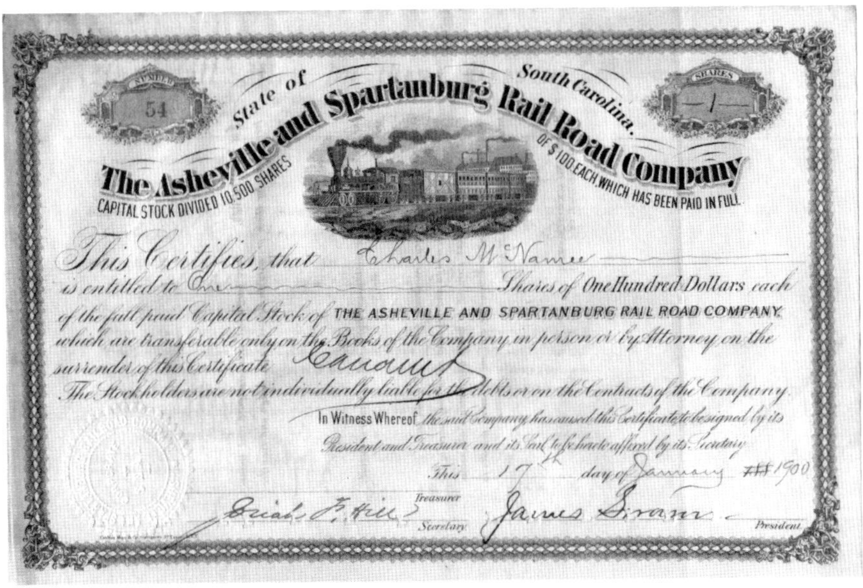

Number 54 — Shares 1

State of South Carolina.

The Asheville and Spartanburg Rail Road Company

Capital Stock divided 10,500 shares of $100 each which has been paid in full.

This Certifies, that Charles M. Namee is entitled to One Shares of One Hundred Dollars each of the full paid Capital Stock of THE ASHEVILLE AND SPARTANBURG RAIL ROAD COMPANY which are transferable only on the Books of the Company in person or by Attorney on the surrender of this Certificate.

The Stockholders are not individually liable for the debts or on the Contracts of the Company.

In Witness Whereof the said Company has caused this Certificate to be signed by its President and Treasurer and its Seal to be hereto affixed by its Secretary.

This 17th day of January 1900

Treasurer — Secretary — President

An Asheville & Spartanburg Rail Road Company stock certificate. *Arthur H. Pearsall Collection.*

Railroad Convention at St. Louis to charter the Cincinnati, Louisville & Charleston Railroad. The City of Charleston responded by forming a committee to begin a dialogue with their counterparts in Cincinnati. Members from South Carolina appointed to this committee included William Drayton (1776–1846), Judge Charles Jones Colcock (1777–1839), Joel Roberts Poinsett (1779–1852), Joseph Johnson (1776–1862) and Mitchell King. King served as chairman of the convention and was directed to appeal to the president of the United States to assign a competent engineer to make a survey of the railroad route proposed from Columbia, South Carolina, to the mouth of the Nolichucky River in Tennessee and thence a survey of the French Broad and Holston Rivers to Knoxville, Tennessee. President Andrew Jackson (1767–1845) granted this request.

Robert Young Hayne (1791–1839) of Charleston was named first president of the railroad venture. His board members included John Caldwell Calhoun (1782–1850), Robert G. Mills (1781–1855), James Hamilton Jr. (1786–1857), Charles Edmondston (1782–1861), Mitchell King, Captain Benjamin Thomas Elmore (1791–1841), Colonel Abram Blanding (1776–1839) and Dr. John Wells Simpson (1796–1881). Former South Carolina governor Robert Y. Hayne, counted among the members of the South Carolina House of Representatives (1814–1818), was Speaker of the House (1818), attorney general of South Carolina (1818–1822), U.S. senator (1823–1832) and mayor of Charleston (1835–1837). He died in Asheville, North Carolina. Mitchell King was elected president *pro tempore* and James Gadsden (1788–1858) succeeded as president of the company.

Under Hayne's term, John Charles Frémont (1813–1890), the "Pathfinder," surveyed part of a route from South Carolina to Asheville and Tennessee and the Ohio Valley. The proposed route would have passed through Sandy Plains and Columbus, around Tryon Peak and through Howard's Gap. After Hayne's death in 1839, plans were abandoned until 1850, when the North Carolina legislature granted charters to companies willing to undertake such projects. Proponents pushed for trunk lines linking the North Carolina Railroad with the Blue Ridge. Crop failure in the mountain region was said to have prompted the move, with corn in the western part of the state having tripled in cost from $0.50 cents to $1.50 per bushel while corn rotted in the fields in the eastern counties for lack of a market.

From 1850 to 1851, a sum of $12,000 was appropriated by the legislature to survey a railroad route from Salisbury to Warm Springs, North Carolina, to the Tennessee line near the French Broad River at Statesville

Zebulon Baird Vance (center, second row to the left of his wife) celebrating a Rough & Ready Guards reunion at his home in Black Mountain. *Photo by E.E. Brown, Asheville; courtesy of Arthur H. Pearsall.*

and Paint Rock. As a result, the Western North Carolina Railroad Company (WNCRC) was chartered in 1855 to build such a line, which would connect the North Carolina Railroad with the Blue Ridge Railroad and Asheville with Old Fort via the East Tennessee & Virginia Railroad. Tracks ran from Charleston to Spartanburg by 1859. Another stretch linked Salisbury and Morganton. Tennessee had built roads from Knoxville to Greeneville until the war crippled further progress. Legislation approved and ratified further surveys on February 18, 1861. James W. Wilson (1832–1910) served as chief civil engineer and president of the WNCRC.

William Bedent "Bede" Smith (1834–1928) of Buncombe County served with the Corps of Engineers that made the first survey of the railroad from Asheville to Spartanburg. Later, Smith helped to survey the first line from Morristown to Wolf Creek, Tennessee, and was working as a member of the construction force of that railroad when the Civil War began. He left to join his second cousin Zebulon Baird Vance's regiment, the "Rough and Ready Guards."

Colonel Samuel McDowell Tate (1830–1897) became president of the Western North Carolina Railroad Company in 1866, but in 1869, he absconded with $4 million in bonds, delaying construction efforts. Dr. John James Mott (1834–1919) succeeded Tate. Litigation and reorganization ensued. The American Civil War—known as the "first railroad war"—had slowed down progress again, after which the state furnished five hundred convicts to work on the line during Reconstruction. Rails reached Old Fort by 1869, and grading was completed to Asheville by 1871. By 1877, tracks had reached Tryon and by 1878, Saluda. In 1879, the same year the railroad reached Hendersonville, the Western Division was abolished and consolidated with the Eastern Division under the name Western North Carolina Railroad Company, with Colonel Thaddeus Charles Coleman (1837–1895) of Weaverville chief engineer of the company. The arduous task involved cuts and fills, culverts, tunnels and trestles with little more than picks and shovels, explosive powder and animal and manpower to conquer the epic task.

By 1886, the stretch between Hendersonville and Asheville had been completed. Laborers carted gravel on hand-propelled flatcars from Henderson County's Balfour quarry to stabilize the track beds. Teams of oxen hauled crossties and rails. Asheville would soon become the future railroad center of western North Carolina.

Iron Horses

Popular locomotives sported names such as Norris, Spitfire, Helios, Cyclops, Tempest, Tornado and Volcano, but in spite of their speedy handles, none of these machines ever achieved impressive velocity, particularly with a cortege of coaches or a drag of freight cars through the mountains' sinuous altitudes. Makers of such beasts included R. Norris & Sons of Philadelphia; Baldwin Locomotive Works of Pennsylvania; Pittsburg Locomotive Works; the Richmond & Danville Railroad's Manchester Shop at Richmond, Virginia; Rogers Locomotive & Machine Company of New Jersey; Hinkley & Drury of Boston; and Lima Locomotive Works Inc. of Ohio. Other models included Mogul, Prairie, Consolidation, Mikado, Berkshire, Decapod, Santa Fe, Texas, American, Atlantic, Ten-Wheeler, Pacific, Hudson, Mountain, Northern and Challenger.

In the News

In March 1906, the *French Broad Hustler* made reference to new construction:

> *The new railroad—a line from Greenwood, S.C., via Greenville to Knoxville, Tenn., by way of Hendersonville, then by way of Canton, N.C., to Newport, Tenn., to Knoxville and the coal fields.*

In August 1908, the *Hustler* printed under the headline "Southern Railway Whistles" the following:

> *Property owners near the depot are loud and bitter in their complaints against the Southern Railway for allowing the unnecessary blowing of engine whistles and ringing of bells at the depot. One property owner there, a former county official, declares it to be a serious nuisance and an entirely unnecessary one. He cites an instance, the other day, of an engine bell on a passenger train, which kept ringing all the time the train was at the depot.*

A further August 1908 account in the *Hustler* read:

> *Another long train this morning contained 11 coaches full of people. The cars were crowded and packed to the utmost capacity. All the excursion trains were pulled into the city with two engines, which puffed and snorted monstrously to get the heavy loads up the mountains, then being several hours behind the scheduled time.*

A January 1909 *Hustler* article reported:

> *Hundreds of excursionists came here* [Hendersonville] *last summer on tickets, which expired on September 1st. On that date owing to the heavy rains, every kind of service on all the railroads in both the Carolinas was demoralized. Bridges and trestles were undermined or washed away—in some sections ten inches of rain fell during the week—and travel was admittedly dangerous.*

By September 1909, the *Hustler* reported that Hendersonville's Columbia Park sported a "handsome new depot scheduled to open May 1st as a regular station of the Transylvania Railroad."

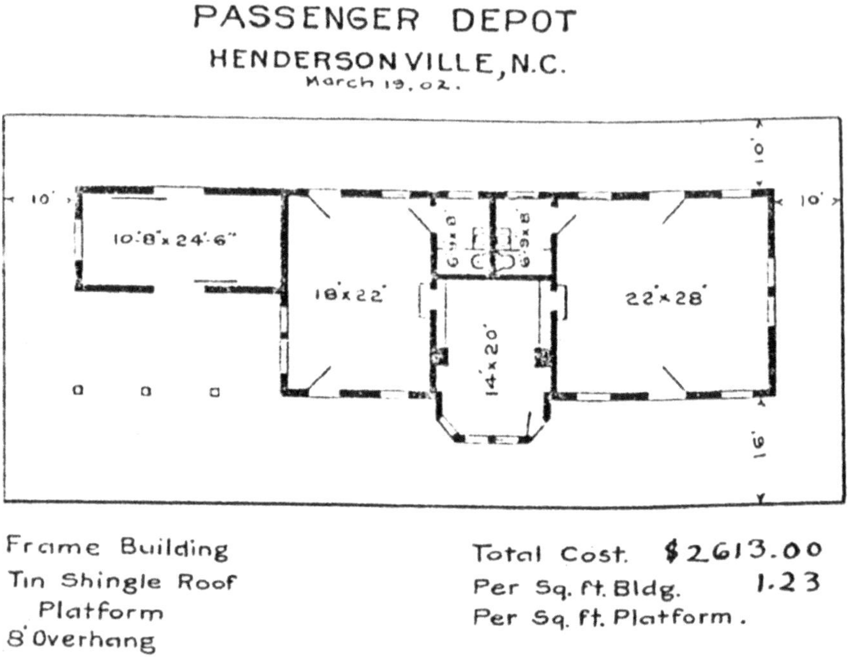

Floor plan, 1902 Southern Railway passenger station at Hendersonville. *Courtesy of Kenneth J. O'Brien.*

A March 1910 issue of the *Hustler* carried news of plans for a new road, improved depot conditions and Southern Railway's agreeing to cement part of the depot grounds.

In December 1910, the *Hustler* carried details on Southern's schedule. The No. 41 from Spartanburg and the No. 42 to Spartanburg would be replaced by the *Carolina Special*, "to be put into service January 2, 1911," with seven stops between Charleston and Cincinnati, with an excursion from Hendersonville to Cincinnati expected to take approximately fourteen hours. Samuel Henry Hardwick (1854–1918) of Montgomery, Alabama, served as passenger manager and James Hall Wood (1866–1933) of Chapel Hill and Asheville, district passenger agent of the Southern Railway.[16]

Plans were announced in March 1911 for a Highland Lake station, with six train stops per day during summers with a roundtrip fare (from the Seventh Avenue depot) of twenty cents. In April, the *Hustler* carried a news blurb about cement floors having been poured at the main depot and longer umbrella sheds added. A piece in a March 1912 *Hustler* read, "The station is still too small to accommodate all the summer tourists. Southern Railway

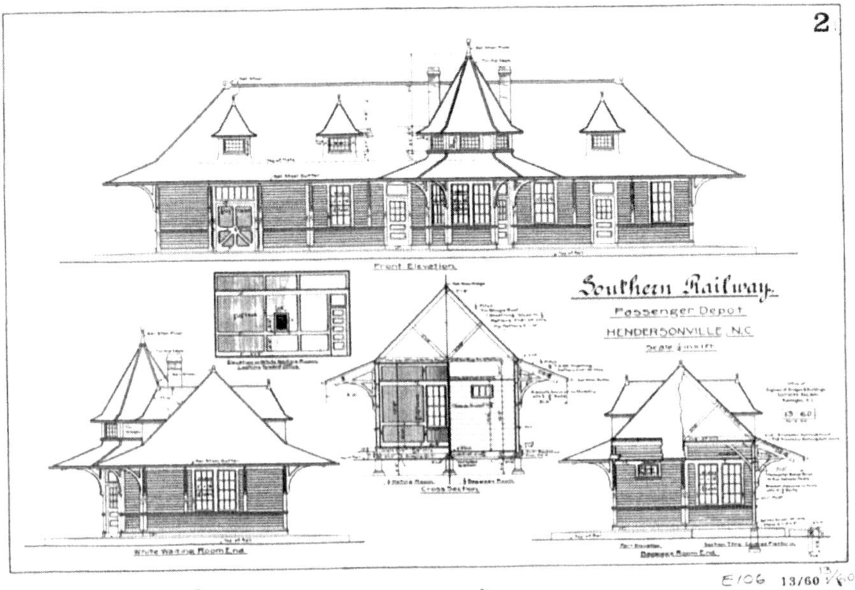

Elevation plan, 1902 Southern Railway passenger station at Hendersonville. The Victorian bay remains as it was designed, but the dormer "eyebrows" no longer grace the rooflines of the depot. *Courtesy of Kenneth J. O'Brien.*

will, in a few weeks, begin construction of a new passenger depot." The new structure, slated for completion by the end of the summer season, "with waiting rooms for both white and colored people to be twice the present size." Improvements also included additional shed space, benches, doubling the size of the baggage room and "plans to macadamize the street around the depot."

A February 1913 *Hustler* article heralded a twenty-foot signboard along the Southern Railway between Hendersonville and Flat Rock that read:

> *You Are Approaching Hendersonville, N.C., "Land of the Sky." The Natural Roof Garden of America. Business • Health • Pleasure.*[17]

August 1913 witnessed "a serious freight-train wreck—but lacking in fatalities" about three miles south of Flat Rock involving freight train No. 50 headed south with fifteen cars. The wreck held up schedules on the line the entire day. All fifteen cars left the tracks, with thirteen having turned over, some badly damaged. The stated cause: "spreading rails." The *Carolina Special* was diverted via Marion.

Wreck near Horse Shoe, July 1895. *Baker photo; courtesy of the Henderson County Genealogical and Historical Society.*

Another wreck occurred on August 12, 1914—a derailment of a Southern Railway train near Tuxedo. The fireman, Bert L. Coley (1881–1914) of Asheville, was killed and nine passengers injured; the accident was attributed to "track conditions." The train had been en route to Asheville from Savannah.

The *Hustler* ran the following information in an October 1914 issue: "Modern Passenger Depot Proposed for Hendersonville." Mentions included talks of building a new depot and converting the present one to a freight depot. Work was to begin the first of the following year, with a target completion date of June 1, but with "concern of the war stalling such building projects."

In March 1915 the *Hustler* shared:

> *Carolina Special Included in 8 All-steel Trains…57 new cars recently placed into service—all steel, electric-lighted, some of the most modern design.*

Around the same time, news stories hinted at the demise of the railroad, with such headlines as "Railroads Alarmed at Big Business of Automobiles," suggesting that privately owned machines were affecting the business of big carriers.

The Saluda Grade

In the mid-nineteenth century, Tommy Thompson's great-grandfather Francis Asbury Thompson operated a post office called Tryon and a stagecoach inn and tollgate on Howard Gap Road—years before the railroad provided a more practical and affordable means of transportation.

Shortly after the Civil War, Lieutenant Colonel Thaddeus Charles Coleman and Captain Charles William Pearson (1841–1915) surveyed Howard's Gap and Pace's Gap for Southern Railway's Spartanburg & Asheville line. As underground springs jeopardized the terrain of Howard's Gap, effecting a shifting roadbed through a proposed route flanking the Pacolet River, Coleman and Pearson selected the steeper and more treacherous, albeit stable, grade through Pace's Gap from Melrose to what would become the town of Saluda. At great expense, including bankruptcies and more than one hundred human lives, the task began in 1876. With the labor of state convicts,[18] ties were laid and rails spiked along what engineers nicknamed the "King of Hills"—the steepest mainline standard-gauge grade in the United States—from 3.7 to mostly 4.7 percent; 5.1 percent on one hundred feet of the grade—a drop of six hundred feet to the mile from Saluda to Melrose (2.7 miles). At the time, this route was considered temporary. And once the

Crest of the Saluda Grade, downtown Saluda. *Photo by the author.*

Left: Captain Charles W. Pearson. *Courtesy of Charles Pearson III.*

Below: The Helper engine and crew at Saluda. Ernest Patterson, engineer, far right. *Courtesy of Charlene Pace.*

climb to Saluda was achieved, there remained the plunge to Green River and the rise to Butte Mountain Gap (2,018 feet, the route's highest point).

With the benefit of convict chain gangs and oxen, the railway was completed in 1878, and on July 4 at 11:00 a.m., the first train chugged up the nearly three-mile grade from Melrose to Pace's Gap. A year later, the line would reach Hendersonville. And two years after that, Saluda would be chartered as a town.

A northbound train required a pusher engine—what locals called the "Helper"—a locomotive built for traction versus speed, with larger cylinders and ten small driving wheels. The Helper propelled the last car of a train as it lurched from Melrose to Saluda. For longer queues, cars would be disconnected and pushed up the grade in sections. Nevertheless, trains experienced wrecks and runaways, plus the perils of traversing fifty hairpin turns, among them Slaughterhouse Pen Cut—a ten-degree curve—and Big Cut.

Officials warned engineers to not exceed eight miles per hour while making descents from Saluda to Melrose. Witnesses describing the process mentioned "ear piercing metal-against-metal squealing" and "brakes wreathed in smoke."

Workin' on the Railroad

Ultimately, eight trains passed through Saluda daily—six of them *Carolina Special* runs between Charleston and Cincinnati with whistle stops at Columbia, Spartanburg, Landrum, Tryon, Saluda, Flat Rock,[19] Hendersonville and Asheville. In 1911, the *Carolina Special* from Charleston to Hendersonville made the run in eight and one-half hours.

Traveling from Charleston to Union Station, South Carolina, the *Special* stopped at Landrum, Spartanburg and Tryon and then at the switching and staging system at Melrose for assistance from the Helper up to Saluda, where cars would be reattached for the continued journey to Hendersonville and Asheville and beyond.

One could say Saluda grew up around the depot, for rails brought visitors and summer residents, creating a need for inns and services. More than that, the railroad directly provided jobs for dozens of townsfolk: switch tenders with three shifts a day (four men each, plus standbys), firemen, spur-track operators (to circumvent runaways), section foremen, coaling and water-station operators, signalmen, station personnel (agents, telegraph operators, clerks), general work crews and maintenance staff, hoteliers, merchants and farmers. The Asheville & Spartanburg provided telegraph service with 47.67 miles of telegraph line installed from Spartanburg to Hendersonville by 1879 and 19.8 miles from Hendersonville to Biltmore seven years later.[20]

The Fall of Saluda's Railroad Heyday

Enter the Great Depression—along with the growing popularity of automobiles—and railway passengers diminished in number. Many of Saluda's hotels and boardinghouses faced financial ruin, and the town experienced a major slump. Following World War II, most railroad lines switched from locomotives to diesel engines—and from whistles and bells to the plaintive strains of horns.

Passenger rail service through Saluda ended in December 1968. In 1983, the town's vintage "Stick-style" depot was relocated 0.2 miles down the street and later restored. Norfolk Southern closed the line through Saluda altogether during the winter of 2001–2.

Across the street from and perpendicular to the now-quiet tracks, browsers find the relocated depot (now a museum) and its neighboring Summer House (a former service station currently housing shops).

> *The train stops in Saluda for five minutes to build air pressure for the brake system and the trainmen run across Main Street to the M.A. Pace Store and grab a soft drink. Two toots on the whistle and they come running, climb aboard and the Special continues on its way to Melrose down the mountain.*
>
> —Western Carolina Tribune, *November 22, 1968*

Childhood Memories

Horace Pace (1925–2013) vividly recalled the days when passenger and freight trains augmented Saluda's scenery. Son of Ransom Taylor "Bud" Pace (1858–1939) and twenty-sixth of twenty-nine children, Horace learned how to make his own amusements. As a youngster, he and his friends gathered up stray chunks of coal between the outskirts of Saluda and Melrose, then sold their boodle to residents for heating their homes. Pace shared:

> *Sometimes, we'd go down to the grease pit and find an old oilcan.*[21] *We'd pour the leftover oil on the tracks and hide behind the bushes, thinking we'd*

enjoy watching the train slip and slide as it inched its way up the grade. But I always got scared, especially when those wheels spun a good bit—that is, until the engineer dumped sand onto the tracks. This helped him regain traction.

Tracking Celebrities

Its remoteness did not shield Saluda from speculators, settlers and public figures. Since the town's railroad days, many have discovered its virtues. The social set vacationed there, and others made Saluda a part-time or full-time home.

Around the turn of the twentieth century, townsfolk thronged the depot to see if they might spot any celebrities debarking the train. Among the first notables to visit Saluda were writers F. Scott (1896–1940) and Zelda Sayre Fitzgerald (1900–1948), Ernest Hemingway (1899–1961) and Sidney Lanier (1842–1881); Lady Astor (Nancy Witcher Langhorne Astor, 1879–1964); William Gillette (1853–1937); and David Niven (1910–1983). Renowned journalist and women's rights pioneer Dorothy Dix (alias of Elizabeth Meriwether Gilmer, 1861–1951) was a regular guest of Saluda's Ivy Terrace Inn. Old-timers remember glimpsing First Lady Grace Coolidge (1879–1957) as she rode through town in a chauffeur-driven open touring car. And, on one occasion Franklin Delano Roosevelt (1882–1945) passed through Saluda from Warm Springs, Georgia, on his return to Washington, D.C.

Saluda Mountain

The big lie exposed: Contrary to years of talk and publication, there is no "Saluda Mountain" as such. There's the city and that's it. For years Southern Railway carried the steep incline on its books as "Saluda Hill," and then, for reasons unknown, began calling it "Saluda Mountain." No peak, no range, no terrain is officially named Saluda. Regardless, it is still America's steepest Class I Grade.

—From "Where Is Saluda Mountain?" by Larry H. Smith, 1989

The Hendersonville Depot

The restored Hendersonville depot sports "Mission" or "Stick-style" architecture in the midst of brick paving and thoughtful landscaping. In 1986, Norfolk Southern Corporation announced plans to donate the structure to the City of Hendersonville and lease the land beneath it to the city. Lovingly restored (beginning in 1991 and again in 2005), the approximately 2,830-square-foot structure now houses railroading memorabilia and the Apple Valley Model Railroad Club's HO-gauge model displays, featuring local and regional railroad history. This structure, built in 1902, was upgraded and appended in 1912.

Buffs fondly recall the "romance" of trains: powerful locomotives pulling into stations under wreathes of smoke, drawing fancy Pullman coaches and dining and observation cars staffed with conductors and passengers nattily dressed. Townsfolk would gather prior to arrival times, hopeful of spotting politicians or celebrated authors or even movie personalities.

Less glamorous aspects of the events would have included live cinders, which on occasion singed onlookers, set a rooftop ablaze or ignited an inferno in a field or woodland.

The Hendersonville Southern Railway Station. *Photo by the author.*

Early-twentieth-century lamentations and news updates in the *French Broad Hustler* decried the deplorable conditions of the depot that preceded upgrades and improved construction and enlargement. Descriptions criticized its confined space, "about the size of a boxcar." Its earthen floor oozed with mud during rainy periods, resembling a "hog-wallow." Ticket windows were segregated, as were waiting areas and restroom facilities. Animal and human excrement defiled its environs. Other reports of early depots in western North Carolina describe them as having been retired boxcars with the trucks removed and furnished with a makeshift counter and a few benches, with no running water or heat.

> *Conditions at Southern Depot Are Almost Intolerably Bad!*
>
> *Conditions at the Southern Railway's alleged depot here are everything they should not be. The little structure about the size of a boxcar is dirty, cold, repulsive.*
>
> *The sanitary conditions have been disgraceful, but through the efforts of Station Agent Bailey* [Joseph William Bailey (1868–1942)] *these conditions are now being corrected. Two new toilet rooms are being added and the old ones repaired.*
>
> *The railway company pays a woman eight dollars per month to take care of the building. The grounds surrounding the structure are even worse than the building. It is impossible to get from the steps of the hotel buses or carriages without wading ankle-deep through mud and water. In the good old summertime the dust is as bad.*
>
> *Architects should be busy drawing plans for a new building—a building more in keeping with the importance of this beautiful town of over 6,000 people, with a summer population of no less than 12,000.*
>
> *With the planting of trees, shrubbery and flowers about the depot the place could be transformed from the very acme of ugliness to a place of beauty, giving incoming tourists a fair impression of a fair town.*
>
> *And to this end, the town of Hendersonville and the Southern Railway, might we cooperate?*
>
> —French Broad Hustler, *January 1910*

Norfolk Southern

The Norfolk & Southern's predecessor, the Richmond & Danville (1847), became a major portion of Southern Railway by 1894. The original railway

A Richmond & Danville locomotive and tender at Saluda. *Courtesy of Charlene Pace.*

ran from Norfolk, Virginia, to Charlotte, North Carolina, with various branches—Aberdeen, Asheboro, Beaufort, Belhaven, Carthage, Columbia, Durham, Ellerbe, Fayetteville, Goldsboro (Atlantic & East Carolina Railway/A&EC), Jackson Springs, Lee Creek, Oriental, Snow Hill (A&EC), Suffolk and Virginia Beach, Virginia. Norfolk & Southern merged into the Southern Railway system on January 1, 1974. Norfolk Southern Corporation, with headquarters in Norfolk, Virginia, currently owns the company.

Founded in 1894 as Southern Railway (headquartered in Washington, D.C.), officials renamed it Norfolk Southern in 1990. In 1982, the railroad and its rival Norfolk & Western merged and created the Norfolk Southern Corporation holding company. In 1982, Norfolk Southern absorbed Norfolk & Western and several other railways, but Norfolk & Western continued paper operations until it was merged into Norfolk Southern in 1997. In 1999, Norfolk Southern acquired over half of Conrail (Consolidated Rail Corporation).

The Railroad to Prosperity

With tracks crisscrossing the western Carolinas, the region boomed as a lumber and agricultural center, milling hub and tourist destination. Livestock and products—particularly tobacco—were more quickly shipped at lower costs from freight depots to eager markets beyond, as were textiles and bricks and other manufactured products.

A Southern Railway System ad for its container cars in a November 1968 issue of the *Western Carolina Tribune* read:

> *Innovations that squeeze the waste out of distribution.*

Whistle Stops in Henderson and Transylvania Counties

Depots besides the main Southern Railway station at Hendersonville and infill depots included East Flat Rock, Laurel Park, Highland Lake, Tuxedo and Zirconia.

The Mullin-Kille & Times-News 1969 *Hendersonville City Directory* stated under "Railroads":

Toxaway Inn depot. *Courtesy of the Rowell Bosse North Carolina Room, Transylvania County Library.*

> *Main line Southern Railway, Cincinnati to Charleston, S.C. Terminus, Hendersonville-Toxaway Division (Southern Railway).*

A 1912 Southern Railway timetable listed stops at:

> *Asheville, Biltmore, Buena Vista, Busbee, Skyland, Arden, Fletchers* [sic], *Hillgirt, Balfour, Hendersonville, Yale, Horse Shoe, Cannon, Etowah, Blantyre, Penrose, Davidson River, Pisgah Forest, Brevard, Selica, Cherryfield, Calvert, Rosman, Quebec and Lake Toxaway—with flag stops at West Hendersonville, Davis, Galloways* [sic] *and Reids* [sic].

Many of the flag stops provided only a waiting shed, versus a depot.

Interurban Railway

An August 1905 issue of the *French Broad Hustler* reported that stockholders of the proposed Appalachian & Interurban Railroad Company had selected W.A. Smith, Esq., as president. Work for such a railway was "under contemplation." Dr. Morse of Chimney Rock was "advised to assist" the executive committees to select competent engineers to survey a route from Hendersonville to Chimney Rock.

A final survey for an "electric road" from Asheville to Hendersonville was made by March 1908, a line that "largely parallels the Southern Railway but is a considerable distance from it." A *Hustler* snippet in 1911 stated that company officials were "still surveying and discussing."

An article in December 1912 referenced C.A. Carlson's "intention to build next year [1913] an interurban line between here [Hendersonville] and Asheville…would entail agreement from townships and property owners and an outlay of at least $300,000." In July 1913, the *Hustler* followed up:

> *To Build Interurban Road from Rutherford Here…delayed due to a lawsuit between the Blue Ridge Interurban Railway Co. and the Hendersonville Light and Power Co.*

In 1917, Henderson County commissioners met to consider a railroad from Hendersonville to Riverview, South Carolina (approximately 114 miles), where the line would connect with the Greenville & Western. The commissioners proposed the name "Henderson County Interurban

Railway Company" and discussed a bond issue and stock subscription. In 1930, commissioners of Buncombe, Henderson, Polk, Transylvania and Rutherford Counties met to consider extending the Seaboard Railway into western North Carolina. None of these notions ever came to fruition.

End of an Era

Western North Carolina saw the last run of the *Carolina Special* in October 1962 and the last passenger train of any kind in December 1968. A headline in the *Hendersonville Times-News* of December 5, 1968, read, "Last Passenger Train Passes Through Hendersonville." This was the No. 28, a diesel engine, one coach and one baggage car with a five-man crew and five passengers aboard when it arrived. Only two passengers boarded at Hendersonville. According to *Times-News* editor Mead Parce, "Southern lost an average of $500,000 annually operating the *Carolina Special*."

The last run of passenger train service through Hendersonville. Pictured here are John Dills (left) and Mead Parce of the *Hendersonville Times-News*. *Photo by Buddy Chapman.*

> *The only remaining passenger train, usually a three-car "mini-train," now running between Asheville and Spartanburg, will be abandoned for lack of patronage by Public Service Commission grant on December 8, 1968, its last run, if true the passing of a nostalgic era in Western North Carolina.*
> —Western Carolina Tribune, *November 22, 1968*[22]

Since the late twentieth century, no passenger rail service has been available in western North Carolina, although Amtrak services the central state.[23] In Henderson County, freight lines are minimal, with none of them running south of the Kimberly-Clark mill at Balfour. Watco Companies LLC, the parent company of Blue Ridge Southern Railroad and headquartered in Pittsburg, Kansas, maintains a small office in Arden, North Carolina. In 2014, the company purchased 91.8 miles of tracks consisting of branch lines that feed into Norfolk Southern's terminal at Asheville, including a line between Asheville and Murphy (Canton Line), a trunk from Asheville to East Flat Rock and one from Hendersonville to Brevard.

Railroading Timeline

Experimental trains, including horse-drawn, wooden and gravity railroads, came to pass from the early 1700s in northern states, leading up to the Leiper Railroad (Delaware County, Pennsylvania, 1810) and the New Jersey Railroad Company, the first chartered railroad in the United States (1815). Although chartered, the latter failed to attract investors and was never built. The earliest railroad charters to be fleshed out included the Mohawk & Hudson (New York, 1826), the Union Canal Company of Pennsylvania (1826) and the South Carolina Canal & Rail Road Company (1827). The first nine miles of tracks in North Carolina would be laid by 1831 and burgeoned in the antebellum period.

1776	North Carolina becomes a state.
1827	South Carolina Canal & Rail Road Company (SCC&RRC) chartered in December.
1830	On Christmas Day, the SCC&RRC inaugurates scheduled passenger service in Charleston.
1831	Petersburg (Virginia) Railroad chartered. Completed by 1833, including nine miles of North Carolina track near Halifax.

1832	Meetings held at Asheville to promote a railroad line following the route of the French Broad River into western North Carolina.
1833	The SCC&RRC completes its line from Charleston to Hamburg, South Carolina, in October. At the time, it boasted the longest continuous line of railroad in the world. North Carolina constructs an experimental railroad less than two miles from the state capitol to a rock quarry east of Raleigh with draft animals conveying the cars. (This was the harbinger of the mighty network of railroads that followed.) The Wilmington & Raleigh receives first charter (amended 1835 to change its terminus to Weldon) of a railroad to operate in North Carolina.
1835	Raleigh & Gaston Railroad chartered.
1836	Railroad Convention held at Knoxville, Tennessee, to discuss and authorize a Cincinnati-to-Carolina route. Construction of the Wilmington & Raleigh road begins (completed in 1840) with nine miles of tracks into North Carolina. The road hooks up with the Richmond & Petersburg and becomes a railroad hub for eastern North Carolina.
1837	Organization of the Louisville, Cincinnati & Charleston Railroad at Knoxville in January. Robert Young Hayne is elected president of the company. The Panic of 1837 affects industry, including the building of railroads, through the mid-1840s.
1839	Robert Young Hayne dies on September 24 at a stockholders' meeting at the Eagle Hotel in Asheville. James Gadsden succeeds him as president of the railroad company.
1840	Raleigh & Gaston Railroad opens its full route in April, with a locomotive-powered train. Wilmington & Raleigh completes connections between Wilmington and Weldon and becomes the longest railroad in the world at 161.5 miles.
1847	Richmond & Danville Railroad (R&D) chartered. Polk County carved out of Henderson and Rutherford Counties. (Repealed in 1849 by the North Carolina General Assembly but re-created in 1855.)

1849	The North Carolina state legislature approves creation of the North Carolina Railroad for a line to run from Goldsboro through Raleigh and Salisbury to Charlotte, connecting with the South Carolina rail system at Charlotte.
1850s	Trains begin converting from wood to coal fuel.
1852	Western North Carolina Railroad Company (WNCRC) chartered. Incorporated in 1855 for the purpose of linking Fayetteville with the coal regions of Chatham (now Moore) County, North Carolina. Charles Beatty Mallett (1816–1872) of Fayetteville serves as second president (1855–1868) of the company. (This line would consolidate with the Mount Airy Railroad Company in 1879 to form the Cape Fear & Yadkin Valley Railway Company.) Work begins on the North Carolina Railroad Company line.
1855	WNCRC incorporates with a capital stock of $3 million for the purpose of tying in with the North Carolina Railroad at Salisbury. A charter is issued to the French Broad Company (subsequently leased after 1879 to the R&D, which would be acquired by the Southern Railway system). The Wilmington & Raleigh incorporates, officially changing its name to Wilmington & Weldon. Capitalists envision a "Greenville and French Broad Railroad," which is never chartered, likely due to the forthcoming Civil War.

Western North Carolina Railroad Company bank notes. *Arthur H. Pearsall collection.*

1856	The North Carolina Railroad joins with the Wilmington & Weldon line and on to Virginia railroads—a 223-mile route. R&D opens a 140-mile line between the cities of Richmond and Danville.
1858	WNCRC completes an eighty-four-mile line between Salisbury from within four miles of Morganton.
1859	The French Broad Railroad from Charleston reaches Spartanburg, South Carolina, with Henderson County's Balis McKendrick Edney (1811–1865), a North Carolina senator, on hand as principal orator for the celebration.
1861–1865	American Civil War: The Union's blockade of the Atlantic shuts off the supply of iron from England to the Southern states. Union troops sabotage Southern rails by prying up and heating them until they could bend. Union soldiers burn bridges, destroy water tanks and tunnels and capture railroad equipment. The Wilmington & Weldon is known as the "lifeline of the Confederacy."
1863	The Pacific Railway Act specifies a federally funded transcontinental railroad to use standard-gauge tracks.[24]
1865	Lieutenant Colonel Thaddeus C. Coleman and Captain Charles W. Pearson, civil engineers, scout the Pace's Gap region (Polk County) for a railroad route to link Spartanburg and Asheville.
1865–1877	The Reconstruction era includes restoration of railroad infrastructure in the South.
1868	Thaddeus C. Coleman becomes assistant engineer for WNCRC's Blue Ridge section.
1870	The Western North Carolina Railroad (WNCR) reaches Marion, North Carolina.
1871	WNCR completes the line from Asheville to the North Carolina–Tennessee line. The R&D leases the North Carolina Railroad.
1872	R&D extends aid to the Atlanta & Richmond Air-Line Railway to complete its road between Charlotte and Atlanta. This line will become a key link in the Piedmont Air-Line.

1873	Incorporation of the Spartanburg & Asheville Company by South Carolina and of the Spartanburg & Asheville Company No. 2 by North Carolina. Christopher Gustavus Memminger (1803–1888) elected president of the company. Ground broken in Polk County for the railroad. When completed the rails will join the WNCR to Tennessee and the Ohio Valley.
1874	Thaddeus C. Coleman chosen chief engineer of the Spartanburg & Asheville line. Coleman advises a longer route around Tryon Mountain but a shortage of funds and unstable geography leads to the steeper grade over "Saluda Mountain."
1875	The State of North Carolina purchases the WNCR.
1876–1877	Workers begin the arduous task of building a railroad route up the Saluda Grade. "Colonel"Andrew Tanner (1820–1898) of Rutherford County,[25] a contractor for the Asheville & Spartanburg, buys land in Pace's Gap and builds Mountain House, the town's first hotel, and supervises convict labor on the railroad.
1877	The Spartanburg & Asheville reaches Landrum's Station (present town of Landrum, Spartanburg County, South Carolina) and Tryon City (today's Tryon, Polk County, North Carolina) as its farthest points west. WNCR completes its line from Morganton to Old Fort.

Downtown Tryon. *Photo by the author.*

Western North Carolina Railroad/Henry's Station as seen from Sprague's Hotel.
Author's collection; stereopticon photograph by Taylor & Jones, Asheville, North Carolina.

1878 On July 4, the first train travels from Melrose to Pace's Gap (Saluda). Only two houses stand within what would become the corporate limits of Saluda. John B. Turner (1834–1923) becomes first postmaster of Pace's Gap. The "post office" occupies a space on the counter of a commissary store. Turner also operates Turner's Shoal Mill, a gristmill near the Rutherford County line on a shoal of the Green River.

1879 On March 11 the 1,832-foot Swannanoa Tunnel is completed, much of it through solid rock with labor provided by convicts. The other tunnels on the route between Salisbury and Asheville: Jarrett's (125 feet), McElroy (89 feet), Licklog (562 feet), Burgin (252 feet) and High Ridge (451 feet). Convicts dig the Point Tunnel (216 feet) over Mill Creek between Old Fort and Henry's Station. Each tunnel is 15 feet tall. During construction, at least eight laborers die due to landslides, cave-ins and blasting accidents. The Spartanburg & Asheville reaches Hendersonville on June 21, with a celebratory arrival from Spartanburg on July 4. The fanfare includes cannon fire, three thousand cheering spectators, a band, color guard and parade, dignitaries, speeches and a barbecue.

The depot at Old Fort. *Photo by the author.*

1880	The line from Old Fort to Asheville completed. More than 90 percent of all locomotives have converted from wood to coal fuel. The Pennsylvania Railroad sells the R&D to the Clyde Syndicate. The WNCR reaches Grey Eagle (Black Mountain).
1881	Pace's Gap chartered as the town of Saluda. Andrew Tanner elected first mayor. R&D acquires the WNCR. Spartanburg & Asheville sells under foreclosure and reorganizes and incorporates as the Asheville & Spartanburg, managed by the R&D. Jonathan L. Williams (1847–1911) serves as first Hendersonville agent for the company.
1882	The line from Asheville to Paint Rock and the town of Pigeon River (renamed Pigeon Ford, Buford and then Canton) completed. The railroad reaches Marshall, Cranberry, Sylva and Linville. The French Broad Valley Railroad Company forms.
1883	Tracks reach Dillsboro and the "Frog Level" district of Waynesville.
1884	The railroad reaches Bryson City.

A Great Smoky Mountains Railroad excursion departs Dillsboro for Bryson City. *Photo by the author.*

1885	Asheville & Spartanburg joins track with WNCR at Sweeten Creek and the Swannanoa River in December.
1886	Rails link Hendersonville to Asheville. The Charleston, Cincinnati & Chicago Railroad reaches Rutherfordton and Bostic. Southern railroad companies agree to coordinate changing the gauge on all their tracks from five feet to four feet, eight and one-half inches. By June, all major railroads in North America use approximately the same gauge.
1887	The Palmetto Railroad completed between Hamlet, North Carolina, and Cheraw, South Carolina. Saluda considered the best-paying station on the Asheville & Spartanburg line. The railroad reaches Spindale and Burnt Chimney (Forest City).
1889	Tracks reach Andrews, North Carolina.
1891	Hendersonville and Brevard Railway, Telegraph & Telephone Company (H&BRT&T) chartered. The R&D reaches Murphy, making a connection to the copper mines at Ducktown, Tennessee.
1892	R&D placed in receivership.

1894	First line on the North Carolina Railroad line leased to R&D. After reorganization by John Pierpont Morgan (1837–1913), the R&D and the East Tennessee, Virginia & Georgia Railroad emerge as the Southern Railway System, chartered on August 22. Southern buys WNCR at auction.
1895	Southern Railway Company (SR) acquires a ninety-nine-year lease on the Piedmont section of the North Carolina Railroad (eastern routes fall to the Atlantic Coast Line and the Seaboard Air-Line Railway). SR absorbs Asheville & Spartanburg on November 11. The railroad reaches Brevard.
1896–1897	R&D sold and conveyed to the new Southern Railway Company.
1898	Spanish-American War, April 25–August 12.
1899	Transylvania Railroad Company (Hendersonville, North Carolina) forms out of the Hendersonville & Brevard Railway.
1900	The Carolina, Clinchfield & Ohio (CC&O) reaches Huntdale.
1902	Asheville & Spartanburg is one of thirty-six corporate entities consolidated as the Southern-Carolina Division. Hendersonville's passenger depot dismantled, moved to the north side of Seventh Avenue and repurposed as a freight depot. A new passenger depot (twenty-two by eighty-seven feet) built at a cost of $2,613.
1904	SR reaches Spruce Pine. A runaway system with safety-track switches is completed on the Saluda Grade.
1906	SR acquires the Transylvania Railroad. The Hendersonville passenger depot adds fifteen feet to its north end and begins construction of a covered passenger pavilion (twenty-five feet, six inches long).
1907	CC&O reaches Spruce Pine. The Southern reaches Franklin.
1908	CC&O tracks completed to Marion. The company later extends a line from Marion to Bostic and on to Spartanburg. The line links remote mountain towns, including Spruce Pine and Linville, to the outside world. Building the CC&O entails the excavation of fifty-five tunnels and eighteen thousand pounds of nitroglycerine mash. Altapass, located in the northern tip of McDowell County, is so named because at over 2,600 feet it stands at the highest point on the CC&O Railroad.[26]

Pullman artifacts: china plate, drinking glass, soap dish, conductor's ticket punch, linen towel and ticket. *Photo by the author; courtesy of the Apple Valley Model Railroad Club and the Henderson County Heritage Museum.*

1911	The *Carolina Special* begins service from Charleston to Cincinnati.
1912	A roundtrip railway fare from Washington, D.C., to Hendersonville, North Carolina: fourteen dollars.
1914	SR sells fifty thousand tickets to Hendersonville during the summer season.
1914–19	United States involved in World War I.
1915	The railroad reaches Hayesville.
1916	An addition extends the south end of the Hendersonville depot and the pavilion is extended as well.
1925	The railroad reaches Robbinsville.
1929–39	The Depression-era economy (following the stock market crash of October 24, 1929) takes a toll on formerly booming railroad towns.
1940s	Heyday of the railroad.
1941–45	The United States is involved in World War II.

1950s	Diesel-electric railcars mostly replace motive power by steam. SR becomes the first major railroad in the United States to convert entirely to diesel-powered locomotives.
1967	The Seaboard Air-Line and Atlantic Coast Line merge on July 1.
1968	Last passenger run conducted through Spartanburg, Saluda and Hendersonville on December 5, by engineman William Franklin "Frank" Clodfelter (1911–1984). Freight service continues.
1970	President Richard M. Nixon signs the Rail Passenger Service Act.
1971	Twenty railroads opt to participate in the formation of Amtrak.
1974	SR acquires the former Norfolk Southern Railway Company, Norfolk-Charlotte.
1975	Final passenger run of SR through McDowell County over the Mountain Division to Biltmore. Final passenger service through Black Mountain.
1982	The holding company Norfolk Southern Corporation created in the merger of Norfolk & Western and Southern.

Working on the railroad in Transylvania County. Thomas T. Hamilton (1896–1974), far right. *Courtesy of Gayle Hamilton Stepp.*

1990	Amtrak initiates the *Carolinian* (New York to Charlotte).
1995	North Carolina inaugurates the state-supported *Piedmont* service.
2001	Norfolk Southern closes its freight line through Saluda.
2009	A steering committee hatches the notion of the Ecusta Trail, a "rail-to-trail" project on the twenty-mile span of the abandoned Watco (formerly Norfolk Southern Railroad and H&BRT&T) line between Brevard and Hendersonville, passing through Pisgah Forest, Etowah, Horse Shoe and Laurel Park.

Toxaway Railroad

Henderson County venture capitalists organized the French Broad Valley Railroad Company in 1882 to build a railway between Brevard and Hendersonville. Fleming Ramseur (1871–1928) first surveyed the route;

The Brevard passenger depot. *Courtesy of the Rowell Bosse North Carolina Room, Transylvania County Library.*

Thomas Chalmers McNeely (1860–1911) next surveyed it. Shortly after construction, the work stopped.

By the early 1890s, McNeely removed to Hendersonville and enlisted the services of civil engineer Thomas Steptoe Boswell (1850–1934). The partners acquired the assets of the French Broad Valley Railroad Company, which had established its first track from Charleston to Spartanburg in 1859. With the acquisition, McNeely and Boswell organized a company to supply a railroad connecting Brevard and Hendersonville. Chartered in 1891 and mostly completed by 1894, this route became known as the Hendersonville and Brevard Railway, Telegraph & Telephone Company (H&BRT&T). Boswell surveyed the grade between Brevard and Hendersonville; after this, construction on the road progressed rapidly, and by midsummer 1895, rails had nearly reached Brevard, opening Transylvania County's abundant forest resources to increased tourism, recreation and industrialism. The company acquired a small American 4-4-0 locomotive to haul construction supplies.

The Brevard line operated independently, after which it went into receivership (December 26, 1896). In 1897, capitalist John Francis Hays (1862–1921) acquired the railroad at auction and reorganized the company as the Transylvania Railroad (chartered 1899). Hays served as general manager of the venture and T.S. Boswell, superintendent. Hays, of New Castle, Pennsylvania, had settled in the area in 1890 for health reasons. In 1898, Hays and his brother-in-law Edwin Clarence Wilson (1856–1903) organized the Transylvania Turnpike Company to construct a road from Brevard to the town of Sapphire. A twenty-mile stretch from Fairfield to Rosman was completed by 1899. Wilson served as resident manager and headed the Brevard Lumber Company.

Of the Jackson County resort area of Sapphire, Arthur Middleton "Chucky Joe" Huger (1842–1925) wrote in *The Overhills of Ottaray*:

> *Of the many healthful, picturesque and altogether delightful districts included in this region none is more attractive than the Sapphire Country, an American lake region that has been compared to the famed English Lake district, which Wordsworth loved and of which he sung.*

Hays led the development of the "Sapphire Country" in Hogback Valley, Jackson County, which became the upscale mountain retreat of Lake Toxaway. With his Toxaway Company, Hays developed lakes, a campground and hotels—including the Fairfield Inn at Fairfield Lake, the Toxaway Inn at Lake Toxaway, the Sapphire Inn at Lake Sapphire and the Franklin Hotel in

Once a popular tourist destination, the Toxaway Inn was damaged by the 1916 flood and sat vacant until 1947, when it was razed. *C.H. Oak Collection; courtesy of the Henderson County Genealogical and Historical Society.*

Brevard. Hays's company also owned the Lodge on Mount Toxaway. Hays paid to install waterlines at Brevard. His Toxaway Company also mined corundum, copper and gold in Jackson County.

Middleton Huger wrote:

> *Lakes Toxaway, Fairfield and Sapphire are the finest sheets of water in this region and Mt. Toxaway is the best viewpoint in this scenic paradise. From its summit the spectator can take in the whole of the Piedmont plateau, while in the distance stand the rugged, picturesque outlines of the Smoky Mountains of Tennessee. More than a hundred peaks are visible from Toxaway, among them Mt. Mitchell, Mt. Pisgah, Old Whiteside, Rabun and many others.*

Once recuperated from the tuberculosis that brought him to North Carolina, Hays dug in as a visionary-entrepreneur. Working with capitalists in Pittsburgh, Hays convinced William Plumer Potter (1857–1918) to fund his railroad venture, of which Potter served as president, according to *Railroad Age*, vol. 27. (Potter was a justice of the supreme court of Pennsylvania.) The syndicate bought the H&BRT&T Company with all its rights and improved and renewed it as the Transylvania Railroad Company. Hays managed the operation, and Andrew Knox Orr (1867–1937) filled the roles of secretary

The Toxaway City (Rosman) depot. *Courtesy of the Rowell Bosse North Carolina Room, Transylvania County Library.*

and treasurer. As general manager, Hays oversaw construction of rail extensions between Brevard and what is now Rosman.

Formed in 1895 (and its title granted on January 4, 1896), the Toxaway Company controlled the line. The 1898 sale included 21.6 miles of track, plus all bridges, trestles and buildings and an inventory of two locomotives and tenders, one first-class passenger car, one combination passenger-and-baggage car, three boxcars, one flatcar and two handcars; all furnishings, furniture and equipment in the buildings; and the H&BRT&T Company. In 1900, Hays expanded the line about ten miles from Brevard to Toxaway City (known at times as Old Toxaway and Estatoe Ford, and renamed Rosman in 1905) and another ten miles to Lake Toxaway in Jackson County. The company added another locomotive and passenger car to its inventory.

By 1904, stations along the line from West Hendersonville to Lake Toxaway included Hendersonville, Yale, Horse Shoe, Cannon, Etowah, Blantyre, Penrose, Davidson River, Pisgah Forest, Brevard, Selica, Cherryfield, Calvert, Rosman, Quebec and Lake Toxaway. Five flag stops dotted the

Trestle at Etowah. *Photo by the author.*

route: West Hendersonville and Davis (Laurel Park) between Hendersonville and Etowah; Fodder Stack between Etowah and Penrose; and Galloways [*sic*] and Reids [*sic*] between Brevard and Lake Toxaway. (Flag stops were points—many times simply a sheltered bench—where a train would stop only if a passenger had raised a flag to let the engineer know they were waiting to board.)

On May 29, 1903, the Southern Railway purchased 249 shares of the Transylvania Railroad Company, gaining controlling interest. By 1906, the Toxaway Company had begun to fail, and it soon dissolved, at which time Southern Railway absorbed the Transylvania lines. Hays did not live to realize his vision to continue a line to Seneca, South Carolina.

According to Laurel Park commissioner and historian A. Paul Hansen:

> *The Toxaway Company operated a rail system on twenty-two miles of track. By 1900, Hays & Co. had extended the line to Rosman (then known as "Old Toxaway") and finally in 1903 to Lake Toxaway. In the same year, the Inn at Lake Toxaway was finished and with the completion of the railroad connection it became a famous and remote resort destination for the influential of the day such as Thomas Edison, Henry Ford, Diamond Jim Brady and many others. By 1905 six trains a day were passing*

> *through Laurel Park (some stopping at Davis Station)*... [on their way to Blantyre (formerly called Irvin), Brevard] *and the final destination at Toxaway. However, by 1906 the fortunes of the Toxaway Company had begun to fail. The clientele had simply moved to new vacation spots with more luxurious inns and the Toxaway Company was soon dissolved. The Transylvania Railroad was sold off to the Southern Railway, which became Norfolk Southern. On July 26, 2014, Watco Companies, L.L.C., began operations of North Carolina's Blue Ridge Southern Railroad, a former Norfolk Southern line.*
>
> *There are many local stories of damage caused by the great flood of 1916 but rarely mentioned is the destruction of the dam at Lake Toxaway that drained the lake there. The Inn at Toxaway closed shortly after the flood and was eventually demolished. It was not until 1960 that the dam was rebuilt but by then the tourists could use Highway 64 to* [reach] *Lake Toxaway and beyond.*
>
> *Passenger traffic was not the only income for the Transylvania Railroad. Carr Lumber Company of Mills River and several other lumber companies had a tremendous impact on the economic development of Brevard. These companies operated their own rail lines to the northwest of Brevard into today's Pisgah National Forest. In 1912 Louis Carr Sr.* [1859–1953] *bought seventy thousand acres of timber rights from George Vanderbilt for $1.5-million. It took an expedition ten days to survey the property. Carr Lumber Company operated about seventy-five miles of track in this acreage hauling out flatcar loads of cut and milled timber to Brevard, Hendersonville and beyond.... When George Vanderbilt died, Mrs. Vanderbilt approached Carr with an offer to sell the seventy thousand acres for five dollars an acre for a total asking price of $350,000. Carr refused the offer (by the time of the offer, considerable sections of the land had been already timbered) and this tract became part of the 500,000 acres sold by Mrs. Vanderbilt to the United States government, which became Pisgah National Forest under the auspices of the Weeks Act of 1911.*

Passenger service to Lake Toxaway via Hendersonville continued until the 1916 flood destroyed the lake's dam. The resort was abandoned before 1930, after which a combination passenger-freighter known as the *Swamp Rabbit* conducted round trips to Brevard until 1932.

The rail line through Transylvania County would later support industries such as Ecusta, Olin and DuPont and Moland-Drysdale Corporation's brick-making operation at Etowah. In 1939, Harry Hans

Straus (1884–1951), an inventor from New York, built the Ecusta Paper Mill on the Davidson River east of Brevard. The company manufactured cigarette papers. Olin Industries purchased the company in 1949, and the plant closed in 2002.

Logging and Mining Trains

Railroads played a major role in the development of logging and acid-wood industries in western North Carolina. In addition to commercial railroads, tramways laced the mountainsides, with skidders and Shay and Climax engines conveying cars laden with timber and ore from logging and mining operations. Regional spur lines included those to operations such as the lumber companies of Carr, Gloucester and Moltz, the Toxaway Tanning Company and the Holden Sawmill. At the time, North Carolina's virgin forests proposed a chief source of revenue for the state. By 1967, North Carolina had been the top lumber-producing state in the South and fifth largest in the United States.

Moltz Lumber Company logging train. *Courtesy of the Rowell Bosse North Carolina Room, Transylvania County Library.*

A Shay locomotive used in Transylvania County logging operations. *Courtesy of the Rowell Bosse North Carolina Room, Transylvania County Library.*

Silvermont, the 1917 Colonial Revival mansion of industrialist Joseph Simpson Silversteen and Elizabeth Mount Silversteen. Designed by New York architect C. Bertram French, the thirty-three-room home is now owned by the County of Transylvania, deeded by Silversteen's daughter Dorothy and home to the county archives. *Photo by the author.*

Lumber mill railroad construction crew. *Courtesy of the Rowell Bosse North Carolina Room, Transylvania County Library.*

Joseph Simpson Silversteen (1879–1958) of Pennsylvania leased thousands of acres in the Rosman, Highlands and Brevard areas, purchased in excess of twenty thousand acres of forest land from George Washington Vanderbilt II (1862–1914) and owned the Toxaway Tanning Company, Gloucester Lumber Company and Rosman Tannin Extract Company.

After having nearly depleted their own forests, a number of speculators from the Northeast and Midwest virtually clear-cut all old-growth timber from the mountains of western North Carolina at the turn of the twentieth century and beyond, leaving behind denuded landscapes prone to erosion. Conservation and reforesting efforts by individuals such as Carl A. Schenck (1868–1955) and entities such as the Biltmore School of Forestry and the Civilian Conservation Corps restored the mountains' forests in the 1930s and early 1940s.

Additional timber moguls included John Francis Hays (of the Toxaway Railroad), who owned the Brevard Tannin Company in Pisgah Forest. Capitalists of Williamsport, Pennsylvania, purchased fifty thousand acres in Buncombe County for its timber. Speculation led to the companies Asheville Lumber, Asheville French Broad Lumber, Craggy Lumber Company at Bee Tree, William M. Ritter Lumber, Bemis Hardwood Lumber, Parsons

Logging train at Lake Toxaway. *Courtesy of the Rowell Bosse North Carolina Room, Transylvania County Library.*

Lumber, Carolina Spruce, Carolina Wood Products Company at Woodfin, Laurel River Lumber and the tannery and extract plant of George L. Adams and Associates. In 1909, Ohioan Peter G. Thompson (1851–1931) established his Champion Fibre Company in Canton, North Carolina, as did the Philadelphia syndicate Champion Paper. The region's chief lumbering interests belonged to George Vanderbilt.

Logging operations replete with camps for workers sprang up around Brevard, Rosman, Clyde, Canton, Biltmore, Morganton, Lenoir, Marion, Hazelwood, Waynesville, Andrews, Murphy, Bryson City and Sylva. Proctor, Hazel Creek, Deep Creek, Smokemont, Elkmont, Sunburst, Townsend and Pensacola counted among the names of these camps.

According to a *Hendersonville Times-News* column by Mead Parce, in their heyday, more than 1,770 timber establishments employed some 11,751 workers in western North Carolina. In 1909, band mills in the region produced four million board feet, or 40 percent of the nation's production for the year. Hendersonville boasted the Pace Wood and Timber Company, which supplied the Mount Mitchell Railroad with crossties. Dock Shuffling Pace (1869–1948) was president of the company and his son Lawrence Justus Pace (1896–1979) secretary and treasurer.

The elder Pace also owned D.S. Pace Real Estate and a mercantile and produce business. He erected a block of commercial buildings on Anderson Street (today's Seventh Avenue East).[27]

ELECTRIC AVENUES

The streetcars ground into the square from every portion of the compass and halted briefly like wound toys in their old familiar quarterly-hour formula.
—Thomas Wolfe, "The Lost Boy"

Beasts of burden provided the motive power for the first streetcars, followed by gas-propelled engines and then electricity. In September 1908, the *French*

Mule-drawn trolleys await passengers at the Hendersonville Southern Railway Station, circa 1890. *Baker photo; author's collection.*

Broad Hustler trumpeted the prospect of mass transit: an electric street railroad in Hendersonville from the depot to Laurel Park, Columbia Park and Osceola Lake—"a proposition seriously considered" by local capitalists, including Robert Marcus Oates (1869–1922). A sum of $30,000 was needed to build the line, which would surely be "an inducement for people to come to Hendersonville." By August 1909, the prospect became a reality when, as quoted by the *Hustler*:

> *A street railway will begin as soon as city council designates the exact locations for the tracks, which will be within ten days. The main line will run from the depot to Anderson to Main to Willow to Lake Osceola. Returning through Columbia Road, through Columbia Park, to Whitted Street to Broad Street to Main. A connecting link will run on Main to Academy, to Washington, to Chestnut, to Ewart, to Whitted, where it will join the main line.*

In October of that same year, Charles T. Blake (1863–1930), a representative of the bond house that would finance Oates's electric streetcar system and power plant improvements, spent a day in an "automobile inspection tour of the country near town." Blake was favorably impressed. In May 1911, the *Hustler* reported that a streetcar run was slated for summer from the depot through Columbia Park to Osceola Lake. In December, the electric streetcar line began a regular schedule from the Southern Railway station to Columbia Park on "well-laid tracks." The one-way fare: a nickel. The motormen were Jule Samuel Rymer (1888–1969) and Albert Issertell Norman (1895–1964); conductors, John Allen Beach (1882–1948) and Albert Norman; and the management, Ulysses Grant Staton (1875–1937) and Dock Shuffling Pace. Staton and Pace first undertook the venture of the Hendersonville Traction Company.

January 1912 brought ice and snow that arrested streetcar operations due to a "severe, cold weather snap," according to the *Hustler*. A streetcar was put out of commission when the temperature reached the freezing point, causing the wheels to slip on the icy rails.

The *Hustler* reported in August 1912 that the Hendersonville Traction Company boasted improved cars with "new motors." By December, the *Hustler* verified rumors that Charles Arthur Carlson (1878–1958) would buy the line from Staton and Pace, with the intention of having two Jackson-Sharpe "pay-as-you-enter" cars delivered from Philadelphia, together with components for his Carlson Gasoline Motor Power Plant about April 1, 1913. Cars would operate on a fifteen-minute schedule on a line extending

A trolley rolling along Fifth Avenue West, Hendersonville. *Baker photo; courtesy of the Henderson County Genealogical and Historical Society.*

between the depot and Columbia Park and down Main Street. Carlson hoped to later build a beltline, which would circle the lakes. The *Western Carolina Democrat* reported on January 1, 1913, "Two electric cars will be in operation on the Carlson Line by March 1st."

A headline in a February 1913 *Hustler* read, "Streetcars to Run After April 1st." During a meeting, stockholders of the Hendersonville Traction Company elected the following officers to its board of directors: Charles A. Carlson, president; Dr. David J. Fuller (1839–1915), secretary and treasurer; Charles S. Calvert (1870–1948), superintendent.[28] The company planned to operate its cars year round. Two "Carlson Truck" cars were to be put into operation after April 1. Reported in the *Hustler*, these cars, measuring forty feet in length, were the "only cars of the kind in the United States."

By June 1913, streetcars were running and bells clanging on Main Street. One car had arrived, and the other was scheduled to be delivered soon from a factory in New York.

Asheville's Electric City Rails

In 1888, the City of Asheville authorized a charter for an electric railway that would include lines from Public Square (now Pack Square) to points within the city, including the depot that served the Western North Carolina Railroad (by February 1889). Edmond D. Davidson (1845–1912) of New York agreed to build the system in collaboration with Frank Julian Sprague (1857–1934), builder of the Richmond streetcar system and known as the "Father of Electric Traction." John W. Barnard (1854–1929) of Michigan and Skyland, who supervised construction, became the company's general manager. Asheville's steepness rendered it ripe for electric versus horsecar operation of streetcars.

Railway companies organized and built streetcar lines to Asheville's neighborhoods and outlying areas, including the Sulphur Springs Resort and Biltmore Village. By 1907, Asheville led North Carolina by carrying three million streetcar passengers, compared to Charlotte and Wilmington, with two million each. By 1915, Asheville's street railway reached its maximum size, operating forty-three cars on eighteen miles of track, including one to the newly opened Grove Park Inn and its surrounding neighborhood. The 1916 flood wreaked major damage on Asheville's streetcar lines, as well as on the major railway systems of western North Carolina.

Following Asheville in establishing electric streetcar service were Winston (1890), Charlotte and Raleigh (1891) and Wilmington (1892). Greensboro,

Streetcars in the "Paris of the South" (Asheville) portrayed in a vintage postcard captioned, "Pack Square looking East, Asheville, N.C." *Author's collection; Souvenir Postcard Co., New York and Leipzig Publishing.*

Durham and Salisbury followed in 1902. Hendersonville employed mule-drawn streetcars until about 1913.

Asheville's street railways were consolidated into the Asheville Electric Company in 1900 and renamed Asheville Power and Light Company in 1912. In 1926, Raleigh-based Carolina Power and Light Company bought the operation. Asheville's electric streetcar system ceased operations in 1934, but it had been streetcars that sparked the dawn of suburbs in the waxing years of the twentieth century.

Jitney buses ("bustitution") took over where streetcars left off. The *French Broad Hustler*, in a March 1915 issue, reported jitneys are "a cheap system of transportation for the sightseeing tourists for the coming summer" at five-cent fares.

From Mule Power to Electrical Energy

Colonel Sidney Vance Pickens (1836–1919) built and operated Hendersonville's first street railway—a mule-drawn streetcar, which, from 1890 to 1902, followed a regular schedule from tracks up the middle of South Main Street to Anderson Street (today's Seventh Avenue East) and the Southern Railway station, with a spur from Main up Shaws Creek Street (today's Sixth Avenue West) to Pickens' Hill (later site of the Park Hill Hotel and then the Elks club). At this popular destination for church picnics, Pickens built an observation tower. Rules on Pickens's streetcar included "passengers must not squirt tobacco juice on the seats" and "no passenger can bring more than one piece of baggage without extra cost." The streetcar line commenced on April 22, 1890. The cost of five cents conveyed a commuter between downtown Hendersonville and the Southern Railway station and a three-nickel fare transported a passenger from town to Pickens' Hill, the latter fare including a climb to the top of the observation tower. Consistent with the writings of Louise Howe Bailey, Pickens's mules were named Kate and Beck; his horse, Major.

After Pickens abandoned his streetcar venture in 1902, town commissioners granted four franchises for street railways. Capitalists built a line between downtown Hendersonville—from the St. John Hotel, just north of the courthouse—to the depot with a spur to Columbia Park (now Lenox Park) with Y-tracks at the railway station and the park for the purpose of cars reversing their directions. Electric trolleys later supplanted gasoline-fueled cars. The franchisees were W.A. Smith's Laurel Park Street Railway Company in 1904;

Colonel Sidney Vance Pickens. *Courtesy of the Baker-Barber Collection, Community Foundation of Henderson County, Henderson County Public Library.*

Hendersonville Lake, Land and Power Company in 1907 with M.C. Toms, president, and Dr. Lucius Broadman Morse (1871–1946), secretary; Robert Marcus Oates and his Hendersonville Light and Power Company in 1909; and the Columbia Land Improvement Company in 1909.

Hendersonville's Dummy Line

At the turn of the twentieth century, William Alexander Smith (1858–1922) established a rail line from Main Street in downtown Hendersonville, which, beginning in September 1905, traveled west on Broad Street (Fifth Avenue West) to Rainbow Lake, the first developed sector of his Laurel Park Estates. In 1911, the line extended from Broad Street, curving right and following what is now Canal Drive, winding up to Crystal Spring Drive and around the north shore of Laurel Park (Rhododendron) Lake. From there, it curved southeast and crossed Hebron Drive onto Lake View Drive, which was extended to include a turn-around loop. The route followed a canal that once linked the two lakes.

Some have noted of this line, nicknamed the "Dummy," that it was thusly called because in its earliest days it could not turn around, instead backing

The "Dummy-Line" train at Fifth Avenue West and Main Street, Hendersonville. *Courtesy of the Henderson County Genealogical and Historical Society.*

from Laurel Park on its return trip to Main Street. But according to Laurel Park historians Knox Crowell and Paul Hansen, the train was so named because it essentially served as a trunk line, traveling to no large destination, connection or city. Initially, a twenty-five-horsepower Davenport "teapot" steam locomotive drove the transport of one fourteen-seat open excursion car. Additional cars, including a flat car, were added at later dates. Tracks were extended onward to Crystal Spring and then across what are now Railroad Drive and Laurel Park Highway. Eventually, the line reached Rhododendron Lake and a loop that allowed the train to turn around. A fountain graced the loop's hub. The train ran on a ten-minute schedule during the tourist season, with stops including the Laurel Park Casino. Another report mentioned:

> *Dummy cars leave Main Street on the hour and half hours, starting at 9:00 a.m. and running to 11:00 p.m., from 11:00 to 12:30 cut out for church on Sundays.*
>
> —French Broad Hustler, *July 23, 1908*

Still another *Hustler* report, from 1911, mentioned a thirty-minute schedule from 9:00 a.m. to 10:00 p.m. The same article referred to a power engine with the ability to take six cars and the engine up the steepest grade in Laurel Park, with "no annoying delays." At the time, promoters and journalists lauded Laurel Park as "Hendersonville's Playground."

Staff of the Laurel Park Street Railway Company included Ransom Lenoir "Ranse" Rhodes (1869–1949), engineer; Walter A. Smith's sons Walter B. (1891–1964) and William A. "Willy" (1889–1936) and Allen Yates Arledge (1892–1966), conductors; and William Pink Carver (1853–1918), fireman. W.A. Smith served as president of the company.

In the opening years of the twentieth century, gasoline-powered streetcars replaced the mule-drawn versions from previous years. Hendersonville received electricity in 1903, but it would be nearly a decade before its streetcars began converting to electric power.

In 1905, W.A. Smith launched the Laurel Park Railroad Company. For seven years, the Dummy Line carried passengers between Main Street and Broad Street to the dance pavilion and lakes that Smith had built at Laurel Park.

As printed in an article in the *French Broad Hustler* on July 14, 1910, the dummy derailed on July 13, causing no serious damage, although service was delayed for one day. By August 1912, the *Hustler* reported a 50 percent gain in traffic on the Laurel Park Street Railway. In October, a report under the headline, "Another Electric Car Line Ready for Operation," read in part:

> *W.A. Smith—prime mover behind the electric line project—preparing to electrify the dummy system. Power plant to be erected at the junction of the Laurel Park Street Railway Company's line and the Southern Railway just this side of Laurel Park. Not less than six cars will be in operation by summer of 1913.*

By December work on the railway "progressed nicely," according to the *Hustler*: "W.H. Bangs of Atlanta was in town to check on the status of the work at the power plant and to put in a generator in connection with the plant."[29]

An advertisement from 1915 listed a one-way streetcar fare of five cents. Trolleys (electric Birney and Brill cars) replaced the old teapot edition. The line continued to operate until 1918, when automobiles began to replace the need for public rails, concluding Hendersonville's streetcar era. The dummy's tracks were removed by 1921. On May 14, 1934, a project of the Federal Emergency Relief Administration was approved for removal of streetcar tracks on Seventh Avenue from the depot to Main Street.

William Alexander Smith

W.A. Smith, born in Georgia and a pioneer citizen of Hendersonville, where he spent most of his life, did much around the turn of the twentieth century to advance the city. Smith served two terms as mayor (1880 and 1882), was a Mason, an attorney, real estate developer, banker and promoter and was elected to the state legislature in 1883. He counted among the members of the board of aldermen, drafted several town charter amendments and served as city attorney and county attorney. He married Ann Hazeltine Jordan (1859–1941).

Smith sold his Ocklawaha Realty Company to the Hendersonville Development Company, in which he remained involved financially.

William Alexander Smith. *Courtesy of Hendersonville City Hall and Lu Ann Welter.*

Around 1898, Smith and James Manning Waldrop (1852–1907) formed Smith and Waldrop. Smith was president of that company and also president of Wanteska, a banking, real estate and trust concern, which consolidated with the First National Bank, which in turn consolidated as the Bank of Hendersonville and changed its name to the First Bank and Trust Company. Smith was also president of the Laborers' Building and Loan Association.

In 1916, Smith organized the Smith-Jackson and Morris Real Estate Company. With Judge Columbus Mills Pace (1845–1925), he bought, for five dollars per acre, ten thousand acres of what now constitutes Laurel Park. At the time, the only access to this property west of town would have been via bridle paths. Smith's vision was "to develop this property into a place of recreation, amusement and a high-class residential section." At his own expense, Smith constructed and maintained Fifth Avenue West, and a desirable residential section grew up alongside the broad avenue.

In 1922, Smith suffered a nervous breakdown and then a stroke, from which he never recovered. His obituary read in part:

> *He has by his incessant boosting caused more people to catch his vision of the future of Hendersonville and thus has caused more new people to locate and construct new business buildings and residences than the balance of its citizens combined. If all of the institutions and improvements were taken from Hendersonville that have sprung directly and indirectly from his influence and activities the town would revert back to a primitive country village with no conveniences or attractions and nothing to make the property owned by its citizens of any appreciable value.*

The Swiss Railway

The Swiss railway at Laurel Park. *Courtesy of Knox Crowell.*

Laurel Park's Swiss incline railway was a counterbalanced cable line with two passenger carts that ascended a sharp slope of approximately one-quarter mile at an elevation of two hundred feet from the vicinity of Crystal Spring and southwesterly to a forty-foot observation tower called High Peak, which stood near a rock quarry on Echo Mountain. The destination, popular with tourists, proffered panoramic views of downtown Hendersonville. The starting point of the grade, off today's Crystal Spring Drive, climbed through what is now Old Laurel Drive to the present location of a cul-de-sac at Smith Drive off Upper Laurel Drive. A coal-fired, steam-generating plant to power the railway stood on Fifth Avenue West and Wash Creek Drive—present site of INdoors, Inc., formerly Raynor Garage Doors and Richardson's Fuel (coal) and Supply Company. The plant also powered the Dummy Line in its latter days.

> *The engine that pulls the car is on a concrete base sunk fifteen feet into the solid rock, and could no more be pulled out of position than the mountain itself.*
>
> —French Broad Hustler, *July 13, 1911*

Advertising lauded Laurel Park as "Hendersonville's Playground in the most beautiful natural park in America." An article in the *French Broad Hustler*, January 17, 1907, mentioned a railway planned for the park.

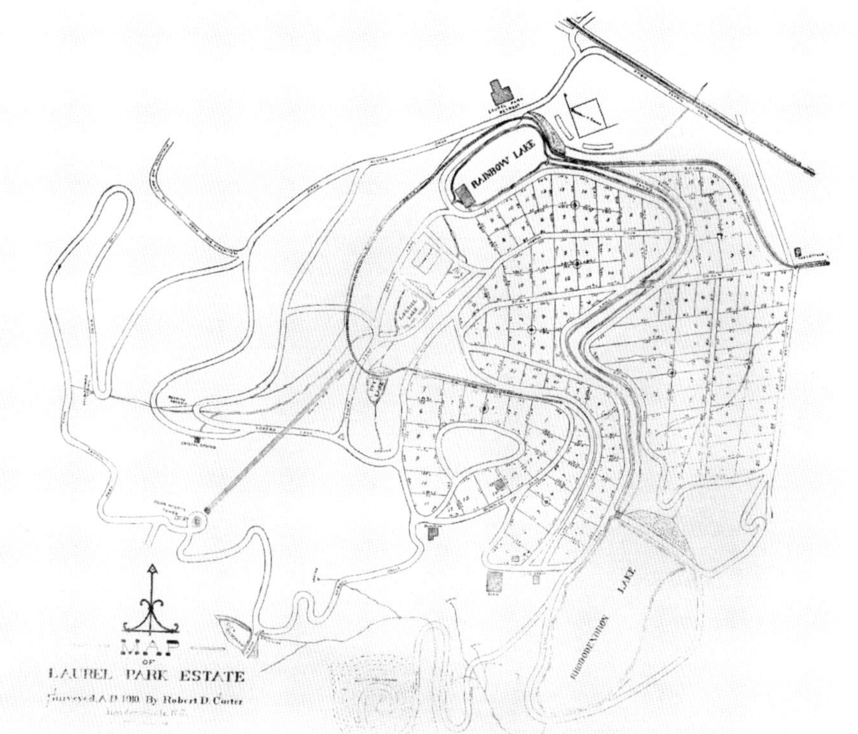
RAINBOW LAKE
RHODODENDRON LAKE
MAP
OF
LAUREL PARK ESTATE
Surveyed A.D. 1910. By Robert D. Carter

High Peak Tower at Laurel Park. *Courtesy of A. Paul Hansen.*

Opposite, top: The homesite associated with 10 Cliff Drive in Laurel Park comprised one of the three levels of W.A. Smith's rock quarry. The modern shared driveway was once the old quarry road. Evidence of drill holes may still be seen in the sheer granite cliff that cradles the home, where koi ponds occupy the pits. The site also included a stone-crusher and a grizzly (rock strainer). Smith employed the gravel for a stretch of the Toxaway railway. *Photo by the author with permission of Stephen Fosberg.*

Opposite, bottom: Laurel Park Estate plan illustrating railways and lakes. *Courtesy of A. Paul Hansen.*

A 1910 map by civil engineer and surveyor Robert Daniel Carter (1877–1956) of Haywood County illustrates the Swiss railway's route from northeast of Ivy Lake and Lovers Lane running southwest to "Park Hights Tower."[30]

As a tactic of attracting young courters, a trail in Laurel Park was named Cupid's Lane. Local legend had it that a coin tossed into nearby Horseshoe Spring would bring luck in love.

The High Peak tower at one end of the Swiss railway stood 2,611 feet above sea level. From it, tourists could "see Mt. Mitchell, Kanuga and Highland lakes, Saluda and other points."

The Gospel of Good Roads

I often hear nowadays, the automobile instigated good roads; that the automobile is the parent of good roads. Well, the truth is, the bicycle is the father of the good roads movement in this country.
—Horatio Sawyer Earle

Hugh Jon Barbour, circa 1898. *Baker photo; courtesy of the Henderson County Genealogical and Historical Society.*

Until the twentieth century, few American roads were paved. Bridges designed for foot traffic and horses and carriages proved too flimsy for heavier conveyances. First-class roads were required to be twelve feet wide and third-class roads wide enough for a single horse and rider. Notions of a national movement to improve roads caught fire as early as 1879 with the League of American Wheelmen (LAW), which officially launched in May 1880. Bicycle enthusiasts, riding clubs and manufacturers met in Newport, Rhode Island, to form such a league with the purpose of lending support to the growing proliferation of bicyclists and horse-drawn vehicles and to protect their

Late-nineteenth-century road construction, Henderson County. *Baker photo; courtesy of the Henderson County Genealogical and Historical Society.*

interests from legislative discrimination. In 1891, New Jersey became the first to pass a law providing for a state to participate in road-building projects. In 1893, the U.S. Department of Agriculture initiated a systematic evaluation of existing highway systems by adopting a state-aid plan. By June 1894, many of the railway companies had made concessions in transporting road materials ranging from half rates to free carriage.

Dr. Chase P. Ambler (1865–1932) led the Good Roads Association of Asheville, which organized in 1899. A nationwide Good Roads Association (a forerunner of the Department of Transportation) formed in 1902 to improve U.S. transportation routes. North Carolina soon formed its own Good Roads Association (NCGRA, founded in Raleigh), creating a sense of urgency to remedy the mostly wretched conditions of county roads.

Before the 1920s, North Carolina's individual counties built and maintained their roads, but with the growing popularity of automobiles, improved roads became essential. At that time, city roads were, in many cases, paved, while rural passageways of dirt or gravel were scarred with craters, dusty when dry, quagmires when wet. A need also existed for the construction of sturdy bridges and culverts.

In 1908, Henry Ford introduced his low-priced, highly efficient Model T. Widespread popularity of this vehicle forced the hand of the federal government to become more directly involved in the development and improvement of roads.

Most importantly, the economy depended on transportation. Leaning on this need, the Good Roads Association produced literature, including *Good Roads* magazine, which boasted a circulation of one million within its first three years. A LAW pamphlet, the *Gospel of Good Roads*, carried the slogan "Provide the fund, levy the tax, build the roads." Advocacy efforts frequently targeted farmers and ranchers, espousing the idea that improved infrastructure would decrease shipping costs, boost industry and diminish rural isolation and poverty. Resounding the battle cry "Get the farmers out of the mud!," lobbyists held road conventions and public demonstrations to entice awareness among the general populace and influence legislators to act on the need for improvement and expansion of rural byways.

The movement gained national attention when President Woodrow Wilson (1856–1923) signed the Federal-Aid Road Act on July 11, 1916. Also, in 1916 the Buffalo Steam Roller Company of Buffalo, New York, and the Kelly-Springfield Company of Springfield, Ohio, merged to form

Early-twentieth-century road crew, Henderson County, with H.E. "Skin" Drake second from left, foreground. *Courtesy of Sindy Drake Hamilton.*

the Buffalo-Springfield Company, a leading compaction business. The industrial giant enabled the United States to embark on a national highway construction campaign that continued into the 1920s.

In 1921, the General Assembly of North Carolina passed a $50 million road-building bond, which created a state highway system to be managed by a State Highway Commission (established in 1917). The General Assembly passed the Good Roads Bill by reason of lobbyist supporters who proclaimed the need for a network of roads to connect the state's burgeoning textile industry and its agricultural centers to national railroads and waterways. North Carolina would soon become known as the "Good Roads State." By 1925, 7,680 miles of hard-topped roads in North Carolina had been made possible through gasoline taxes, automobile license fees and federal government highway bonds.

Parentage of Good Roads

Prominent figures in the Good Roads Movement included Horatio Sawyer Earle (1855–1935)—also known as Horatio "Good Roads" Earle, the "Father of Good Roads" and "By Gum" Earle—of Vermont and Michigan. Earle, a Michigan state senator and highway commissioner, served as chief consul of the League of American Wheelmen, for which he chaired a committee to form a Good Roads committee. He also founded the American Road Makers (later renamed American Road Builders Association). Activist Harriet "Hattie" Morehead Berry (1844–1940) of Hillsborough, North Carolina—a leading campaigner in North Carolina's Good Roads movement—served as secretary of the Good Roads Association from 1918 into the 1920s and became known as the "Mother of Good Roads." The *Raleigh Observer* hailed Berry as the "best woman politician in the state" in 1921. In 1986, the North Carolina Department of Transportation (NCDOT) named a twelve-mile segment of Interstate 40 for Berry.

North Carolina governors Locke Craig (1860–1924) and Cameron Morrison (1869–1953) were known as "Good Roads governors." Other leaders of the movement included geologist Joseph Hyde Pratt (1870–1942); Pleasant Henderson Hanes (1845–1925), first president of the NCGRA; and Henry Branton Varner (1870–1925), second president of the NCGRA and publisher of the *Lexington Dispatch* and the magazine *Southern Good Roads*.

The Federal-Aid Road Act of 1916 created the Federal-Aid Highway Program, under which funds were made available on a continuous basis to state highway agencies to assist in road improvements. But the United States entered World War I before the program commenced. At the dawn of the Roaring Twenties, the Federal Highway Act of 1921 authorized the Bureau of Public Roads (BPR—forerunner of the 1967 Federal Highway Administration) to provide funding to assist state highway agencies in constructing a paved system of two-lane interstate highways. During the 1930s, the BPR assisted state and local governments in creating Depression-era road projects that would employ many citizens in need of work. When America entered World War II in 1941, interests diverted toward providing roads for military purposes. Following the war, the nation's roads stood in disrepair, and congestion had become problematic in major cities. In 1944, President Franklin Delano Roosevelt signed legislation authorizing a network of rural and urban express highways—the National System of Interstate Highways. This legislation, however, lacked funding. It was not until President Dwight D. Eisenhower (1890–1969) signed the Federal-Aid Highway Act of 1956 that the Interstate program progressed. From its start, this project was hailed as the greatest public works project in history.

North Carolina convict road crew. *Author's collection.*

Carolina on the Move

A majority of the Justices being Present the Court orders that John Davis, Richard Allen Snr [sic] *& Boyd McCrary or a majority of them be appointed Commissioners to Let out to the Lowest Bidder the making of a Road & Bridgs* [sic] *passing through the whole Length of the Main Street of the Town of Hendersonville Intersecting the Turnpike Road in the manner Reported by the Jury of Review as heretofore made said Commissioners are not authorized to Excede* [sic] *the amount of fifteen Hundred Dollars for the Entire Cost of Said Road the Contractors for making the same to be Paid out of Funds arising from the sale of Town Lots after the Contractors for the Court House and Jail are first Paid.*

—July Session 1842, Court of Pleas and Quarter Sessions, Henderson County, North Carolina

Asheville's streets were first paved in 1890 with brick cobblestones baked in the kiln at Limestone (Fletcher).[31] In Hendersonville, macadamizing commenced on Anderson Street (Seventh Avenue East), Main Street and Maple Street in 1902, and asphalt followed in 1912, as well as the extension of the paving program to other streets, including Broad (Fifth) and Chestnut (First Avenue). Street railway companies were required to pave between rails and a foot of both sides of the track, and in the latter stages, revenue was simply not sufficient to meet these costs.

William Franklin Edwards (1848–1921), an architect and city planner, helped shape the cityscape of Hendersonville. His work included building the 1904–5 Henderson County courthouse designed by Richard Sharp Smith (1852–1924) of Smith & Carrier Architects, Asheville. Edwards won the contract to pave Main Street in 1910—the first time the grand passageway was macadamized. Early paving efforts were typically limited to cities and townships with neglectfully shoddy rural roads.

In North Carolina, the Good Roads Movement first came to light in counties such as Mecklenburg and Buncombe with large towns or cities, but even in cities roadwork was scattered. Certain county commissioners, once reluctant to raise taxes or invest heavily in roads and bridges, were at last motivated to act and approved the building of roads surfaced with macadam (crushed stone), sand-clay, gravel, concrete and later, asphaltic materials. Officials likewise contracted out to build bridges and culverts. Many other North Carolina counties, particularly those in isolated rural areas of the mountain and coastal regions, found they did not have the resources necessary for road and bridge improvements and construction.

This convinced activists that federal and state governments should play a role in the financing and construction of statewide highway systems.

By the waning years of the nineteenth century, the need for paved roads and navigable bridges beyond city limits became glaringly evident with the speculation and development mania in western North Carolina and with the uptick in automobile ownership in the early 1900s. Farmers complained about the deplorable state of transporting goods. Speculators and other promoters were desirous of passable conduits as a measure of enticing industry, new residents and visitors to what they touted as a superlative destination resort. Hendersonville's broadsheet of the day, the *French Broad Hustler*, carried numerous letters to the editor and articles concerning the need for improved roads. Samplings follow.

> *The roads of Henderson County are in such a truly deplorable condition that the people are about desperate. They are no longer worthy of being called roads, they are simply beds of soft sticky mud, dangerous to life and limb, and impossible to travel in many places. It's like hauling a heavy load to try and drive over the best of our roads at this time, and the thousands of summer visitors have been deprived of one of their chief sources of pleasure. People do not wish to be tied down to the city. They want to get out and see the many points of interest surrounding the town, and to do so with any degree of pleasure decent roads are necessary.*
>
> *As to the farmers getting their produce to town, many of them are in despair. On almost every road leading to town there are stretches, which are almost impassible, and the farmers are now waking up to the necessity of good roads in Henderson County.*
>
> *The Flat Rock road will serve as an illustration. Horses are compelled to walk, in many places knee-deep in mire, all the way from the railway track. One or two places are simply dangerous to life and limb. The people living on that road are now circulating a petition and expect to go down into their own pockets, also in order to get a road by which they may get to town. As it is now they feel they might as well live 10 or 15 miles out in the country.*
>
> *E.W. Durant Jr., of Charleston, S.C., whose summer home is on the Flat Rock road, is fixing part of the alleged road at his own expense. Mr. Durant claims that $200 would put the road into passable condition for the present.*
>
> *To use a slang phrase, Mr. Durant is "sore." He has been the moving spirit in the Flat Rock Country Club, where $10,000 has been spent on*

the clubhouse, golf links, tennis courts, etc., and it has been impossible for people to reach the grounds. He has talked up the beauties, the advantages, both health and pleasure, of Flat Rock and Hendersonville, and when his friends come many of them expecting to invest money in summer homes, they find themselves hemmed in by a sea of mud.

Mr. Durant feels that he cannot, in fairness, recommend this country to any more of his friends in the south.

It is highly desirable that this class of people be convinced of the advantages of Hendersonville, Flat Rock and the surrounding country. The admirable clubhouse and the golf links at Flat Rock, combined with its far-famed natural beauty, would prove a sufficient argument to many wealthy people to build summer homes there and in this city, but, as Mr. Durant says, with such roads as we have to offer, people might come once and ever after stay away. (September 27, 1906)

Editor Hustler*: While the good road agitation is on, I have plans for a change in our public road system, which I herewith offer for consideration of your readers. The establishment of a perfect road system in our county would reduce the team labor on the roads 50 percent, would reduce the labor of keeping up the roads 75 percent and increase pleasure on them 90 percent. It is economy on our part to change, but we should change to the right thing. It is about as easy to build a road at the right place as at the wrong place and we have already lost too much labor and turned too much land into gullies by running our roads up and down steep hills. Experience has shown that it pays to build railroads on good grades.*

With the disadvantage of the mire and the inferiority of the horse to the powerful engine, does it not seem much more important that we should reduce our dirt roads to good grades? The fact that railroads are running through our country on good grades is proof that good grades can be found yet our wagon roads run up and down hills so steep that a team cannot draw more than half a load on them and the water rushes down them with a fury that sweeps them into gullies making it an everlasting burden to keep them in repair. The labor lost in keeping these washouts refilled and the hauling labor lost on account of their steep grades, would in a few months rebuild all the roads and put them on perfect grades.

Why should we continue to waste so much labor, when labor spent rebuilding the roads would reward dollars for cents? Law regulates the building, rebuilding and keeping up of public roads. This makes it necessary to reform the law before the roads can be reformed. If the law was made right the people would volunteer of their own accord to make the roads right. All that is needed to bring the desired changes in our present road law that authorizes the County Commissioners, when a majority of the men along any line of road who are required to work on public roads petition them to rebuild their road, to send a competent engineer with an instrument, to lay out the road where it should go, on grades not to rise or fall more than four feet to the hundred.

When the road is laid out let the commissioners notify the justices of the peace of the township or townships in which the road is situated to meet and proportion the hands who are required to work on roads according to the work required and appoint overseers and require them to work their hands a certain part of each month until their part of the road is made according to law.

When the road is complete, let the commissioners receive it and give every man who has done a share of the work a permanent release from working on public roads any more in the state and let the road out to the lowest bidder to be kept up at the expense of the county. It costs but little to keep up roads intelligently built on good grades. I know pieces of road that have been in use for 25 years without a lick of work being struck on them. In this way the people can enjoy the benefits of a perfect road system without hardly noticing the difference in their taxes.

In order to get good roads and get released from working on public roads the men who are obligated to work the roads will volunteer to rebuild their roads and if the legislature will give them the privilege, they will soon work a revolution in our public road system that will prove satisfactory to our people and honorable to our county.

—J. T. Anderson, January 3, 1907

The committee appointed at the mass meeting, last Saturday, met at the Court House, on the 28th, and drafted a new road law. This will be submitted to a mass meeting of our citizens, which has been called to meet at the Court House, on Saturday, January 5th, at one o'clock. After it has been discussed thoroughly, the bill will be forwarded to Raleigh and the Legislature will be asked to enact it into a law.

It is highly important that everyone attend this meeting. There is nothing more important now before our citizens, and next Saturday will be the time for all interested to make their objections known to any part of the new law.

There is much discussion all over the county, just now, as to good roads.

Many of our citizens take the position that ordinarily the roads of the county are excellent the greater part of the year, and all that is necessary is an intelligent working of them.

One prominent citizen and heavy taxpayer says the overseers should and may be indicted under the present law for failure to properly do their duty as public officers.

It is hard to find a man who will advocate a bond issue for the purpose of good roads, although everyone admits that good roads, which may be traveled at ALL seasons of the year, rain or shine, is now a prime necessity.

Attend the meeting next Saturday and express your sentiments. (January 3, 1907)

Paved roads in Henderson County would do more to increase the material property of both town and county than any other one thing, except possibly the location of mills here. It would mean more than lakes or railroads. It would build both town and county, increase the valuation of all real estate, make Hendersonville a more desirable summer and winter resort and thereby offer the farmers a better and higher market for all their produce. Better one mile of paved road than one hundred miles of mud holes. (March 5, 1908)

At any rate, by 1910 at least some progress had been made, as the following words attest.

Editor Hustler*: I am happy to say that most of the objections to Henderson County have now vanished, and as a very good judge of good roads said the other day, this county is coming to the front in good roads sentiment. We are having the best grades of any county in the state made on our new roads, thanks to Mr. P.F. Patton, who is one of the best managers of roads and of landowners over whose land the roads must be built, that any county may boast of. And Captain Ben Souther is one of the best dirt road builders I have ever seen. Everybody in the county is singing the praise now while they are alive, which is good. They are building their own monuments in the work they are now doing.*

Sometimes Mr. Patton meets an obstruction in the way of some landowner who does not know the value of good roads to a settlement. Now, my brother, if I am talking to or about you, see here: I, with the help of Mr. Patton, have just persuaded a neighbor to have a road made through his property. I tried to buy the right of way, but he refused to have the road except by a legal process. He said he could get 10 an acre for that land, which I thought too much, but just as soon as the road was made and the travel turned on he sold his land for 63 per acre. You can do the same thing.

Mr. Editor, I want you to go to Bat Cave or Hoopers Creek and see the best roads and the best-pleased people you ever saw in your life![32]

—R.M. Pryor, June 30, 1910

But as revealed in the following article, there was still much work to be accomplished on improving the road situation.

The Henderson County good roads association met Saturday and discussed fully the best way to proceed in order to give satisfactory results and accomplish the most in the way of good roads in the shortest time.

Those present from various sections of the county stated before the meeting that the sentiment for better roads is now ripe, and that the citizens are ready to support the good road movement. It was clearly shown to the association that the dynamo only needs to be started and then the better roads movement would assume perpetual motion. With this end in view the association adopted the following resolution first suggested by Judge Ewart and amended by G.W. Conner and W.A. Smith.

Moved and passed, that a mass meeting be called on the first Monday in September in conjunction with the county commissioners meeting to discuss the making of good roads, and that a committee of six be appointed to report on the law and necessary machinery.

Chairman C.M. Pace appointed the following to compose this committee, after which the meeting adjourned until the first Monday in September.

Messrs. R.C. Clark, W.A. Smith, Judge Ewart, Judge Blythe, G.W. Conner and W.F. Edwards. (August 25, 1910)

"I believe," said a merchant of Hendersonville, this morning, "that the Commercial Club ought to introduce a resolution about good roads at their next meeting. Let the resolution represent the sentiment of the Commercial Club, if it is adopted after a full and fair discussion. Then let that resolution be the basis for a good roads campaign, which shall wake the echoes in the mountains. There is no time to be lost. We want good roads and we want them now." (November 27, 1910)

The Buncombe County Good Roads Association, one of the most effective organizations of its kind in the South, and which has done a work in which is simply invaluable for the good of roads of the county, favors the sand-clay method of road construction to the exclusion of macadam.

Buncombe County has many miles of superb roads, but some of them are getting in bad shape, and it is claimed the cost of repairing them and keeping them in good condition is excessive. After an actual experience with this method of construction, Engineer Toms, in charge of roads in the county, endorses sand-clay in preference to macadam, and the directors of the Good Roads Association have adopted his report as theirs.

If Henderson County is ever to have good roads here, is a point that will require careful consideration—sand-clay or macadam. It is not too early now to discuss the different methods. It is not too early now to try and bring roads agitation to a head in some form or other. (November 27, 1910)

The Evolution of Hendersonville's Main Drag

A Majourity [sic] *of the Justices Being Presant* [sic] *they proceeded to the Election of a County Survayor* [sic] *Which Terminated in the Choice of Charles DeChoisuel* [sic] Esqr.
—July Session 1841, Court of Pleas and Quarter Sessions, Henderson County, North Carolina

After Charles de Choiseul (circa 1821–1862) was elected county surveyor in July 1841, a crew laid out Hendersonville's streets, including the one-hundred-plus-foot-wide swath that cut through the heart of it.[33] From its origins as a broad and dusty or—given the season—muddy, earthen roadbed, Main Street witnessed all from macadam to asphalt and horses and mules and hitching posts to Tin Lizzies, trolleys and marching bands. Gas lamps phased out in favor of electrified versions, and at one time, strings of Christmas lights spanned its wide way—switched on only during the holiday season. And hotels, private residences and picket fences gave way to office buildings, banks, department stores, eateries and parking lots. Shade trees once graced its median, followed by light-rail tracks and then parking spaces. City planners reconfigured parking patterns, and Main offered four lanes of cruising—and at times a speedway—for youngsters. Main Street was arbiter to all from boom times to near-ghost town status to today's thriving tourist destination flanked with boutiques, restaurants and museums. And it has seen all, from the blazes that incinerated its earliest hotels, the Carolina Theatre and the Belk department store to the fanfare of festivals and parades—and turkeys being tossed across it from the roof of the Skyland Hotel.

Hendersonville's Main Street prior to its serpentine reconfiguration. *Courtesy of the Henderson County Genealogical and Historical Society.*

Main Goes Serpentine

Hendersonville City Council minutes from September 4, 1975, reflect a summary of a visit made by commissioners Ray Blanton Shealy (1926–2000) and Joel Wright (1922–2008), city attorney Francis Marion Coiner (1923–2004), Donald Bethea Keith (1914–2004), Kermit Edney (1924–2000) and James "Jimmy" Edney (1931–) to Grand Junction, Colorado, to inspect a project similar to the layout proposed for reworking Hendersonville's Main Street. Mayor Boyce A. Whitmire (1905–1985) named the following members to the Downtown Committee to oversee the project's fruition: Joseph Egerton "Jody" Barber (1923–2001), R. Charles Waters (1938–), Mary Barber (1922–2008), Kermit Edney, D.B. Keith, Emory Jackson (1939–) and Sam H. McGuirt (1937–).

> *Downtown was drying up. The anchors—Penney's and Belk—were leaving and our goal was to help the little guys survive. Kermit and Jody were the driving forces behind this venture. Mary Barber was the "glue."*
>
> —*R. Charles Waters*

Hendersonville chief of police William Vernon "Bill" Powers (1920–2010) served as project manager. Mary Barber represented the Garden Club. Luther Smith (1947–) oversaw the landscape design, and David Quinn, a planning consultant from Asheville, supervised the overall design. The group met frequently at the Barbers' home in Laurel Park. Edney, Barber and Keith took on an off-street parking lot project funded in part by two hundred stockholders, including the Duke Power Company and downtown merchants.

The layout with reconfigured curbing began on November 21, 1975. In 1976, contractors buried conduits for power lines under Main Street. Beginning in 1977, the four-lane thoroughfare was transformed into a "serpentine" pattern, reducing its vehicular flow to two lanes, allowing for perpendicular and parallel parking spaces and broad walkways and piazzas with planters. The goal: to slow vehicular traffic and encourage pedestrian traffic and commerce in a "park-like" atmosphere. The mid-block planters were fashioned from concrete sewer pipes veneered with epoxy and pebbles and the corner planters of cinderblock veneered with brick. The "serpentine" configuration was completed in 1978 and dedicated on June 30.

The opening of the Blue Ridge Mall in 1983 took a toll on Hendersonville's Main Street,[34] as department stores relocated from

Revitalizing Hendersonville's Main Street, 2012. *Photo by the author.*

Streetcar rails unearthed during the excavation of Hendersonville's Main Street. *Photo by the author.*

downtown to the new shopping center. Downtown promoters saw continued revitalization as an important element in drawing merchants, tourists and shoppers to the heart of town.

A three-year project beginning in the winter of 2010 further enhanced the beautification and "shopping-and-dining experience" of Hendersonville's Main Street. The massive undertaking included updating antiquated infrastructure and landscaping. Excavations prior to resurfacing exposed trolley tracks and rail-tie remnants and early twentieth-century artifacts. New curbing and sidewalks were poured, a brick stage replaced a gazebo-style bandstand that once stood between Fourth and Fifth Avenues alongside Main Street's east sidewalk and mid-block pedestrian crossings were installed. New brick-veneered planters replaced older ones and a band shell was added to South Main Street near the visitors' center.

Over the years, modifications to Main Street have been met with both applause and objection, and to this day many natives have expressed their displeasure with the tight intersections and overall serpentine flow with the familiar mantra, "I don't recognize my hometown."

SPANNING THE AGES

Assessing tolls per person, animal and conveyance, early settlers employed canoes, rafts and other flat-bottomed vessels to ferry travelers, livestock and goods on channels that crossed their land. These landholders oftentimes upgraded the crossings with crude bridges. With the passage of time, the building and maintenance of county roads and bridges fell under the supervision of courts of pleas and quarter sessions, a charge assigned in 1868 to county commissioners until 1921, when the State of North Carolina assumed responsibility.

Early Ferryboats and Bridges

To transport drovers and other travelers, Swan Pritchett Burnett (1779–1837) ran a ferry at Del Rio, Cocke County, Tennessee. Philip Hoodenpyle (Philippus Hoodenpijl, 1757–1833) operated a ferry at Warm Springs (known now as Hot Springs) and had charge of a toll road—Jewel Hill Road—from the Hopewell Turnpike to Warm Springs, North Carolina, and Newport, Tennessee. Of this pass in December 1812, the Methodist circuit-riding bishop Francis Asbury (1745–1816) wrote, "Why should we climb

A ferry being drawn by a windlass on the French Broad River. *Author's collection.*

over the desperate Spring and Paint mountains when there is such a fine new road?" Such crossings came into play for drivers of livestock from Tennessee through North Carolina to South Carolina markets.

Regional landholders with toll crossings included:

- Colonel Samuel Chunn, a bridge in Madison County.
- William Curtis Anderson (1881–1964) ferried timber across the French Broad River in Madison County.
- Colonel William H. Garmon (circa 1806–1854), a ferry (later a bridge) near Craggy in Woodfin. The flood washed away Garmon's bridge in 1852, and Union soldiers burned its replacement in 1865.[35]
- James Mitchell Alexander, a ferry and bridge.
- John A. Davis (1762–1823), a ferry.
- David Kimsey/Kimzey (1755–1828), a ferry.
- James Madison Henderson (1817–1903), a ford superseded by Sams' Ferry.
- Captain Edmund Sams (1750–1845), the above-referenced ferry—purportedly the first operated on the French Broad River. Sams, first coroner and a justice of the peace in Buncombe County, sold his operation to John Jarrett (1776–1845) and Jarrett sold to James McConnell Smith, who built a bridge across the ferry route in 1833–34 (near today's Craven Street in Asheville, supplanted by an iron bridge in 1881). A law enacted in 1883 prohibited crossing "faster than a walk" over this new double-track, iron bridge in Asheville.
- Richmond Pearson (1852–1923), a bridge straddling the French Broad River in Asheville, built 1893. The 1916 flood washed it away, after which a reinforced concrete bridge replaced it.
- Edward Edwin George Carrier (1839–1927), a lumber baron, erected a bridge across the French Broad River in Asheville in 1899.

By 1798, John Davis operated a ferry across the French Broad River near the mouth of Newfound Creek. In 1801, the county of Buncombe established the following rates of ferriage:

> *Wagons and team and driver, fifty cents; two-wheeled carriage and team with driver, twenty-five cents; rider and horse, six cents; a footman, six cents; loose stock, two cents per head.*

At that time, a ferry operator might have employed a windlass—a system of ropes, pulleys and winches—to draw the flat-bottom rafts across the channel. Other operators used poles to maneuver their ferries. Still others drew the conveyances hand over hand with cables.

Smith's Bridge, Asheville, 1916 flood. *Courtesy of Knox Crowell.*

According to Forster Alexander Sondley, James McConnell Smith owned the first bridge across the French Broad River in Buncombe County. Initially operating a toll ferry, Smith later built a toll bridge across the expanse. The entrepreneurial Smith owned Asheville's popular Buck Hotel, which he built in 1825. (Smith served with Bartlett's Tennessee Regiment of the Union army, and although he was said to have been illiterate, he was a minister of the gospel.)

Those crossing Smith's bridge put out fifty cents for a four-horse wagon, thirty-seven cents for a three-horse wagon, thirty-one and one-half cents for a two-horse wagon, twenty-five cents for a one-horse wagon, fifty cents for a four-wheel carriage of pleasure, thirty-seven and one-half cents for a buggy of pleasure, twenty-five cents for a "gig or sulky of pleasure" or a cart, twelve and one-half cents for a "slide of truck," six and one-quarter cents for a man and horse, three cents for loose horses or mules, two cents for a footman and two cents per head for cattle. Fares were slightly less for empty equipages. Other toll takers collected fifty cents per wagon and team, twenty-five cents per two-wheeled carriage and team, six cents for a horse and rider and two cents per head for loose stock.

A map drawn by surveyor William Trout in 1878 reveals the following bridges, fords and a ferry crossings on the French Broad River from Buncombe through what are now Henderson and Transylvania Counties:

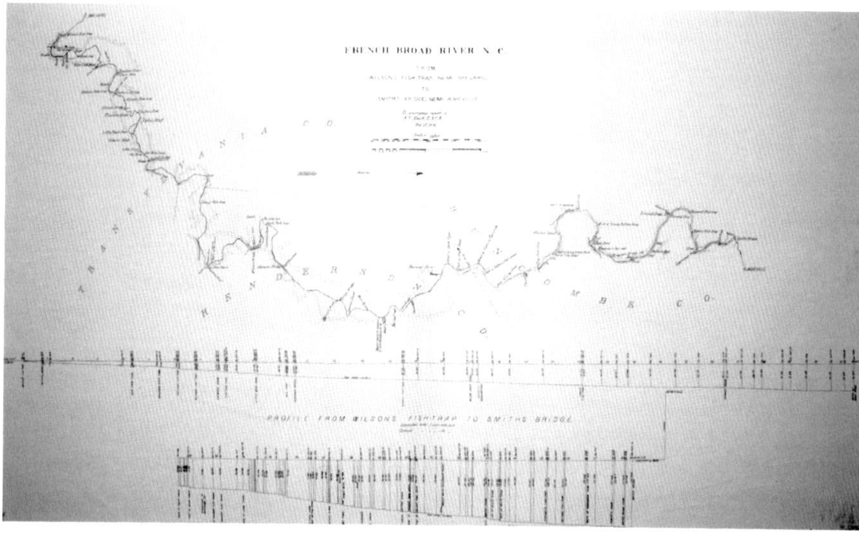

Surveyor William Trout's 1878 map of the French Broad River through the counties of Transylvania, Henderson and Buncombe. *Courtesy of Nancy Roberts, William E. Trout III and the Henderson County Genealogical and Historical Society.*

As seen from the Blannahassett Island Bridge, the Madison County seat of Marshall on the French Broad River. Courthouse (1907) designed by Richard Sharp Smith. *Photo by the author.*

Wilson's, Patton's, Allison's, Shuford's, McClain's, Johnson's, King's, Alexander's, Tennant's and Smith's bridges; Tennant's ferry; and Graham's, Clayton's, Old, Long Shoal, Taylor's and Patton's fords.

Early twentieth-century photographs depict a covered bridge over the Pacolet River at Morgan Chapel in Polk County. This crossing fell within the plantation of Henry Clay Morgan (1843–1909).

The Blannahassett Island bridges span the French Broad at Marshall, the county seat of Madison.

King's Bridge

Revolutionary War veteran Samuel King (1746–1828) took his pension in land, choosing acreage in Buncombe County (now the Mills River section of Henderson County) at the confluence of the French Broad and Mills Rivers. For King, this topography struck a familiar chord with his native Virginia.

Today's King's Bridge harks back to Samuel King's tenure on the fertile bottomlands flanking the French Broad River. His home stood in the general vicinity of the Regional Water Authority of Asheville plant now located on Haywood Road (NC Highway 191) northeast of School House Road. Grandview Lane, just southwest of this land and for the most part paralleling Haywood Road, runs largely on the alignment of the *original*

King's Bridge, over the French Broad River. *Photo by the author.*

NC Highway 191—with the section from the current NC Highway 191 to the ninety-degree turn (0.7 miles) having been constructed when the DOT realigned the highway in the mid-1950s. The current bridge (280 feet long by 28 feet wide), rehabilitated in 2013, rides over remains of the 1955 bridge. Ruins of the 1905 bridge abutments may be seen beneath the current bridge (NCDOT No. 129, steel stringer, five-span girder), which carries the highway today.

King descendants maintain that their ancestors—Samuel King's son Joseph King (1770–1849) and Joseph's son Benjamin King (1817–1883)—operated a ferry and built later a bridge at what is now a dead-end section of alligatored roadbed beyond the curve of Grandview Lane. King descendants and others speculate that this was the location of the first "King's Bridge," built by Samuel King's son Joseph.

King's Bridge was one of the few spans that survived the effects of the 1916 flood through Henderson County. Fanning's Bridge washed away, as did the bridge on the Brevard highway near Horse Shoe.

> *Rugby is on a boom so far as bridges are concerned. An iron bridge is being built over the French Broad at Kings bridge and we have a new bridge over the branch at the foot of Summey Hill, not before we needed it, however.*
>
> —French Broad Hustler, *October 26, 1905*
>
> *The meadow this side of the King's bridge is still a solid sheet of water and when at its highest reached up into the grove near Henry Lane's home on the Haywood road. Several families in this section lost nearly all their crops.*
>
> —French Broad Hustler, *July 20, 1916*

Written histories cite James Andrew Miller (1750–1808) as having built the first bridge over the French Broad River in what is now Henderson County. From *Revolutionary War Soldiers of Western North Carolina*, vol. 2:

> *There is some tradition that* [James Andrew] *Miller had previously owned a portion of the three thousand acres on the French Broad River granted to him about 1790.*

The Indians assisted him in constructing a raft of logs, and later when he built the first bridge, they lent a hand in helping to place the logs. The first bridge over the river was some distance from the present one—King's Bridge, near the Ladson home, and close to where the original building of French Broad Church was erected. At one end, the bridge was anchored on a natural abutment of rock, which still stands there in the river.

James Andrew Miller, his wife Rebecca Alexander Brank Miller (1745–1825), a grandchild of the Deaver family, and others are buried in the Old French Broad Baptist Church Cemetery—not far from where Andrew built the first bridge across the river.

Arguably, Miller built his bridge some distance southwest of the Haywood road, since he originally owned that land.

More French Broad Crossings

Additional bridges spanning the French Broad within Buncombe County include Asheville's Carrier Street Bridge, Pearson Street Bridge, West Asheville Bridge (built 1911, the only bridge in Asheville to survive the 1916 flood), Captain Jeff Bowen Bridge (formerly called Smoky Park Bridge, opened in 1950), the Interstate 40 French Broad River Bridge and the Alexander Bridge. In Transylvania and Henderson Counties, spans include the Patton, Crab Creek, Blantyre, Etowah School Road and the McClain Bridges—the latter once kept by Captain John Wellington McClain (1792–1879) across the French Broad between present-day Etowah and Horse Shoe (U.S. Highway 64 West).[36]

Johnson's Bridge carries Banner Farm Road across the French Broad River north of U.S. Highway 64 West (Brevard Road) at Horse Shoe. This bridge's provenance is attributed to Captain Hugh Johnson (1793–1876). In line with the Henderson County Court of Pleas and Quarter Sessions, Hugh Johnson was paid to make repairs to McClain's Bridge in 1848.

The namesake of Fanning Road and Fanning's Bridge over the French Broad River in the town of Mills River was the Reverend Francis M. Fanning (1812–1881) of Virginia, a Methodist circuit-riding minister. Fanning's son Joshua Soule Fanning (1842–1899) was postmaster at Gypsy in 1888.

Butler Bridge over the French Broad River, Mills River, at Butler Bridge Road was named for George Washington Butler (1838–1925) and Edmund Butler (1812–1895).

McDowell Bridge carries Old Haywood Road (NC Highway 191) over McDowell Creek and was named for Charles Gordon McDowell (1817–1907), a descendant of General Charles Quaker Meadows McDowell (1743–1815).

Davenport Bridge

The Davenport Bridge carries the Boyleston Highway (NC Highway 280) over the Mills River, south of Jeffress Road. The current bridge would be the third span, having been moved from the first and second locations. The first, built by Clarence DeCourcey Davenport (1848–1926), is locally called the "191 Mills River Bridge." The second bridge (from 1955) was named for James Theodore Davenport (1871–1946). The third bridge (No. 205, SR1764) opened in 1992. In 1993, the Henderson County Board of Commissioners adopted a resolution, prompting the North Carolina Board of Transportation to honor James Davenport and the Davenport family for their service to Mills River and Henderson County by naming the 1993 bridge "Davenport Bridge."

Davenport Bridge construction, Mills River, 1954. *Courtesy of Jim Davenport.*

Poinsett Bridge

The oldest surviving bridge in South Carolina is named for Charlestonian Joel Roberts Poinsett (1779–1852), a prominent politician and diplomat. This span is the only surviving one of a series of three arched bridges, retaining walls and forty-four stone culverts completed by October 1820 as part of a toll road from Columbia, South Carolina, to the South Carolina/North Carolina line. Constructed of locally quarried stone fitted without mortar, the Poinsett Bridge spans 130 feet over Little Gap Creek (a tributary of the north fork of the Saluda River and currently called Callahan Branch after Gresham Callahan). In what is now the Poinsett Bridge Heritage Preserve in the Greenville County watershed district just south of Henderson County, this bridge features a Gothic arch rising to nearly 14 feet from the bedrock to its apex.

Poinsett first saw the region of western North Carolina in 1816 on a journey from Washington, D.C., to the Ohio River, to Greenville, South Carolina, and back to his home in Charleston. As secretary of war in President Martin Van Buren's cabinet, Poinsett submitted to the senate a survey report by Lieutenant Colonel John Jacob Abert (1788–1863) of the

Poinsett Bridge, South Carolina. *Photo by the author.*

Corps of Topographical Engineers dated October 7, 1837, in Flat Rock, North Carolina.

According to some historians, Robert Mills (1781–1855)—architect-engineer of the Washington Monument—designed this bridge, which the South Carolina Board of Public Works constructed under the supervision of Joel Poinsett, who served as president of the board.

Poinsett Bridge was one of the first completed elements of the State Road (known also as "Saluda Mountain Road," a link in the Buncombe Turnpike) that would tie Charleston and Columbia to western North Carolina and eastern Tennessee. The South Carolina State Road ran from Charleston to Holly Hill, Cameron and Columbia; up the western shore of the Broad River to Spartanburg, Greenville, Sandy Flat, Tigerville and Callahan Mountain; alongside Little Gap Creek, the North Saluda River and Hodges Creek; and up the Saluda Gap.

The many who traveled the old South Carolina State Road and over this bridge included drovers and merchants conveying crops to market. Convoys of livestock and wagons hauling goods southward commonly followed this route. Mode of carriage determined toll fares, as did the number and type of animals either pulling conveyances or being herded along the road.

Later, seasonal resorts and health sanitariums mushroomed throughout the mountains, attracting South Carolina planters and their families. Years before the Civil War the road carried caravans of carriages and wagons, as groups of planters moved their families and servants up to the mountains to escape the Lowcountry's oppressive summer heat, humidity and malaria. While economic activity eventually declined on the State Road—many avoiding it in favor of toll-free roads—Lowcountry planters favored this route. This road and its bridges would also bear the traffic of stagecoaches, cavalries and cannons.

The bridge, now part of a protected heritage site, remained in use into the 1950s. It no longer serves as part of a traffic conduit.

A DAR marker on the south side of the Poinsett Bridge reads:

> *This bridge on the state road from Greenville to Asheville was built in 1820 by Abram Blanding, Acting Commissioner, Board of Public Works, Joel R. Poinsett, President.*

Peter Guice Bridge

Peter Guice/Guise was born in Buncombe County to parents who settled there soon after the Revolutionary War. Guice family members received land grants on both sides of the Green River, and Peter built the first bridge over the river in what became Henderson County.

Drovers, traders and settlers used an ancient Indian trail along Howard's Gap to cross the Blue Ridge from South Carolina to Tennessee—a principal route used by settlers and traders to enter what is now Henderson County from the south. Drovers moved livestock to markets through the mountains along this corridor, which supplied the principal pass through the region.

Young Peter Guice realized the need for a bridge and way station, both of which he constructed. He also ran a gristmill and blacksmith shop. Guice's inn served as an overnight stopover with accommodations and provisions for drovers and their livestock. The wooden toll bridge—much lower than

Installation of the closing girder for the eastbound-lane structure of the Peter Guice Memorial Bridge. *Courtesy of William B. Zeeveld, project engineer for the American Bridge Division of U.S. Steel.*

the present ones, built around 1820—added a measure of convenience and safety. Peter Guice's son, Joseph Elexander Guice (1821–1900), repaired the bridge and took over operations and was succeeded by his son William Dockery "Dock" Guice (1854–1924) and grandson Joseph "Joe" Ripley Guice (1883–1918). Joe replaced the original bridge, which had washed away during the 1916 flood.

A new highway was built, after which a stretch of Howard Gap Road fell into disuse, rendering Guice's wooden bridge to also fall into disrepair. When North Carolina highway engineers laid out I-26, they learned the old bridge crossing at Green River first constructed by the Guice family proved the logical locale over which to erect two colossal steel-frame/concrete bridges. Work commenced in 1967 and was completed in 1972. The height of 225 feet qualifies these as the third-tallest bridges carrying an interstate in the eastern United States. Cost of construction: $3,758,028.

William B. Zeeveld (1938–), project engineer for the American Bridge Division of U.S. Steel Corporation, shared, "The steel, fabricated in Ambridge, Pennsylvania, was railroaded upright to Zirconia.[37] With no roads to the construction site, a crew needed to forge a path in order to transport the material, which was loaded flat and hauled through the woods. Some of the girders, one-hundred-feet long by fourteen feet deep, weighed twenty-eight tons."

The present, dual Peter Guice Memorial Bridge (NCDOT No. 112EB and No. 108WB, I-26/U.S. 74), rehabilitated in 1997, honors the builder whose original bridge crossed the river at the same location.

Twentieth-Century Bridges

The first bridge built under the supervision of the North Carolina State Highway Commission, carrying NC Highway 42 over the Tar River in Edgecombe County, was erected in 1916 by the Roanoke Bridge Company for $15,641.81, according to *North Carolina Roadways* of January–February 1951.

According to a NCDOT "Bridge Location Map" index key, 2015, 381 citations (no names but numbered and keyed with routes listed) register 40 culverts, 18 pipes, 8 overhead signs, 2 "cntlvr" signs, 3 railroad bridges and 310 road bridges (including city bridges) in Henderson County.

North Carolina Route 1852 Bridge, Lake Summit. *Photo by Rick Lanier; author's collection.*

Route 1852 Bridge

Two bridges span Lake Summit at Tuxedo, one of them abandoned. Completed in 1921, the pin-connected Pennsylvania "Petit" through-truss bridge measures 228 feet long by 23 feet wide—the widest deck of any truss built in North Carolina before 1950. The bridge, carrying Old Summit Lake Road/SR1852, features twelve panels subdivided with intersecting diagonals. Traffic crosses the adjacent bridge completed in 1985 (NCDOT No. 63), a steel stringer, multi-beam span.

Lake Lure Flowering Bridge

An abandoned bridge (1925) of reinforced concrete spans the Rocky Broad River in Rutherford County. The 155-foot bridge was closed to traffic in 2011 and outfitted in 2013 as a garden.

High Bridge

Between East Flat Rock and the Henderson/Polk County line, the seven-span, steel-plate-girder and reinforced concrete High Bridge carries U.S. Highway 176 (Spartanburg Highway) over the Green River Gorge near Lake Summit. Featuring open spandrel arches, the bridge stands 138 feet from crown to bed and measures 712 feet long by 30 feet wide.[38] Early newspaper articles trumpeted this bridge as a "great engineering marvel," claiming that its structural arch "conforms to no laws of arcs, curves." Additional descriptions included, "[A new structural arch] which conforms to no mathematical laws of arcs and curves and one which was designed entirely from the graphs of strains and stresses and in the proper sense is not an arch or curve at all since at no point has it focal or a center point of radius. It is neither a simple arc, a multi-centered arch nor parabola." A *Times-News* reporter wrote of it:

> *A towering symbol of North Carolina's progressive, trail-blazing spirit...situated about five miles from Hendersonville on the highway to Tryon and Spartanburg. It was built at a cost of $113,000 in order that*

Second High Bridge construction. *Photo by Brad Jones; courtesy of the Henderson County Genealogical and Historical Society.*

Arthur and Dovie Hamilton Staton at the original High Bridge. *Courtesy of Gayle Hamilton Stepp.*

> *these few miles may conform to the high standard the state has set for itself, and in order that a main artery of travel into the most beautiful section of the state might be as beautiful as possible and as nearly perfect for material use as engineering skill could devise.*

Herbert E. Howes (1881–1962) and George Lynn Sarsfield (1861–1947) surveyed the site in 1926. The resulting 1927 span incorporated 3,014 cubic yards of concrete, 320,000 pounds of steel and 5,300 pounds of plates and bolts, weighing "a million or more pounds." State engineer W.F. Hunter (1878–?) of Raleigh designed the arches. E.A. Woods and Company of Andrews, North Carolina, built the bridge, which J.H. Anderson directed as superintendent of construction, assisted by Neely J. Cromer (1895–1955), resident engineer. Benjamin Fred Teague (1890–1936) inspected the project. The bridge was designed to carry the standard load of "two fourteen-ton trucks, live weight, passing, and the amount of dead weight that its spans would bear."

The original span was outfitted as a parking lot and pedestrian observation deck alongside the current traffic bridge (NCDOT No. 375), completed in 2001, which supplanted the 1927 bridge (NCDOT No. 120). The route follows the Saluda Grade.

ALL IN A DRAY'S WORK

With progress and growth came the call for transporting people and goods. The produce-market center of Hendersonville's early years—the Jockey Lot at Main Street and First Avenue East (Chestnut Street)—served also as a parking facility for horses, oxen, mules, buggies, carriages and wagons and supplied a hub for gossip and politicking. Business mogul Flavius Goodson "Flave" Hart Sr. (1852–1940) owned the lot.

To serve the demands of a growing town, there existed from its formative years at least fifteen livery stables in Hendersonville and no fewer than two at Flat Rock, as well as others throughout the county. Many of the hacks delivered luggage by horse- or mule-drawn wagons to hotels and boardinghouses and conveyed freight from the Southern Railway station to merchants. Certain liveries offered repair services and blacksmithing. One such enterprise operated where the building that houses Flanagan's Printing stands today alongside Third Avenue West—in the days when Third was called College Street. John Lafayette Orr (1855–1920) and his son Glover T. Orr (1878–1936) operated a livery on Fifth Avenue East.[39] Ezra Johnson "John" Francis (1875–1958) and his wife, Minnie Belle Potts Francis (1883–1980), operated a thriving livery business on South Main Street.

Draymen moving produce from Flave Hart's Jockey Lot to the Southern Railway station at Hendersonville. *Courtesy of the Baker-Barber Collection, Community Foundation of Henderson County, Henderson County Public Library.*

Hacks at Brevard. *Courtesy of the Rowell Bosse North Carolina Room, Transylvania County Library.*

William J. "Will" Turner (1882–1929) owned a draying operation at 209 North Second Avenue West and later the Star Dray Company on Maple Street in the depot district. In addition to hauling, the entrepreneurial Turner dealt also in wood, coal, crushed stone, sand, brick and grading. Turner bought out a livery business formerly conducted by Henry Franklin Finnegan (1887–1917),[40] as indicated by a notice in a *French Broad Hustler* of March 1915. Turner purchased the Star Dray Company, organized in 1906 by Sam Y. Bryson (1877–1925), in 1914. After Turner's death, Horace Dewitt Morris (1884–1936) and Daniel E. Patty (1893–1954) took over the business. Turner and his family lived in Hyman Heights.

In Hendersonville's depot district, William Alexander Keith (1880–1947) owned the Hendersonville Buggy Company, and William Claude Turner (1856–1919) ran a stable on Locust Street. On King Street stood Brookshire's Stable, owned by James B. Brookshire (1874–1930).[41] Thomas Andrew "Tom" Jackson (1868–1934), John Henry Lane (1883–1928) and Hiram Tillmon Brock (1881–1917) founded the latter business before Brookshire and his partner Voltaire Condorsed Volney "Vol" Shepherd (1869–1946) took it over. Brookshire bought out Shepherd. Brookshire's sons Ernest R. (1894–1971) and Otto A. Brookshire (1897–1954) succeeded their father in the business. T.A. Jackson also owned the Hendersonville Livery and Transfer Company.

Marcus M. Patton Arledge (1856–1938), John Livingston (1869–1919) and Samuel Lee "Sam" Corn (1883–1959) operated stables in

The Star Dray Company building on Seventh Avenue East, Hendersonville. *Photo by the author.*

Hendersonville hacks with luggage. *Baker photo; courtesy of the Henderson County Genealogical and Historical Society.*

Hendersonville, as did John Wesley Smathers (1861–1943) and George Whitfield Liverett (1896–1957). Nicholas Adolphus "N.D." Hollingsworth (1869–1910) kept a livery stable on Depot Road (today's West Blue Ridge Road) in Flat Rock.

Henderson County's hacks and chauffeurs included John Frank Hisaw Israel (1875–1957), Rufus D. "Rufe" Anders (1882–1953), Beeman Gregory (1858–1926) and Smiley McCall (1907–1976). Gregory, a porter (listed as "mulatto" in census records), hacked for the Hodgewell Hotel. Sam Corn of the Corn Transfer Company owned one of Hendersonville's first engine-powered trucks, a Model T one-ton vehicle.

Some of Hendersonville's grand hotels, including the Wheeler and Kentucky Home, boasted their own liveries.

The 1921 *Miller's Directory* listed the following under dray services:

- BLUE RIDGE GARAGE, corner of Main St. and First Ave. E., opposite [Confederate] monument; mechanic, automobile supplies, oils, gasoline, vulcanizing repair work a specialty.
- CAROLINA OIL & SUPPLY CO., Fourth Ave. E. on railroad tracks; coal, wood, feed, draying and storage.
- FRANK BROWN, Patton Ave., near Third Ave. W.
- GEORGE CORN, N. Main (Hyman Heights).
- H.C. BIGGERS, 352 Rhodes.
- HENDERSONVILLE TRANSFER CO., 703 N. Main.
- JAMES B. BROOKSHIRE (stables, sales and feed), King St., corner of Second Ave. E.
- J.M. DERMID, 224 Third Ave. E., corner of Grove St.
- LUTHER LATHAM, 717 Seventh Ave. E.
- M.A. HARDEN, 324 First Ave. E.
- MITCHEL ANDREWS, Flat Rock (stables, sales and feed).
- M.N.P. ARLEDGE, 215 S. Main St.
- PINK DRAKE, 358 First Ave. E.
- SAM CORN TRANSFER CO., 416 King St.
- STANLEY SEXTON, 721 Seventh Ave. E.
- WILE TRANSFER CO., 325 N. Main: All kinds of draying, hauling and storage. Trunks, freight, baggage. Prompt service. Long-distance hauling, Geldest J. Wile [1893–1949] and Charles Scronce Corpening [1896–1941], proprietors.
- WM. GRIFFIN, Oak near Sixth Ave. W.

Hendersonville's "Depot District" with the Seventh Avenue Buggy Company. *Courtesy of the Henderson County Genealogical and Historical Society.*

The 1926–1927 *Miller's Directory* listed Valentine & Co., "Crushed Stone & Sand," supplying, no doubt, surfacing for the well-traveled roads of the county.

Eventually, hacks and dray companies gave way to machine shops, service stations and automobile dealerships.

Local Boy Makes Good

Author Frank Lockwood FitzSimons wrote:

> *Alonzo Shipman was connected with Kanuga Lake long before it became a conference center for the Episcopal Church. Mr.* [Smiley] *McCall said that of all those early hack drivers Alonzo Shipman was the most successful. When the automobile began to take the place of horse-drawn vehicles, Mr. Shipman switched to automobiles for transportation of people. From a start with one automobile for transportation, Mr. Shipman eventually developed Queen City Trailways, an interstate bus system.*

Alonzo C. Shipman (fourth from left) and Jake Hughes (second from right) with their team at Southeastern Stages, Augusta, Georgia. *Courtesy of Southeastern Stages, Inc.*

Arguably, Smiley T. McCall (1907–1976) was confused about the details of Mr. Shipman's success. Research turned up Alonzo Curtis "Lon" Shipman (1900–1989), born in Henderson County, North Carolina, died in Fulton County, Georgia. As a youth, Shipman worked as a hack for George Erwin Cullet Stephens (1873–1946) at the Kanuga Club in south-central Henderson County. With his brother Seldon Edgar Shipman (1896–1981), Lon founded a bus company in Hendersonville in the mid-1920s. Seldon exited the company in the late 1920s. Seldon also operated Shipman Taxi Service from Main Street.

In the early 1930s, Lon took on Jacob William "Jake" Hughes (1898–1987) as a partner in Augusta, Georgia. Lon served as president of what would be the merger of three independent bus companies, which he and Hughes named Southeastern Stages Inc., incorporated in 1933 and headquartered in Atlanta. Today, Lon's granddaughter's husband, Mike Dickson (1965–), serves as president of Southeastern Stages, which logs an average of three million miles per year.

Queen City Coach Company, founded in 1928, joined National Trailways, a nationwide association of independent operators and companies. Shipman's Southeastern Stages was not one of the seventy coach companies absorbed by Trailways. Lonnie Adam Love (1894–1969) founded Queen City Coach Company in Charlotte, North Carolina, in 1928, and that company is now a part of Trailways.

> *Alonzo Shipman was my great-uncle. He and my grandfather Seldon Shipman founded the company in the mid-twenties (it had a different name at that time). My grandfather exited the business in the late 1920s and my great-uncle moved the company from Hendersonville to Augusta. In the early 1930s Alonzo took on a partner named Jake Hughes. Together they came up with the name Southeastern Stages. They incorporated in 1933. Today Alonzo's grand-son-in-law is president of the company.*
>
> —*Shane Shipman (1968–)*

> *The two founders of Southeastern Stages, A.C. ("Lon") Shipman and J.W. ("Jake") Hughes, devoted their efforts to making the new company a major participant in the growing intercity bus industry. The eventual interlining of passengers with Greyhound Lines and other regular scheduled carriers at various transfer points provided expanded service to travelers and the company began to really grow. Today, Southeastern Stages operates daily scheduled service between cities in the Southeast including: Atlanta, GA; Asheville, N.C.; Charleston, S.C.; Columbia, S.C.; Myrtle Beach, S.C.; Savannah, GA, and Fayetteville, N.C. Our nationwide operating authority allows us to provide charter services to destinations throughout the U.S. and Canada.*
>
> —*Southeastern Stages, Atlanta, Georgia*

Buses, Taxicabs and Truck Lines

The Model-T Ford, when used as a taxicab, was nicknamed "jitney bus." Such were touring cars operating on fifteen-minute schedules in Hendersonville, basically replacing the "dummy" train and streetcars until street rails were discontinued by 1918 due to increasing ownership of private automobiles. "Jitney" was slang for a nickel, the original fare to ride such conveyances. Some have noted that Charles C. Collins Sr. (1901–1982) was Hendersonville's first bus driver.

Miller's Directory, 1926–1927, listed:

> *Red Bus Line, Inc., office, Rose Pharmacy Main St., operating buses on a regular schedule between Asheville, Hendersonville and Black Mountain; and Potts' Auto Service, F.C. Sheldon, proprietor, Taxi.*

The 1939–1940 issue of the directory included the Union Bus Terminal:

> *Ames Hotel Building, 415–417 N. Church St.*
> *City 10¢ Taxi: We specialize in all mountain tours, B. Jackson Jr., manager, 432 N. Church St.*

Former Greyhound Bus Lines Terminal, 337 Seventh Avenue East, Hendersonville. Built around 1930 by the Pure Oil Company, this building served as Bella Dura Pure Oil Service Station, Fisher's Purol Station and the Chicken Shack. *Photo by the author.*

John L. Loy (1894–1953) founded City Bus Company in the early 1940s. The Mullin-Kille & Times-News 1969 *Hendersonville City Directory* stated, under "Intercity Bus Service":

> *Intercity Passenger Bus Lines serving Hendersonville include Greyhound, Queen City Coach and Carolina Scenic Trailways.*

The directory listed Greyhound and Trailways Bus Lines in the Union Bus Terminal at 707 North Main Street. Cyril Earl Livingston (1907–1992) served as manager.

The same publication conveyed the following under "Trucking Concerns":

> *Serving Hendersonville with regular scheduled service: E.T.&W.N.C., McLean, Dance, Ryder (Great Southern Division), Overnite, Central Motor Lines, Blue Ridge, Pilot, Mason & Dixon, Associated Transport, Johnston Motor Lines, Silver Fleet, Frederickson, Akers Motor Lines, Bowman Transportation and Carolina Freight Line…Youngblood Truck Lines and Clay Hyder Truck Lines have their main terminals in Henderson County.*

The Mullin-Kille & Times-News 1969 *Hendersonville City Directory* listed the following taxicab companies and services:

> *Blue Bird Taxi Co. (combined with City Cab Co. and Deluxe Cab Co., limousine service to airport; 622 N. Main St.; Bill Deaver and Mrs. Mayo C. Deaver, owners)*
>
> *Deaver's Cab Co. (airport trips, sightseeing trips; 621 N. Main St.; Mr. & Mrs. Bill O'Kelly, owners).*

Additional listings included Bradley's Cab Service, Carolina Taxi Service, Checker Taxi Cab, Independent Cab Co., Johnson's Taxi Service, Radio Cab Co., Robinson Cab Service, Skyland Taxi and Terminal Taxi. Garland Jackson (1898–1968) was one of the city's many taxi drivers.

Devil Wagons and Speed Demons

Automobiles came on the scene when electricity and Grafonolas were still curiosities.[42] The first horseless carriages counted as luxury items piloted

William Mulvaney with his Willys Overland coupé. *Courtesy of Helen Ingle.*

mostly by wealthy men as a hobby. In 1900, just one in every 9,500 Americans owned one—40 percent of them steam-powered, 38 percent electric and 22 percent gasoline-powered. The hobby caught on. By 1901, the number of car owners had increased to nearly 14,000 and by 1915, 1.75 million pleasure cars plied American roads. The year 1901 also witnessed the first appearance of license plates on American vehicles—and production of steam-powered automobiles by the White Sewing Machine Company of Cleveland, Ohio.

Jean Joseph Étienne Lenoir (1822–1900) of Belgium built the first successful gasoline-powered automobile in 1858, but four decades elapsed before automobiles would be made available to the general public. In 1901, Ransom Eli Olds (1864–1950) opened the first automobile factory in Detroit, which produced 425 cars on an assembly line in its first year. An R.E. Olds product, the Curved Dash Olds—a two-passenger, gasoline-powered runabout model—sold for $625.

Other early cars included the Riker electric automobile and the Locomobile steam automobile in 1900; the Autocar, Pierce Motorette and the White Steam Stanhope in 1901; the Franklin in 1902; the Cadillac, Curved-dash Olds and Winston Touring Car in 1903; the Columbia electric automobile in 1904; and the "Flivver" in 1908.

Tourists on a mountain excursion with their Graham-Paige. *C.H. Oak Collection; courtesy of the Henderson County Genealogical and Historical Society.*

Known as "Tin Lizzies," the "Flivver," or Model T, was the brainchild of Henry Ford (1863–1947), whose vision was to build and supply "a motor car for the great multitude." In an era when a good horse could be bought for \$150 to \$300, a Flivver would set a buyer back about \$850. With improved methods of mass production, stripped-down models sold for \$300 or less by 1925. Ford produced nine models, including eight prototypes: the A, B, C, F, K (the "Brush"), N, R and S—and the T, each of them available in any color the buyer desired, providing the color were black. The Model T was voted "Car of the Century" in a 1999 election overseen by the Global Automotive Elections Foundation.

William Crapo "Billy" Durant (1861–1947) and Frederic Latta Smith (1870–1954) gave Ford a run for his money by cofounding General Motors in 1908. The new company combined Buick, Cadillac and Oldsmobile.

In the very early twentieth century, the *Western Carolina Democrat* and *French Broad Hustler* conveyed lamentations about newfangled automobiles, which included the phrases, "devil wagons," "reckless disregard of public safety," "Main Street, a speedway." The devils in the wagons—"who think their rights are supreme"—would have most likely been Lowcountry gentry and other outsiders—visitors to and summertime residents of western North Carolina. Those visitors and part-timers included John Frampton Maybank (1870–1941) and his brother Dr. Joseph Maybank (1868–1942) who, together with a cousin and a Mr. Mullens, made a road trip from Hendersonville to Charleston in 1914. The *Charleston News and Courier* carried a story about the foursome having made the 265-mile journey "at 19 mph in just 17 hours, including layovers." The *French Broad Hustler* carried the same story under the headline "New Automobile Record."

According to the *Hustler*, the first automobile made its appearance in Hendersonville in 1902. The brief included a photograph, which did not identify the make of the vehicle or its passengers. Many have claimed that John Wesley Smathers, a liveryman, owned one of the first automobiles in Hendersonville. And shortly thereafter, stables and liverymen would begin giving way to garages and auto mechanics.

In 1902, the Reverend Reginald Norton Willcox (1873–1929) of England moved to Edneyville and worked with Episcopal missions and the churches of St. Paul's and St. James. Initially, Willcox's own feet or the back of his trusty mare Bess provided his primary modes of transportation as he trekked unpaved byways between his priestly calls. Under his watch as president of the Greater Hendersonville Club, Willcox appointed a committee to promote auto events with parades and an auto endurance run from the deeper South to Hendersonville for the 1913 summer season. At the time, Willcox owned a motorcycle, and in 1914, he purchased a Hupmobile—said to have been among the first cars owned in Henderson County.

In one of the earliest touring cars to be driven through the region, colleagues Harvey Samuel Firestone Sr. (1868–1938), Henry Ford (1863–1947) and Thomas Alva Edison (1847–1931) visited entrepreneur Captain Marion Columbus Toms (1843–1917) and textile mogul Joseph Oscar Bell Sr. (1866–1939) in Tuxedo for two days in the summer of 1906 during a tour of western North Carolina.

In the *Henderson Gold Leaf*, April 20, 1911, this news appeared: "The Henderson Loan and Real Estate Company just purchased a two-passenger Hupmobile for the use of the company."

John P. Patton (1853–1921) also owned one of the first cars in Hendersonville. Patton ran a blacksmith shop and learned to repair and maintain automobiles. An advertisement in a 1921 issue of the *Watauga Democrat* touted the Hupmobile with such accolades as "easy handling, snappy pickup and above all, downright reliable." Either of two models, a five-passenger touring car or a two-passenger roadster, could be had for $1,650.

As stated by his daughter, Louise H. Bailey of Flat Rock, William Bell White Howe III, MD (1881–1948), a country doctor, made house calls on a motorcycle before he purchased his first Buick touring car.

In June 1910, a group of six—Nora McCrery, Eads Poitevent, H.E. Vincent, S.B. Merrick, Pink King and E.M. Bobb—unloaded a Chalmers-

Detroit "60" 1910-model motorcar in Hendersonville with the intention of touring Henderson and Buncombe Counties in the automobile, according to the *French Broad Hustler*. With automobiles being such novelties at the time, another report from the *Hustler* mentioned "Messrs. Frank Loughran, Richie Loughran and W.C. Hawk passing through Hendersonville en route to Greenville in Loughran's big touring car."

In the same year, Carl Thompson (1893–1990) set a record for having traveled in an Overland touring car from Spartanburg to Hendersonville in four hours and twenty-three minutes. The route included Howard's Gap. Meanwhile, a Stanley Steamer had already set a speed record of 127 miles per hour in 1906.

In 1915 McGraw-Hill published *The Gasoline Automobile*, the first do-it-yourself manual for car owners. The book included tips on driving, maintaining and repairing the newfangled conveyances.

Automobile manufacturers, capitalizing on the new trend of motoring, designed and fabricated all from affordable to extravagant in driving machines. Early models included the open-top Winton, REO Flying Cloud and Royale models, Stearns-Knight cars and Mormon convertibles, Pierce Arrow 66, Packard Phaeton, Oakland, LaSalle, Auburn, Cord and Willys Overland Touring Car.

In the midst of this newfound mania with horseless carriages, most of western North Carolina drivers still employed horse-drawn buggies,

"Rapid Transit." *Baker photo; courtesy of the Henderson County Genealogical and Historical Society.*

surreys, basket phaetons and wagons[43]—the horsepower frequently spooked by the occasional passing of a motorized vehicle. Livery stables maintained a brisk business, including that of William Gaston Gullick (1844–1924), who specialized in repairing and painting buggies, carriages and wagons.

By July 1912, North Carolina had passed a new law for a five-dollar state license for automobiles. The state returned three dollars of each fee for building and maintaining county roads.

The Novelty of Speed

"Speed Maniacs Arouse Wrath of Ruralities," screamed a headline in the *Hustler* in September 1912. Jessie William Merrimon (1849–1938) of Balfour told the reporter, "At least 100 machines traverse the Asheville-Hendersonville road daily." Merriman described the drivers as "joy riders" in "buzz wagons," driving recklessly, "some of them as fast as 35 mph!"

At the time, the speed limit on Hendersonville's Main Street was ten miles per hour, and one gas pump stood in front of the Clarke Hardware Company building, between Fifth and Sixth Avenues.[44]

A flapper with her Stutz coupé. *C.H. Oak Collection; courtesy of the Henderson County Genealogical and Historical Society.*

Herbert Ladd Towle (1874–1954) penned a column for the February 1915 issue of *Scribner's* magazine titled "The Woman at the Wheel." Towle, a sexist by modern standards, described women as fragile creatures who cared not to stray far from home and their domestic chores. With a sense of astonishment, he remarked on the throngs of women suddenly taking to the roads—not exclusively in petite models but also in large roadsters. He reasoned that modern appurtenances had made driving more facile for the fairer sex, with features such as automatic spark advance, electric gear shifts and the advent of the power tire pump. The most advanced driving feature, he suggested, would have been a pedal-actuated "foot-plunger" (an electric or pneumatic starter) in lieu of the old-fashioned hand cranks. Even still, he explained, should the delicate driver encounter a flat—and albeit with the convenience of a power tire pump onboard—she would wait for a male protagonist to come to her rescue.

Wheeling and Dealing

Harry David Blomberg (1904–1991) owned Harry's Cadillac-Pontiac—originally Harry's Cadillac-LaSalle, founded in 1923, and currently known as Harry's on the Hill—Asheville's first new car dealership and western North Carolina's first Cadillac dealership.

For a city of moderate size, Hendersonville hosted multiple automobile dealerships over the years. In the 1920s, such companies included Brock, Groome, Hendersonville Hudson (South Main near Alamance), Hendersonville Willys, Hermes, Johnson, Kaystone, Logan, Thompson and Wetmur.

Joines Motor Company occupied a brick building on Hendersonville's East Allen Street at King Street. Shadrack Rufus "Shade" Joines Sr. (1886–1955) owned the company, where he sold and serviced Ford automobiles, trucks and tractors. Joines owned another dealership in Brevard. Francis Sampson Wetmur Sr. (1869–1956) of the Wetmur Motor Company later sold Fords from Joines's location next occupied by Chipman-LaCrosse Hosiery Mills,[45] the Robotyper Corporation and then the Henderson County School Administration and Henderson County Land Planning Department.

Shipman Motor Company began as Shipman Brothers Garage (Ming and Seldon Shipman) on First Avenue East near Main Street. Mingus Lafayette "Ming" Shipman (1894–1959) operated the company, selling and servicing Fords at 633–639 North Main Street, a corner that would later host a number of automobile dealerships.

Boyd's Gulf Service and Boyd Pontiac Company, 1946. *Courtesy of Cam Boyd Jr.*

L.C. "Bubba" Boyd Sr. (1915–2000) bought a Gulf service station at 200 Fourth Avenue West at Church Street in 1932. He soon added Studebaker sales, followed by Pontiac and Cadillac. In 1948, the dealership relocated to North Main Street at Five Points and U.S. Highway 25 (901 Northwest Main Street), where it flourished for more than sixty years before relocating to the Spartanburg Highway's "mile of cars" in 2013. Currently known as Boyd Chevrolet Cadillac Buick (adding Chevrolet in 2011), the dealership has been owned and operated by three generations of Boyds. Lewis Campbell "Cam" Boyd Jr. (1944–) sold the Five Points property to the Henderson County school system. L.C. "Les" Boyd III (1973–) currently serves as president of Boyd Chevrolet Cadillac Buick Inc.

> *Dad's favorite part of business was the trade—trading cars for property, rugs, dogs, horses, antiques—anything on which you could put a value. Sometimes he made money; sometimes he did not. He was a true trader and an absolute character with a lot of good friends. He was one of the original one hundred people who started the Hendersonville Country Club and was a charter member of the Hendersonville Rotary Club—past president with twenty-five years of perfect attendance. He was a Mason, a Shriner and an Elk and was appointed by Governor Hunt to sit on the state school board. He served on the Hendersonville High School Board. He was one*

of eight people who started the Home Bank and Trust Company, which became a part of Bank of North Carolina and later the Bank of America. He accomplished a lot and gave back to our community whenever he had the opportunity.

—L.C. Boyd Jr.

In the building currently housing the Brunson's furniture business, 400–6 North King Street at Fourth Avenue East, Kaystone Motors opened in the 1920s with Buick models. Ralph R. Orr (1902–1962) and Everett O. Mitchell (1905–1977) operated Auto Sales Company and Automotive Machine Company from this building during the late 1930s and early 1940s. The latter company sold used and new cars and trucks and featured Plymouth and Dodge products.

City Motor & Sales Company Inc., owned by James Edward Smith (1908–1971), president-manager, occupied 631 North King Street and sold Chrysler and Plymouth models. James Hoyt Lampley later served as president with Clyde L. Jackson (1923–1989), manager. The dealership also provided sales and service.

James Hoyt "Tappy"/"Pappy" Lampley (1891–1975) served as superintendent of the Hendersonville City Water Works, where he picked up the nickname "Tappy." In 1934, Lampley acquired half interest in and was president of City Motor & Sales Company. In 1935, he bought the remaining half interest, renamed the business Lampley Motors, incorporated in 1937 and moved the business to 609 North Main Street. In 1945, Lampley built a one-story Quonset hut–style brick structure with a semidomed roof (101–11

Site of the former Lampley Motors Inc. dealership. *Photo by the author.*

North Church Street) where he sold and serviced Chrysler and Plymouth models. In 1953, he moved the dealership to Main Street at Seventh Avenue. In 1954, he sold the Chrysler-Plymouth franchise to William Fitzhugh "Pete" Folsom (1909–2004) and relocated to smaller quarters on Kanuga Street, where he sold used vehicles. Pete Folsom Motor Company, at 447–49 South Main Street (new and used cars at the site of present-day Auto Zone), added Dodge to its line. Folsom sold the business to John F. "Bud" Egolf Jr. (1920–2005) in the 1970s. Egolf subsequently moved to Duncan Hill Road. Lampley's Church Street building later housed Everett Gusta "Gus" Thomas's (1901–59) Thomas Motor Company (1954–59), Grose's Corner auto sales and service (1962–67), Superior Rug Company (1969) and then the Henderson County Technical Institute (1971).[46] The most recent occupant, the Next to New resale shop, vacated the building in 2015.

Philip Homer "P.H." Grose Jr. (1925–) opened Grose's Corner at the Shipman Motors building on Main Street and 122 Seventh Avenue West in 1957. Grose sold used vehicles and also owned a filling/service station and body shop. In 1962, he added Lincoln and Mercury models to his line and GMC trucks in 1964 at his new location in the Lampley Motors building on Church Street. Grose, first to sell Lincolns in Hendersonville, moved his "Corner" to his new building at 1105 Spartanburg Highway in 1967. He also sold Saab. The Motormasters—a classic car restoration company, owned by Grose's son P.H. Grose III—and Scot King Auto Sales currently occupy the space.

In the late 1940s, Blair-McLeod Motors—the franchise agency for Studebaker-Packard sales and service—operated at 305–7 North Church Street, moving later to 220 South Main Street. Lawrence Andrew Blair (1897–1991) served as president and manager and Blair's son-in-law John Franklin McLeod Jr. (1924–2007) as secretary-treasurer. In 1971, John Franklin "Frank" McLeod III (1952–) joined the business. The company added Rambler, Land Rover and Mercedes-Benz to its line. It was the first dealership in the area to sell Subaru. The business operated until 1976.

In 1957, Roderick Woodrow "Pete" Stokes (1917–2003), Charles Reginald Rouse Jr. (1924–1994), Herbert McLemore (1931–2013) and others opened a dealership, originally selling Mercury products and later picking up Lincoln, Chrysler and Plymouth models. Reggie and Pete of Rouse-Stokes Motors Inc. bought out their partners. Originally located at 119 South Main Street (presently occupied by Never Blue restaurant), the business moved to the Shipman Motors building. Rouse opened a Toyota and Jeep dealership on the Asheville Highway in 1966.

Hunter Chevrolet Company at Five Points. *Photo by Lucile Stepp Ray; courtesy of the Henderson County Genealogical and Historical Society.*

Hunter Chevrolet Company, owned by Tom Hunter (1913–1999), opened in 1940 at 119 South Main Street and also sold Allis Chalmers tractors. In 1945, the dealership moved to the Shipman Motors building, next to North Main Street at Five Points, and then to 2520 Asheville Highway. Grady J. Vaughn (1913–2015) sold Lincoln and Mercury models from the space on South Main Street. Dixon Motor Company (Albert T. Dixon, 1899–1968) occupied the space from 1939 to 1940.

Additional dealerships in Hendersonville included:

- GARRETT MOTOR COMPANY opened in 1955. Owned by Cecil C. Garrett (1924–1998), the company carried tractors and used vehicles, operating from Dana and Tracy Grove Roads (Garrett Ford Tractor Company) and 1253 North Main Street, later moving to Duncan Hill Road. In 1972, Bryan Easler (1935–) bought into the business, and the partners, doing business as Garrett-Easler Ford, added Ford products to their line. Easler bought out Garrett, and the company gave rise to Mac Easler Ford (now Four Seasons Ford, owned by Roger Gregg) and Easler Toyota on Spartanburg Highway, headed by Stephanie Easler (1961–).
- T.L. OSBORNE INC., Oldsmobile and GMC trucks, 127 South Main Street, 780 North Church Street and 1325 New Spartanburg Road, owned by T. Lee Osborne (1891–1963).

- H&H Motor Company, new and used cars, 101 North Church Street.
- Fletcher Motor Company, owned by Lloyd Cornelius "Pete" Youngblood (1908–1978) in Fletcher. Pete's son Larry "Joe" Youngblood (1944–2009) took over the business as Fletcher BMW. Youngblood sold to Don Elliott (with car dealerships also in Texas), who formed Sunshine Chevrolet and later moved to Long Shoals Road. Fletcher Motors sold and serviced Chevrolet and BMW vehicles. Joe sold the BMW dealership to Field's Automotive (out of Chicago), which operates on Airport Road.

A Benevolent and High-Velocity Practitioner

Remembered as a generous and compassionate fellow, James Steven Brown (1866–1958) began his illustrious career as a doctor of obstetrics by making house calls in a buggy drawn by his mare Dolly. Dr. Brown succeeded his buggy with a Ford Model T and thereafter with an assortment of automobiles, some of which he wrecked. He owned one of the first telephones in the area. Brown was born in Mount Ulla, North Carolina, and after attending medical school at Northwestern University in Chicago he practiced in Salisbury for ten years before settling in Henderson County in 1906.

Louise Howe Bailey (1915–2009), whom he delivered, recalled an occasion when Brown barreled south on Church Street, hit a curb and rolled his car onto its side. "He got out and walked the rest of the way to his appointment," Bailey said, "with the wheels of the car still spinning." On another adventure, Brown's car plunged over an embankment, somersaulting and landing in the muck of Dulus Stepp's recently drained millpond. Other old-timers enjoy retelling the tale—whether or not true—of Dr. Brown having negotiated with a car dealer for a trade-in. When asked to inspect the vehicle he had intended to trade, Brown told the salesman he would need to drag the millpond to see it.

> *Dr. Brown had brought a new era to the medical community in Henderson County when he came with obstetrical instruments and chloroform and a use of them that established him as the leading obstetrician in western North Carolina. Some other doctors have delivered triplets, but Dr. Brown perhaps holds the record for having brought three sets of them into the world. Before Patton Memorial—Henderson County's first hospital—was built in 1913, he took seriously ill children into his large stone house that stood on the Greenville Highway south of town.*
>
> —*Louise H. Bailey*

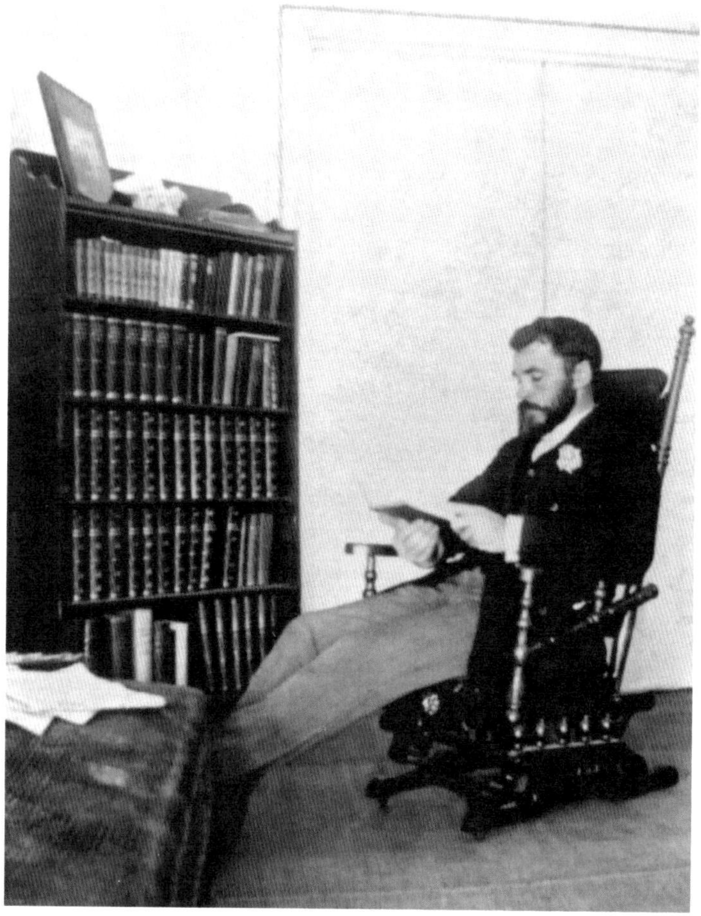

Dr. James Steven Brown in his study at Salisbury. *Courtesy of Mary Campbell Beshere and the Henderson County Heritage Museum.*

Old-timers recall that Dr. Brown willingly helped when needed—even those laboring mothers and other patients who could not afford to pay for his services. He traveled on all manner of roadbeds, including those mired in mud and pocked with ruts. Dr. Brown practiced medicine for sixty-five years, and his home at times doubled as a pediatric ward. In 1948, the American Medical Association awarded a gold medal to him for having "won universal recognition for exceptional service as a general practitioner." And *Ripley's Believe It or Not* listed Brown for having delivered twins on his ninety-second birthday. Brown's granddaughter Sarah Cannon (1950–) shared that he brought "at least 6,547 babies" into the world during his lengthy and impressive medical career.

A doctor's buggy, Mountain Home and Farm Museum. *Photo by the author.*

Following his surgery and a period of hospitalization Dr. Brown wrote:

> *After three long months they let me wobble out under regulatory restrictions, i.e., never more to drive a car (and I haven't driven much over 50,000 miles since); see no night patients (and I have seen only those who needed a doctor's help); do no more obstetrics (but my count has increased from 5,786 to 6,080). Thanks to three excellent surgeons, with kind help from a skilled dietitian and a lovely nurse...and my ever-present Guardian Angels, I have no ambition to retire from work while there are any good deeds for me to do.*

The Barbers of DeVille

According to Mary Louise Barber (1949–), "Mother's Caddy took part in several North Carolina King Apple and Christmas parades in Hendersonville." One year, Mary's father, Jody Barber, rode in the back seat as grand marshal of the King Apple Parade. His grandson Burt acted as chauffeur.

The celebrated car lives on through massive restoration efforts by retired Laurel Park dentist Arthur H. Pearsall (1951–). Sleek, long, low and stylish, the 1969 Cadillac DeVille convertible sports a lacquer veneer of "Colonial Yellow," tan ostrich-grain leather upholstery, a 472-V8 engine and an eight-track stereo tape player. Additional features include front disc brakes and a Turbo Hydra-matic transmission.

In 1969, Hendersonville's Boyd Automotive sold the brand-new beauty for "around $4,000" to Jody Barber's wife, Mary Evelyn Douglass Barber (1922–2008). The original catalogue describes the vehicle as "open-air motoring at its finest." The Barbers' daughter Mary Louise next owned it. Boyd Chevrolet Cadillac Buick resold the vehicle in 2010 to Arthur Pearsall for $20,000 and Pearsall put another $55,000 into restoring the classic Caddy. Pearsall occasionally takes the DeVille—top down—for

Dr. Arthur Pearsall with his vintage Caddy DeVille. *Courtesy of Arthur H. Pearsall.*

spins on the back roads of Henderson County and has piloted it in King Apple Parades.

And then there's that car buried in Tuxedo…

Blue Ridge Parkway

Stretching 469 miles between the Shenandoah and Great Smoky Mountains National Parks, the Blue Ridge Parkway is the longest, narrowest and most frequently visited national park in the United States. In concept since 1933, construction of the "Appalachian Scenic Highway" actually commenced on September 11, 1935. The first section, a twelve-mile span near Cumberland Knob, North Carolina, opened a route to the North Carolina–Virginia state line.

Impressed with the work of the Civilian Conservation Corps (CCC) on the Skyline Drive through Shenandoah National Park, President Franklin D. Roosevelt endorsed the concept of constructing the parkway to link the two parks with an approved allotment of $16 million for the project. The route would follow the rims and contours of the crest of the southern Appalachians through Virginia and North Carolina.

During a devastating economic era, Roosevelt emphasized regional financial stimulus goals and saw the massive project as a tactic for providing much-needed jobs. Another motivating factor was the increasing availability of automobiles and a new generation of motoring vacationers.

Lead architect Stanley William Abbott (1908–1975) drew his inspiration from the works of renowned American landscape architect Frederick Law Olmsted (1822–1903)—whose work included New York's Central Park and Asheville's Biltmore Estate. Abbott's vision for the project was to create as little scarring as possible and design and blend the roadway into its natural surroundings—to "fit the parkway into the mountains as if nature has put it there." Skilled rock masons and other construction specialists from all over the United States participated in building tunnels, bridges and walls. Constructed in various stages, the bulk of the labor force consisted of local residents.

Under an authorization by federal public works administrator Harold L. Ickes (1874–1952), private contractors with federal contracts carried out most of the construction. On June 30, 1936, Congress formally authorized the project as the Blue Ridge Parkway and placed it under the jurisdiction of the National Park Service. Various New Deal public works agencies carried out some of the labor, with the Works Progress Administration performing a share of roadway construction. Crews from the Emergency Relief Administration implemented landscaping and development of parkway recreation areas. Personnel from four CCC camps executed roadside cleanup and plantings, the grading of slopes and improvement of adjacent fields and forestlands. Part of the process included negotiations with property owners for rights of way by the states to be turned over to the federal government to be administered by the National Park Service.

Construction progressed until World War II—when funds were diverted for the war effort—save for some work performed by a band of conscientious objectors.

The parkway ascends to 6,047 feet at the Richland Balsam overlook near Waynesville, North Carolina (Milepost 431), and descends to just over 600 feet at the James River in Virginia. It commences at milepost 0 near Waynesboro, Virginia, and terminates at milepost 469 near Cherokee, North Carolina. The parkway, passing through two national forests—Pisgah and Nantahala—boasts more than two hundred parking areas and overlooks, twenty-seven tunnels (with twenty-six of them in North Carolina), 168 bridges and six viaducts. The route covers 217 miles in Virginia and 252 miles in North Carolina.

The last phase of construction, commencing in 1968, entailed designing and fabricating a seven-mile stretch around North Carolina's Grandfather

Lucy Ann Barker admiring views from the Hominy Valley pullout alongside the Blue Ridge Parkway. *Photo by the author.*

Mountain, including a 1,200-foot suspended deck known as the Linn Cove Viaduct. Dedicated on September 11, 1987, the completed parkway runs from the southern terminus of Shenandoah National Park's Skyline Drive in Virginia at Rockfish Gap to U.S. Route 441 at Oconaluftee in the Great Smoky Mountains National Park near Cherokee, North Carolina.

Robert E. Lee Dixie Highway

First planned in 1914 to link the Midwest with the South, the Dixie Highway became part of the National Auto Trail System. Constructed from 1915 to 1927, the result actually produced a network of connected paved roads. The Lincoln Highway—the first coast-to-coast, east-to-west route across the United States—inspired the idea. Indiana-born Carl Graham Fisher (1874–1939), an auto parts and auto racing magnate, headed the formation of the Lincoln Highway Association and later organized the north-to-south Dixie Highway.

Dixie Highway plaque, Pack Square, Asheville. *Photo by the author.*

In the highway's early years, individuals, businesses, local governments and states supplied funding for its construction. The federal government provided subsidies until 1927, when the Dixie Highway Association disbanded and the U.S. Route system took over. Red striping with the white letters "DH" marked the pavement, the DH logo also emblazoning adjacent utility poles.

State commissions for the highway project settled on a split route with the purpose of serving more communities. The decision begot a 5,786-mile network passing through Michigan, Illinois, Indiana,

Ohio, Kentucky, Tennessee, North Carolina, South Carolina, Georgia and Florida.

The Carolina route abridged the distance between Knoxville, Tennessee, and Waynesboro, Georgia, on the eastern route. This sector now follows U.S. Route 25 West and U.S. Route 25 and traverses Asheville, North Carolina; Greenville, South Carolina; and Augusta, Georgia, in its approach to the eastern route and to Savannah, Georgia. Much of the eastern route—and the entire Carolina route—became U.S. Highway 25.

Two articles in the *Brevard News* of November 25, 1921, mentioned connectors to the Savannah Road. One of the articles, under the headline, "State to Build New Highways," included a reference to "the Asheville to Murphy highway now being built." A list outlined 110 miles of grading and gravel construction in Haywood, Cherokee, Jackson, Macon, Transylvania and Clay Counties.

The name "Dixie Highway" endures in various locations along its original route. In the late 1920s, the United Daughters of the Confederacy placed bronze plaques on granite pillars to mark the highway in western North Carolina to honor General Robert E. Lee (1807–1870). The markers stand in Hot Springs, Marshall, Asheville, Fletcher and Hendersonville, North Carolina, and on the South Carolina and Tennessee state lines. Another monument stands in downtown Greenville, South Carolina.

Appalachian National Scenic Trail

Conceived by forester Benton MacKaye (1879–1975), the Appalachian Trail was begun in the eastern United States in 1923 as a system to connect a series of farms and wilderness work-study camps for city-dwelling hikers. The marked hiking trail—the longest of its kind in the world, completed in 1927—stretches approximately 2,300 miles and passes through the states of Georgia, North Carolina, Tennessee, Virginia, West Virginia, Maryland, Pennsylvania, New Jersey, New York, Connecticut, Massachusetts, Vermont, New Hampshire and Maine. Comanaged by the National Park Service, the U.S. Forest Service and the nonprofit Appalachian Trail Conservancy, the route is maintained by trail clubs and multiple partnerships. Approximately sixty miles of the trail run through North Carolina's Madison County.

Interstate 26

Interstate 26 appeared in the original (1956) interstate highway plans running between Charleston and Asheville. The route was first mapped as an "under-construction highway" from U.S. Highway 25 near Hendersonville north to NC Highway 280 (current NC Highway 146). The first segment opened in 1966 beginning at NC Highway 280 to the U.S. Highway 25 connector near East Flat Rock in Henderson County. In 1969, I-26 was extended north to Interstate 40, and the South Carolina segment was extended to NC Highway 108 near Columbus.[47] In 1973, I-26 was extended from the U.S. Highway 25 connector to Saluda. Three years later, I-26 was connected. The segment from Saluda to NC Highway 108 was completed in 1976. In 2003, officials planned to extend I-26 to the Tennessee state line, where a freeway existed and the highway was routed over I-240 and stretched along U.S. Highway 23 to the north—its current routing.

One of the most challenging sections through which to build I-26 was in Howard's Gap. Numerous landslides along Miller Mountain and Tryon Peak delayed work, and special engineering had to be completed to continue work on the highway through this geography. The most crucial issue encompassed controlling the soil and water on the mountains and surrounding areas, remedied by adding several miles of underground pipes to drain water along the roadbed.

In 2013, the NCDOT reopened the idea of widening I-26 from Asheville to Flat Rock. The project had been planned since 2003 but was halted by legal challenges.

The I-26 connector has been planned to start in 2018. The project would upgrade I-240/I-26 from the I-40 interchange to Patton Avenue in Asheville. The project would also improve the Brevard Road, Amboy Road, Haywood Road and Patton Avenue interchanges, along with constructing a new freeway from the Patton Avenue interchange across the French Broad River and then to U.S. 19/23/70/future I-26 south of Broadway Street in Asheville. The total project length: 5.1 miles (8.2 kilometers).

Another project, north of Patton Avenue to U.S. 19/23A, would upgrade existing standards to interstate standards by replacing bridges and adding highway width and shoulders. The project, needed so that I-26 may fully be labeled along that stretch, is currently in development. The estimated cost: $184 million, with right-of-way acquisition slated for 2018.

III
Afloat

The highest steamboat in America.
—*Advertising slogan for the paddleboat* Mountain Lily

Broad but Shallow

The world's third-oldest river—after the Nile in Egypt and the New River near Boone, North Carolina—the French Broad may be more than 250 million years old, predating the Blue Ridge Mountains. The river begins just west of the Eastern Continental Divide and flows for 218 miles in a huge semicircle through western North Carolina, starting north to south, northeast through Transylvania and Henderson Counties, north through Buncombe and northwest through Madison County. The Broad is one of only two rivers in the United States that flows in a generally northward direction. After snaking through Warm Springs (Hot Springs) into Cocke County, Tennessee, the river joins the Pigeon and Nolichucky Rivers, meets the Holston River and flows into the Tennessee River, which empties into the Ohio and Mississippi Rivers and the Gulf of Mexico.

Albeit shallow, the Broad indeed spreads wide along much of its loop. Coastal Carolina longhunters, as they penetrated the mountains of western North Carolina, purportedly named this river for its breadth and for the reason that it flowed north into what was then French territory. In the 1700s, the French occupied much of the territory west of the Blue Ridge, where

The French Broad River. *Photo by A.F. Baker's London Art Galleries; courtesy of the estate of Louise H. Bailey.*

the river drained. The name stuck, even after France lost its share of interest in the country.

Formed by the junction of North Fork and West Fork in southern Transylvania County near the town of Rosman, the French Broad flows northeast into Henderson County, where it arcs northwest and courses through Buncombe and Madison Counties. The river flows through the city of Asheville, where it picks up the Swannanoa River and continues north into Tennessee. After leaving North Carolina, the French Broad proceeds west for 102 miles, joins the Holston River to form the Tennessee River near the city of Knoxville and eventually flows into the Mississippi River.

The Cherokee names for the French Broad River vary, with the most common being *Tah-kee-os-tee*, meaning "racing waters." Others, such as *Peo-li-co*, *Agiqua* and *Zillicoah*, referred only to segments of the river. Euro-Americans originally knew it as the Broad River—the way it was inscribed on a 1766 map of Indian Nations. By 1776, however, the word "French" had been added.

Many have cited *Agiqua* ("long man") as the Cherokee name for the river, but linguist Garfield Long says "long man" would be *Ganvhidv Asgaya*. Some writers stated that the rapids below Asheville were called *Tahkeyostee* ("where they race") and tributaries of the Broad, "chattering children." Long said he had never heard the latter, but he added that "chattering children" would be *diniyotti alinohedi*.

The 1916 deluge swelled the Broad to a flood table of 23.1 feet. Dams burst, lakes overflowed and, with careless abandon, floodwaters swept away bridges, roads, railways, homesteads, entire farms, railways and people.

The French Broad River has a North Carolina watershed of 2,830 square miles with a total length in the state at about 70 miles. For much of the twentieth century, the river was environmentally threatened, but through several public and private initiatives it has recovered and become an important natural and recreational resource. The river basin encompasses twenty-four municipalities, with a total population of about 400,000 in the early 2000s.

THE *MOUNTAIN LILY*

The French Broad Steamship Company began with the notion of a paddleboat intended to carry passengers and freight on a stretch of the

Model of the paddleboat *Mountain Lily* by Knox Crowell, Henderson County Heritage Museum. *Photo by the author.*

French Broad River. If successful, this plan would open the Broad as an important line for commerce where rails did not connect centers of trade. The vessel was the brainchild of Colonel Sidney Vance Pickens of Hendersonville, an entrepreneur and veteran of the Civil War, described in the *French Broad Hustler* as "one of Hendersonville's most honored citizens." Pickens's scheme involved linking Brevard, Hendersonville and Asheville by water. Pickens was president of the company, and R.W. Allen (1818–1905) served as secretary and treasurer. Corporate records from September 25, 1880, list Squire Jonathan Williams (1847–1911) and Albert Cannon (1845–1924) as partners in the venture.[48]

Born near Weaverville in Buncombe County, Pickens attended college at Tusculum, Tennessee, and studied law in Asheville. He was a lieutenant with Joseph "Fightin' Joe" Wheeler's company in the Civil War. In 1871, Pickens and his wife, Cornelia Sarah Davis Pickens (1847–1928), settled in Hendersonville, where he practiced law and promoted tourism. Their home stood alongside South Main Street at Caswell Street, and his offices occupied 116 South Main Street. In 1883, Pickens established the first bar association in western North Carolina and initiated the Henderson County chapter of the Confederate Veterans Association in 1899. The Pickenses were active in the Methodist church.

With his cousin Congressman Robert Brank Vance (1828–1899), Pickens managed to pull political strings in Raleigh. Vance and Pickens secured an appropriation to improve the proposed route for Pickens's steamboat, initiating a dredging project by the U.S. Army Corps of Engineers to clear the channel between Brevard and Hendersonville, with a projected cost of $44,000. When the corps began the work of blasting shoals, removing reefs, constructing jetties and deepening sections of the riverbed, Pickens announced his plan for building a steamship to ply the waters of the mountain.

In the spring of 1881, Pickens and his partners hosted a benefit replete with much fanfare. Brass bands, a barbecue picnic, hard liquor and speeches coerced the guests to buy stock in the company at twenty-five dollars per share. All 160 shares were sold.

Completed by the summer of 1881 and christened the *Mountain Lily*, the conveyance measured ninety feet long and sported staterooms and two decks to accommodate up to one hundred passengers. Painted white with green trim, the riverboat featured two caged paddlewheels and twin twelve-horsepower steam engines to drive them. John Luke Porter (1813–1893), who designed ironclads for the Confederacy, built the *Mountain Lily*. Pickens promoted his ship as the highest steamboat in America. On its maiden voyage on August 2, 1881, the *Lily* conveyed a band, freight and one hundred passengers, mostly friends and colleagues of Pickens.

The French Broad Steamship Company proved unsuccessful in ever showing a profit, with the ply never reaching beyond Penrose or King's Bridge. The freight depot, ticket office and loading dock stood on the east bank of the Broad on land purchased from Richard Ledbetter (1819–1903) near the present location of Johnson's Bridge in Horse Shoe (across the French Broad at U.S. Highway 64 near today's Banner Farm Road).

The shallowness of the Broad hindered the ship's navigation, even after laborious attempts had been made to dredge the less navigable sections. Additional setbacks included unpredictable variations in the river's flow, extreme drought, low-hung bridges and obstacles presented by logjams, beavers and muskrats. When the water level was high enough, the company attempted alternate ventures—endeavors including short tourist runs and floating parties—each of them not nearly as successful as Pickens had planned.

A flashflood in 1885 pulled the ship from its moorings at Horse Shoe, sweeping it upstream, where it became mired in a mudflat near King's Bridge—a span across the river on what is now NC Highway 191 (Haywood Road). Pickens abandoned the venture and sold the boat for salvage, including its engines and boiler, to operate a sawmill. Her bell was hung on the property of Riverside Baptist Church and later in the church's belfry. For many years ,the decaying hull could be viewed near King's Bridge.

The *Mountain Lily* snagged on a sandbar near King's Bridge, French Broad River. *Courtesy of the Rowell Bosse North Carolina Room, Transylvania County Library.*

More intensive dredging and/or locks may have solved navigation issues on the Broad. The National Archives holds an original set of survey plans for a length of the French Broad between Brevard and Asheville, North Carolina, submitted by William Trout in 1878. The detailed map included locations of bridge sites: Wilson's, Patton's, Allison's, Shuford's, McLain's, Johnson's, King's, Alexander's, Tennant's and Smith's. Trout labeled the following fords: Graham's, Clayton's, Old, Long Shoal, Taylor's and Patton's, as well as Tennant's Ferry. Tributaries included Davidson's River, Mills River and a number of creeks. The minutiae depicted ripples, bluffs, reefs, shoals, granges, a sawmill, fish-traps and even a site labeled "Soap-pot," near "Gash's land" and a "fish-trap." Trout's map accompanied a report of S.T. Albert, USACE, replete with elaborate plans for locks of timber, iron and stone construction, which were never implemented.

Horse Shoe First Baptist Church

Riverside Baptist Church, organized on September 16, 1888, held its first services in Colonel Pickens's freight depot at Horse Shoe. With twenty-nine charter members, Elder Daniel Buryman Nelson (1832–1895), who led in the constitution of the church, was elected first pastor. The Reverends George Washington Mace (1825–1899) and Jacob Lafayette McCarson (1850–1926) assisted with the constitution. Members built a sanctuary in 1898 (near the location of the current church) and renamed it Horse Shoe Baptist Church (between 1905 and 1907). Herbert Phiefer Houlk (1891–1954) veneered the building with river stones in 1947.

The *Mountain Lily*'s bell called the faithful to services until 1924, when members gave it to William Bennett Case (1843–1933) and bought a new bell for $42.51 from the Davenport Store in Mills River. Additional pastors of Horse Shoe Baptist Church included James Jefferson Gray (1860–1932), Elijah Marion Allison (1839–1923), Thomas Clingman Holtzclaw (1860–1938) and Ernest G. Ross (1883–1939).

In 1985, members renamed the church Horse Shoe First Baptist and constructed a new building of brick in 1993.

Try and Try Again

Further efforts were initiated to improve navigation on the French Broad. Under the authority of the River and Harbor Act, the U.S. Army Corps of Engineers (USACE) made an examination of the river in 1874 and 1875.[49] The examination continued in 1875 from the Henderson-Buncombe County line to the river's junction with the Holston.[50] The corps surveyed the river from Brevard to the head of Buck Shoals—about thirty miles.[51] The report included plans for locks, lateral and short-wing dam groins and channel excavation for a cost of $121,500. The work reportedly resulted in only somewhat improved conditions for navigation, and the project was abandoned in 1885. Allen Granberry Thurman (1813–1895), a U.S. senator from Ohio, denounced the project, declaring that a catfish could not navigate the shallow depths of the French Broad River.

Steam-powered paddleboats on the French Broad did not end with the fate of the *Mountain Lily*. Writers of old in this region chronicled only that particular ship, but at least one other was launched locally—in 1907, explicated by reports in the *French Broad Hustler*, which debuted a brief of the venture on February 28, 1907. The *Hustler* made a mention of a Mr. McBee

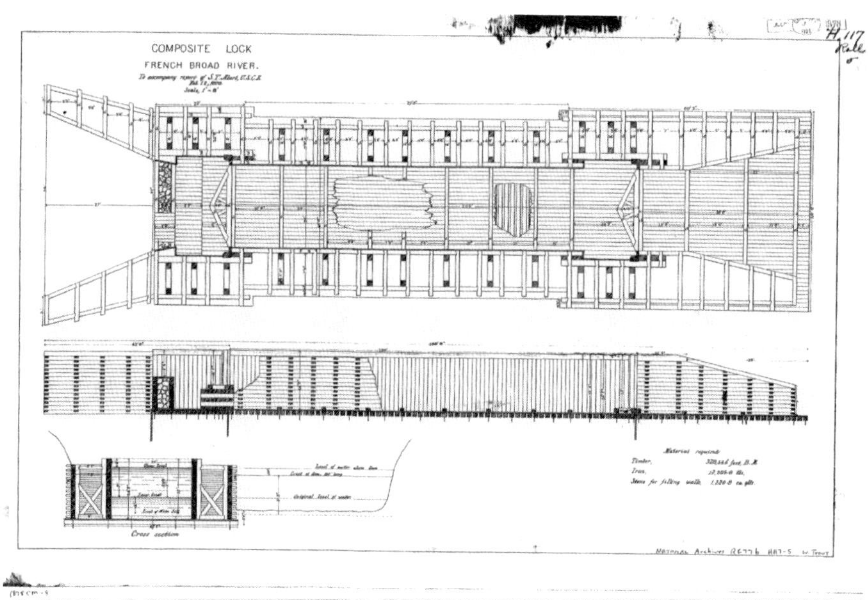

Surveyor William Trout's plans for locks on the French Broad River, 1878. *Courtesy of Nancy Roberts, William E. Trout III and the Henderson County Genealogical and Historical Society.*

and a Miss Eastman running a steamboat on the French Broad River. This boat was smaller than Pickens's *Mountain Lily*. Like the *Lily*, this later boat was meant to ply between Brevard and Asheville.

STEAMERS ON THE FRENCH BROAD

Last Sunday the new steamboat running on the French Broad passed Horse Shoe for the first time. She carried a good load of passengers and made a brave showing as she went up the river. She is about 89-feet long and 20-feet wide, was built under the direction of a man from Norfolk, Va., and is owned by Miss Eastman and Mr. McBee of Horse Shoe. The new boat runs from Fanning's Bridge up to Davidson River, and covers a distance of about fifteen miles.

There is a decided possibility of Asheville men building and operating a steamboat to run from Asheville to Long Shoals. Passengers will then be transferred around the shoals, a distance of a few hundred feet, and re-embark on the boat now running. For picturesque scenery and natural beauty, the trip is unsurpassed, it is said, anywhere in the world.

This steamboat line is one of the novelties of the world, as there is probably only one being operated at a higher altitude than the one now making regular trips past Horse Shoe. It is really a steamer line in regular operation on top of the mountains, and aside from the beauty of the trip, possesses the charm of a decided novelty. If the Asheville men carry out their part, it is expected it will be a paying proposition from the start.

—French Broad Hustler, *March 7, 1907*

In spite of the *Hustler*'s characteristic puffery concerning new enterprises, the ship co-owned by Eastman and McBee was, like its predecessor the *Mountain Lily*, ill-fated. The *Hustler* carried reports on November 12 and 19, 1907, detailing a court case between Sophy Harrison Eastman (1874–1942), a wealthy divorcée from Chicago (residing at the time in Fletcher), and Colonel V.E. McBee and their co-venture, Buck Shoals Company. Eastman charged McBee with fraud, unreliability and insolvency. McBee accused Eastman of abuse. The *Chicago Daily Tribune* also carried the story.

Further research concerning Ms. Eastman revealed the following. Born Sophonisba "Sophy" Grayson Harrison in Germany, she grew up in Chicago, a daughter of the Windy City's mayor Carter Harrison (1825–1893), and was the sister of her father's successor as mayor, Carter Harrison II (1860–

1953). She was married first to Barrett Eastman (1869–1910), second to Baker Everett "Rider" Edwards and third to Albert Rowland Thomson (1884–1943). In 1900, she bought Buck Shoals, the estate of humorist Edgar Wilson "Bill" Nye (1850–1896), in Skyland. Newspaper reports described the home as "palatial." Eastman involved herself in business with Colonel V.E. McBee, who lived with her for a time at Buck Shoals. The two named their venture after the impressive estate. When Eastman attempted to sue McBee for fraud, McBee in turn alleged accusations that led to Eastman's arrest. A piece in the *Chicago Daily Tribune*, dated November 7, 1908, included the following:

> *Sophie* [sic] *Harrison arrested on a warrant issued by a county magistrate charging her with the violation of a state law, which forbids "the living of a man and a woman in a house unattended by other females, they being not married or not relatives."*

To vindicate Ms. Eastman, her attorney arranged for a quick marriage between his client and Baker Everett Edwards (1869–1932), her beau of the moment—a dashing young man from Norfolk, Virginia. The wedding took place in a back room of the lawyer's office.

Further newspaper articles portrayed Sophy as attractive, sporting haut couture and with blue eyes. One report mentioned her nonchalantly and daintily nibbling chocolates during court proceedings.

Vardry Echols McBee Jr. (1879–1910), a prominent railroad man, had been general superintendent with the Richmond & Danville Railroad at Columbia, South Carolina.

IV

Aloft

North Carolina, for the present at least, may claim not only the first horizontal flight but the first vertical one as well.
—Thomas C. Parramore, First to Fly, *2002*

Firsts in Flight in the Old North State

In the breadth of a century, aviation facilities in the Old North State advanced from a beach in the Outer Banks and a few level cornfields to nine commercial airports—four of them international—and numerous general-aviation airports, seventy-five of them public and nearly three hundred privately owned. Goaded by a sense of adventure and freedom, the earliest feats of flight entailed state-of-the art science—for the era—and North Carolina led the field. The initial heavier-than-air, powered flight took place over the Outer Banks in 1903, and the first helicopter hovered a few feet within Carteret County's airspace in 1907. But the state's aviation history did not stop with Wilbur Wright's record flight at Kill Devil. Nor did it begin there.

The Wright brothers of Dayton, Ohio, perfected gliding flight by 1902 after having experimented with flying machines since 1896. They traveled back and forth from Ohio to the diminutive fishing village of Kitty Hawk near Kill Devil Hills in 1900, 1901, 1902 and 1903. With the aid of Outer Bankers, including the Wrights' hosts Captain William J. "Bill" Tate (1875–

A Morane-Saulnier Type N (French monoplane fighter aircraft) replica, Western North Carolina Air Museum, Hendersonville. *Photo by the author.*

The Wright brothers' 1903 *Flyer* stands before their camp at Kill Devil Hills. *Author's collection.*

1953) and his family, the brothers tested, crashed, retested, rebuilt and perfected their gliders until one was "right" for a gasoline engine. In the interim, affable Outer Bankers built for the Wrights a hangar and machine shop near a sandy test strip, where the Ohioans conducted countless experiments to master controlled flight. The Wrights hunted gulls, gannets, geese, fish hawks and buzzards and analyzed the birds' anatomy for the intricacies of avian maneuvering. Before their successful motorized flight, the brothers had conducted over one thousand brief tests with gliders.

On December 17, 1903, Orville Wright (1871–1948) piloted the first successfully powered airplane—the *Wright Flyer*—for approximately 12 seconds, covering approximately 120 feet over Kitty Hawk Beach. Later that day, his brother Wilbur (1867–1912) kept the ship airborne for 59 seconds for a distance of 852 feet, marking aviation history with the first powered flight.

James Henry Gatling (1816–1879) of Hertford County, North Carolina, built the first American airplane—the *Gatling Flyer*—in 1873, thirty years before the Wright brothers' historic flights over the Outer Banks. Gatling's craft was a hand-cranked monoplane. Dr. Daniel Asbury (1816–1882) of Anson County crafted a steam-propulsion monoplane in 1881. Jacob Aaron "Jake" Hill (1862–1927) of Winston fabricated a dirigible (steerable balloon) in 1902, and William Luther Paul (1869–1946) of Carteret County designed and built a twin-rotor helicopter—the *Bumblebee*—in 1907. Leonardo da Vinci had sketched plans for the first manned helicopter in 1493, and several inventors—such as Frenchmen Paul Cornu and Louis Charles Breguet with his brother Jacques—had built similar machines by 1907, but unlike those gyroplanes, Paul's *Bumblebee* successfully lifted off the ground.

Perhaps North Carolina's first air disaster that ended in death involved an exhibition balloonist who drowned at Charlotte's Lakewood Park on Saturday evening, September 2, 1911. The *Charlotte News* reported on September 3, 1911, "Between six hundred and eight hundred spectators" looked on amidst a pyrotechnics show as W.L. Brown (1893–1911)—an aeronaut from Cincinnati—fell from a balloon and into the lake. The day before, Brown had admitted that he could not swim.

According to the *Albany Journal*, on December 28, 1911, Thorny Andrews flew his Curtiss pusher No. 12 from League Park Station (a baseball field and fairgrounds) in Albany, Georgia, for a distance of ten miles over the city and on his return flight dropped a locked pouch of mail to postal officials waiting below.

Thorny Andrews

Thornwell Hamwood "Thorny" Andrews (1876–1931), a skilled auto mechanic, was the first commercial pilot of North Carolina and the first to fly over Charlotte. Glenn Hammond Curtiss (1878–1930) taught him to fly. Thorny's father owned a Studebaker horse-buggy dealership in the Queen City.

In 1907, Andrews and Homer Moses Chamblee (1881–1939) opened the Greensboro Auto Company at 103 South Davie Street—Greensboro's first automobile agency and garage. In 1911, entrepreneur Lindsey Hopkins (1879–1937) of Reidsville opened the Lindsey Hopkins Aviation Company in Greensboro, paid for Andrews' flight lessons in White Plains, New York, and hired Andrews as a pilot a few months before his historic flight and mail drop above Albany. Hopkins sponsored aviation exhibitions across the country. Andrews later bought Hopkins's 1911 Curtiss pusher biplane.

Thorny Andrews. *Courtesy of James Andrews "Jim" Meyer.*

One of only about two dozen professional pilots in the United States at that time, Andrews was first to fly over Charlotte, in 1912. He landed his biplane—in six hundred feet, traveling at forty miles per hour—on Charlotte's old fairgrounds. It would be a good many years before the Queen City gained a major airport, but this piece of aviation history stands preserved at the Carolinas Aviation Museum in Charlotte.

Considered to be one of the most daring pilots of the time, Andrews flew in many air show competitions nationwide. He crashed only twice in his entire career as a pilot, the first time in Albany. Expected to make a second airmail flight, after dropping the first pouch of mail, Andrews collided with a fence upon landing and destroyed his plane. He escaped with nothing more than a broken arm but a year later narrowly escaped death in a crash at Gordon, Nebraska.

Thorny Andrews married a divorcée named Elizabeth Hunter Gonzales in Danville, Virginia, on September 25, 1913. The couple had divorced by 1930, and Thorny, at age fifty-three, was living with his father and stepmother in Charlotte. His father, Francis Hamwood "Frank" Andrews (1852–1944), owned a music store and in 1880 was listed as a harness maker in the Mecklenburg County census records. His mother was Elizabeth Sarah "Bessie" Stinson Andrews (1851–1930). Thorny Andrews died of pellagra.

Frances Davis Andrews Meyer, mother of Hendersonville's aviation pioneer Oscar A. Meyer Jr., was Thorny Andrew's sister.

Georgia Ann "Tiny" Thompson Broadwick (1893–1978) of Granville County, North Carolina, became the first woman to parachute from a plane on June 21, 1913.

In 1928, Viola Gentry (1906–1959), the "Flying Cashier" from Richmond County, set the first non-refueling endurance record for women at eight hours, six minutes and thirty-seven seconds. She learned to fly in 1924 and was the first woman from North Carolina to pilot an aircraft. A longtime friend of Amelia Mary Earhart (1897–1937), Gentry once worked as a cashier in a restaurant.

Other North Carolina aviation pioneers included World War I pilot Kiffin Yates Rockwell (1892–1916) of Asheville, the first American to shoot down an enemy plane. Rockwell founded the Lafayette Escadrille. Robert Opie Lindsay (1894–1952) of Reidsville shot down six German planes, qualifying him as an ace. Robert Morgan (1918–2004) of Asheville flew the *Memphis Belle*, a World War II B-17. And several members of the Tuskegee Airmen Unit—the most highly decorated outfit in the war—hailed from the Old North State. North Carolina pilot graduates of the Tuskegee Flight School include Cecil L. Browder, Fred L. Brower Jr., Willie L. Byrd Jr., Marshall S. Cabiness, James Y. Carter, John H. Chavis, Conrad H. Cheek, Quinten V. Cheek, Lewis W. Craig, Spurgeon N. Ellington, Willie H. Fuller, Vernon V. Haywood, George W. Helm, Aaron Herrington, Andrew Johnson Jr., Andrew D. Marshall, Harvey L. McClelland, Clinton B. Mills, David J. Murphy Jr., Francis B. Peoples, Clarence E. Reynolds Jr., Robert C. Robinson Jr., Graham Smith, Reginald V. Smith and Arthur Wilburn. Lieutenants Craig, Robinson and Wilburn and Flight Officer McClelland hailed from Asheville.

Hubert DeVault McLean (1895–1929) of Gibsonville, Guilford County, piloted the first airplane brought to Asheville. He enlisted in the Aviation Corps in January 1915 and was appointed sergeant in the Fifteenth Aero Squadron, Signal Corps, on October 1, 1917, at Hazlehurst Field, Mineola, New York. He was stationed at Rockwell Field, San Diego, California, in 1919. McLean also served as an instructor pilot at Mitchel Field, New York. He was chosen as one of four pilots to make the first transcontinental flight attempted by the U.S. Army under the leadership of Major Albert Daniel Smith (1887–1970) and bears the distinction of having been the only pilot to return with the same plane.

Shortly after World War I, McLean served as a border patroller using DH-4 airplanes along the United States–Mexico border. Lieutenant Hubert D. McLean was in command of a detachment first at Eagle Pass and later at Del Rio. One of his subordinates was Second Lieutenant (later General) James Harold "Jimmy" Doolittle (1896–1993). Lieutenants McLean and Doolittle were recommended for permanent commission in the Air Service, Regular Army, on the same letter (July 2, 1920). McLean retired from the army in 1921, joined the Mexican Gulf Oil Company and organized an aerial motor transport company in Mexico, which became part of the Aviation Corporation of America. He was flying the payroll in a Fairchild for outlying camps when his plane hit a wire as he dipped to make the drop. The two passengers lived. Because of bandits, payrolls had to be transported and dropped by air. At McLean's funeral, the sizeable floral arrangement was in the shape of an airplane. It was said that over five thousand people attended the service. The McLean Brothers Airport of Gibsonville, North Carolina, is named for Hubert D. and David Finley McLean (1904–1934), both of whom died in air crashes.

Master Sergeant William Avera "Bill" Winston (1896–1948) of Wendell, Wake County, was one of Charles Lindbergh's flight instructors. Lindbergh was a cadet at Brooks Field at San Antonio, Texas, where Winston, stationed as a flight instructor, reputedly held the record for flying time in the army at that time with close to thirty-five hundred flying hours. About his experience at Brooks Field Lindbergh said:

> *Barnstorming had made me a skillful pilot, far more skillful than my Army instructors in selecting and operating from "strange fields" for instance. Military training taught me precision and perfection of flying techniques.*

When he entered the service, Lindbergh already knew the basics of flying. The army made him a more accomplished pilot, and he attributed this skill to Bill Winston. Bill said of Lindbergh:

> *He was a likeable chap, never trying to impress that he knew it all, always eager to learn. I let him fly by himself the first time we were up. It was easy to see that he was a natural flyer.*

Charles Dewey Sumner's World War II fighter plane *Bat Cave*. *Courtesy of Richard Barnwell.*

As a pilot for Pan American Airlines, Winston flew over three million miles and was one of the first pilots to cross the Atlantic Ocean more than one hundred times.

Lindbergh flew the first solo nonstop flight across the Atlantic Ocean on May 20 to 21, 1927. In his *Spirit of St. Louis*, he flew 3,600 miles in thirty-three and a half hours. Lindbergh was born in Detroit, grew up in Little Falls, Minnesota, and attended the University of Wisconsin–Madison.

Charles Dewey Sumner (1898–1955) of Bat Cave, Henderson County, nicknamed his World War II fighter plane *Bat Cave* for his hometown. Sumner's rank was Seaman Second Class, United States Regiment/Headquarters Fifth Naval District, North Carolina S2 U.S. Navy Reserve, World War II. He was married to Pauline Freeman Sumner (1898–1968), and lived in Mills River (listed as "farmer" in the census records) in the 1940s. The Sumners are buried at Bat Cave Baptist Church Cemetery.

And Hendersonville, North Carolina, boasted an aviation prodigy named Oscar Meyer.

Henderson County's Aviation Pioneer

One could say Hendersonville's first airstrip spanned a stretch of First Avenue West, because that is where a homegrown, aspiring pilot learned to fly. As a youngster, Oscar August Meyer Jr. (1913–1998) would find a willing driver to tow him or a buddy behind a motorcycle or car. In a pair of roller skates, Oscar or the friend would grab hold of his glider and taxi down the avenue until reaching a velocity that, when the passenger jumped, would lift him from the ground and into flight. But Oscar wanted much more.

> *We never spent a nickel for gasoline. Nearly everybody in Hendersonville who owned a good-looking car was eager to show it off in front of our glider.*
>
> —*Oscar A. Meyer Jr.*

It would not be an exaggeration to describe Oscar Meyer as a whiz kid. He showed all the earmarks: introspective, quiet, gentle, inventive and, like most boys, in possession of a trenchant infatuation for science and all things mechanical. The *Asheville Citizen-Times* reported on Sunday, September 13,

Oscar Meyer. *Courtesy of James Andrews "Jim" Meyer.*

Oscar Meyer's son Jim. *Courtesy of James Andrews "Jim" Meyer.*

Oscar Meyer with his wind wagon. *Courtesy of James Andrews "Jim" Meyer.*

1931, that Meyer (eighteen years old at the time) "enjoyed tinkering around a machine shop since he was a small boy."

Meyer's son Jim shared:

> *From the age of ten, he built model airplanes and gliders. He built a wind wagon, motorized his bicycle before upgrading to a motorcycle, and at fourteen he crafted a "boy-sized" biplaned hang glider with tricycle wheels for landing gear. At age sixteen, he built his first airplane and taught himself to fly. The craft was a Heath Parasol with an open cockpit, an engine from a Chevrolet and tires from a motorcycle.*
>
> *At twelve years old, Oscar owned a single sport model 1922 Harley-Davidson. He gave me my first motorcycle ride on another one of his Harleys when I was five years old. He sat me on the gasoline tank in front of him, and I held on to the handlebars like a little monkey. I still remember that experience and started riding motorcycles when I was ten. He instilled a passion within me to enjoy motorcycles. To date, I have taught over three thousand students the art of motorcycling and hopefully have instilled the same passion within them, thanks to Dad.*

LURE OF THE SKY

With the help of his buddies Grant Louis Zickgraf (1913–2001) and Thomas J. "Tommy" Stocks (1914–1997), Oscar cut his aviation teeth by building that glider, which he and his friends named a "skating glider." The boys spent eleven months assembling the craft.

Aviator and inventor—and Oscar's childhood friend and, later, a flight student—Guy Edwin Dixon Jr. (1920–2014) said:

> *One would skate down a hill and jump up into the air and the glider would move you a few feet. Oscar had the idea of pulling the primary glider with a rope from his motorcycle. So Tommy would fly the glider and Oscar would pull it with the motorcycle. They got along pretty good until they got into a severe crosswind...the glider...drifted to the side of the street and hit a telephone pole. That was the end of the glider.*

Oscar's buddy Grant recruited passengers for membership in the boys' glider club for a fee of fifty cents. Each membership entitled the bearer to one flight, with no limit to the number of memberships.

The width of city streets, electrical wires and poles and other obstacles limited any quantifiable altitude or distance. Meyer refined his agility to taxi first in his wingless fuselage on Hendersonville's streets before attaching the wings and perfecting his technique on sod runways.

Some of young Oscar's heroes included his uncle Thorny Andrews; James Edward "Doc" Owen, DDS (1896–1964), an Asheville dentist and barnstormer; Major Louis Milton Bourne Jr., U.S. Marine Corps (1891–1935), the first to fly nonstop from the United States to Nicaragua (1928); and Lieutenant Alfred Isaac Boyd Jr. (1909–2010), a daredevil pilot. Oscar's first formal flight instruction came only after he had "designed, built and test-flown six aircraft for a total of several hundred flights over a period of seven years," stated Sandy Hudson Jr.

Garland O. Goodwin (1930–), one of Oscar's flight students, said:

> *Ellen* [Ramey] *Fain Bowen [1904–1995], daughter of the founder of the Hendersonville newspaper* [James T. Fain Sr.], *was Oscar's and my English teacher. She said that all Oscar ever did in her class was draw airplanes.*

When his uncle Charles Stinson "Charlie" Andrews (1892–1979) of Charlotte gave him a three-dollar set of blueprints for a Flying Flivver light plane from the Storms Aviation Company, Oscar set about building the monoplane in a neighbor's—Dr. Guy Dixon's—garage on Third Avenue. These were the same plans used in 1928 by Newell Eldon Storms (1887–1953) of Asheville. Named the *Meyer's Special*, this plane cost $110 in materials, including white pine wood; plywood gusset plates (for added strength); Sears, Roebuck & Company bed sheets; and nitrate dope. Taking one year to complete, the craft weighed 680 pounds, including its engine. Oscar whittled the propeller from poplar and installed his wind-wagon's 1928 model Chevrolet engine (forty horsepower) with overhead valves. Assigned the CAA (Civil Aviation Authority) identification number 10212, the monoplane featured a wingspread of thirty feet and wing cord of six feet and was twenty feet long. The untipped propeller—as well as all of Oscar's other homebuilt versions—measured six feet with a pitch of three feet. (Some of Meyer's later props featured cloth tips.) The only instruments were an ignition switch and an oil-pressure gauge. There were no brakes, no steerable nose or tail-wheel and no self-starter. The flying speed was seventy miles per hour, and the land speed was twenty-five miles per hour.

Not permitted at first to fly his *Meyer's Special* from the Asheville Municipal Airport, Oscar learned to taxi on roads in his neighborhood. "He took the wingless fuselage out onto the streets and learned to taxi this partial airplane by trial and error, guiding it with the rudder, and taxiing up and down the streets of Hendersonville," according to Guy Dixon Jr. Soon after, Oscar would fly the length of the airport's sod runways of approximately 3,500 feet. He and his friend Grant sold tickets for rides in the two-cockpit glider, towed aloft by an automobile at the airport. As was typical for the time, none of Oscar's homebuilt planes featured brakes. A tailskid was standard. For longer flights, Oscar and his friends employed a cornfield skirting Hendersonville's Bat Fork Creek. In 1932, this was the less-than-auspicious provenance of Meyer's flying field and the Hendersonville Airport.

Oscar August Meyer Sr. and Frances Davis Andrews Meyer. *Courtesy of James Andrews "Jim" Meyer.*

After having taken a number of flights in the Chevy-powered plane, part of the engine's cowling blew up and lodged in the wing struts, impelling the plane to the ground. Oscar survived unhurt. He rebuilt the craft and installed a 1931 Model-A Ford engine.

Oscar Meyer was the only child of Oscar August "Ock" Meyer Sr. (1879–1950) and Frances Davis Andrews Meyer (1880–1966). Oscar Sr. managed the Hendersonville district of the Southern Public Utilities Company and oversaw construction of the Green River-Tuxedo hydroelectric plant, dam and the 324-acre Lake Summit, Henderson County's largest lake. When a Duke Power Company subsidiary—Blue Ridge Power—purchased the power site in 1929, Meyer remained as manager. Frances Meyer was a trustee of the board of the Hendersonville Library. The couple and their son first lived near the construction site in Tuxedo and then on Fleming Street, Oakland Street and Druid Hills Avenue.

Oscar Meyer Jr. said, "Before Blue Ridge Power Company had an office we used our living room as one. People used to come to the house to pay their light bills." His father retired from Duke in 1940.

Prompted by his father to attend engineering school, young Oscar enrolled at State College (North Carolina State University at Raleigh) but stayed for only one year, believing he knew more than his professors did about aircraft.

In 1932, Oscar bought his first airplane for $600, a used Ox-powered Bird. Passengers (up to two at a time) could ride for one dollar a head—or for five dollars, "if they wanted the fancy stuff," Oscar said. When all eight cylinders froze and busted that winter, Oscar replaced the engine with a used Axelson radial engine, which arrived "in a million pieces." The aspiring pilot set about assembling the pieces and fashioning custom gaskets. He soon earned the reputation as an accomplished aircraft mechanic.

In the early 1930s, Oscar flew round trip to Raleigh with two breakdowns on the way and two more on the return trip. He embarked on the flight with his friend Grant in the dual-cockpit plane with an OX-5 engine. Neither of the two knew a thing about navigation but fulfilled the itinerary, at last, with the aid of a compass purchased along the way. With each engine quit and malfunction, the boys managed to alight safely—on an airstrip and on three different agricultural fields. They made their own repairs, rehydrated the radiator and continued their journey. When the crankshaft failed, the engine quit for the last time, and the boys landed in a field near the small town of Biscoe, Montgomery County, North Carolina. Oscar phoned his father, asking to have a spare engine trucked to him. Three days later, with

Oscar Meyer with his Axelson. *Courtesy of James Andrews "Jim" Meyer.*

the spare installed, Oscar and Grant flew back to Hendersonville with no further breakdowns.

LOFTY INSPIRATION

Kermit Edney (1924–2000) suggested, "the famed daredevil stuntman Roscoe Tanner" [*sic*]—Roscoe Turner (1895–1970)—likely inspired young Oscar Meyer to fly. Meyer's son James Andrews "Jim" Meyer (1945–)

maintains that his father's uncle Thorny Andrews, in fact, inspired Oscar Meyer Jr. in his call to aviation.

Turner's Flying Circus barnstormed across the southeastern United States. On August 28, 1921, pilot Harry J. Runser (1890–1981) flew Turner over Laurel Park (Rhododendron) Lake, with Turner planning to parachute from the plane and put down in the water. He instead landed in the woods, about a half-mile distant, on a slope of Echo Mountain. The craft was named *Cloudland Express*, a two-seat JN-4 Canuk—a Canadian modification of the Curtiss JN-3 "Jenny." Turner, who often flew with his pet lion Gilmore as a passenger, went on to achieve the status of three-time winner of the Thompson Trophy air race.

Barnstorming

Flappers, hip flasks, splashy living and the bravado of daring young flyers all coincided with the Jazz Age and the Roaring Twenties. For $150 or less, unlicensed pilots bought light planes, such as surplus "flying Jennies" (Curtiss JN-4s) left over from World War I; taught themselves to fly; and performed dangerous aerial stunts that included spins, dives, loop-the-loops, barrel rolls and wing-walking above crowds of voracious spectators. A newfound mania for aerial exhibitions fanned the flames of flying circuses, which were all the rage until the passing of the Air Commerce Act in 1926, calling for the licensing of planes and pilots. Establishing safety regulations by 1927 led to the decline of barnstorming. Charles Augustus Lindbergh (1902–1974) "Lucky Lindy" counted among the U.S.'s audacious barnstormers.

> *The slow roll (compared to the "barrel roll and "snap roll") is so difficult to perform in those old birds that World War II squadron commanders had to forbid their fighter pilots from doing "victory rolls" because too many of them lost their lives when they flew into the ground trying to complete a slow roll. I lost a friend, and years later the world lost one of the few P-38s still flying, from attempted slow rolls near the ground. This is why a waiver of the rules is required for air shows.*
>
> —*Garland O. Goodwin*

In 1911, barnstormer Lincoln Beachy (1887–1915) of California performed aerial stunts over Asheville in a Curtiss biplane. Touted as the "quintessential daredevil," Beachy later died from injuries sustained in a crash in San Francisco.

The earliest flying patches in Henderson County consisted of level fields, including one bordered by Mud Creek, Kanuga Road and Erkwood Drive. Revealed in the writings of Frank L. FitzSimons Sr., this was known as the "McAdoo place,"[52] and it served the barnstormers Runser and Turner when they took off for their botched attempt at an intrepid stunt in 1921.

FitzSimons also wrote of a barnstormer he called "Speedy Colquist [*sic*]." On July 18, 1926, three local teenagers met pilot C.D. Colquitt in a field and were disappointed to learn that only two of them would fit in the ship. The *Independent* of St. Petersburg, Florida, reported on Monday, July 19, 1926:

> *Two Killed Taking Airplane Joyride*
>
> *Hendersonville N.C.—Taking a joyride in a commercial airplane "for excitement," two Hendersonville youths, Mack Colt and Robah Bland were fatally injured and their pilot was seriously hurt when the plane went into a tailspin and fell five hundred feet to the ground here late Sunday.*
>
> *The boys died two hours later at a hospital. The pilot, C.D. Colquitt of Thomaston, Ga., sustained a broken leg and facial cuts.*
>
> *The party had been in the air only seven minutes when the plane crashed.*

The teens were Mack Colt (1905–1926), Robah Bumpass Bland (1905–1926) and Arthur B. Shepherd (1906–1970). Shepherd lost a coin toss and stayed on the ground, only to watch the plane crash, fatally injuring his two buddies. The pilot, Calvin Drake "Speedy" Colquitt Jr. (1898–1928), survived with injuries.

On November 17, 1928, Speedy crashed a plane in Tampa and died the following day. His death certificate stated the cause of injury: "Fracture of skull due to aeroplane accident."

HENDERSONVILLE'S FIRST AIRPORT

With his father's help, Oscar Meyer Jr. acquired the cornfield property at Bat Fork. Deeds describe the acreage as "bottomland…swampland…flood zone…cornfield…Bat Fork Creek (Memminger Creek)…Johnson Drainage Ditch near Barker Heights in East Flat Rock." Meyer Sr. bought the land from Preston Fidelia Patton (1878–1967) and his wife, Sadie Smathers Patton (1886–1975), in 1933. Deeds included the wording "Glade Road over King's Creek…bridge…and Tracey Grove Road." Frank L. FitzSimons Sr., register of deeds at the time, recorded the transaction.

On that farmland, Oscar laid off a strip approximately 150 feet wide and 1,500 feet long and cleared it for the purpose of a runway. With an old steamroller and a road-scraper, "and a lot of picks and shovels," according to Guy Dixon Jr., "we all began to build a landing strip by hand." After leveling the runway, Oscar and his friends raised a wooden hangar. Oscar purchased a used Bird with an OX-5, water-cooled engine—surplus from World War I. The boys rebuilt the plane and installed a new Axelson 150-horsepower radial engine. Dixon wrote:

Meyer's Flying Service operation at Hendersonville. *Courtesy of James Andrews "Jim" Meyer.*

Our first flight was with Oscar in this new rebuilt Bird aircraft, which was quite exceptional. Our first flight instruction came sitting on the lap of Oscar in the Curtiss Robin, three-passenger airplane that we had rebuilt the previous year.

Oscar Meyer received his flying license and aircraft and engine mechanic's license in 1936. Oscar's son, Jim, wrote:

One of the first pilot's licenses offered, even before the FAA existed. There is no date on the license issued to him. In the October 1978 issue of Flying *magazine an article about Oscar listed "1936" as the year he obtained his license. The CAA was put into law in 1938. Back in the day when Dad first flew there were no federal interventions. At that time you did not even have to have a driver's license.*

In 1936, I finally got under the thumb of the CAA. The inspector just walked down the flight line and licensed all my airplanes. I got my commercial and my A&E.[53] *It was a cold day, and the inspector stayed inside by the stove while I went out and flew my exam in an open-cockpit Travel Air. Nobody from the feds ever rode with me.*

Over time, Meyer added larger hangars, a maintenance and repair shop, two T-hangars, 1,200 more feet of runway length and 100 more feet of width. James Blaine Brooks (1924–2004) worked as Meyer's chief flight instructor.

Form ACA 962
DEPARTMENT OF COMMERCE
CIVIL AERONAUTICS ADMINISTRATION
WASHINGTON

THIS IS TO IDENTIFY
Oscar (First name) August (Middle name) Meyer, Jr. (Last name)
who has been approved to serve as an airport officer at the following-named landing area by the Civil Aeronautics Administration:
Hendersonville (Airport)
Henderson (County) Hendersonville, (City) N. C. (State)
(Signature) Civil Aeronautics Administration Inspector.

(Signature) Fingerprinting Officer.

Oscar August Meyer Jr. (Signature) Airport Officer.

Place of birth Charlotte, N. C.
Date of birth 1/29/13
Color eyes Blue, hair Brown
Weight 130 lbs. Ht. 5 ft. 9 in.
FINGERPRINTS—RIGHT HAND
RIGHT THUMB

Oscar Meyer's first CAA license. *Courtesy of James Andrews "Jim" Meyer.*

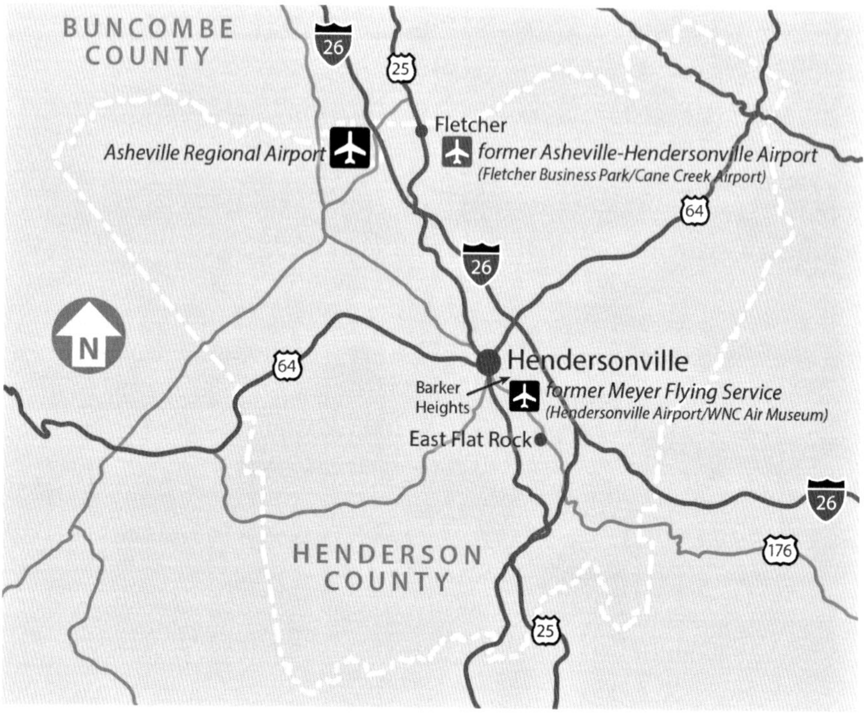

Map courtesy of Knox Crowell.

Tommy Stocks worked as an aircraft mechanic and flight instructor and later moved to Spartanburg, South Carolina.

An advertisement for Meyer Flying Service in a *Miller's Directory* stated:

> *Fly from Hendersonville Airport: Passenger Flights • Charter Trips• Student Instruction •Hangar Facilities; Spartanburg Road (2 miles south).*

Meyer's airport included a flying school, charter flights, a filling station, repair shop, rentals and sales. The enterprise made a good living for the man. In addition to selling fuel, making repairs for others and providing flight and ground instruction, Meyer taught countless people to fly in a Cub. The airstrip was considered a mecca for barnstormers. Clarence Duncan Chamberlin (1893–1976), who was trying to beat Lindbergh across the Atlantic, flew out of Meyer's airport. Nationally renowned barnstormer and aerobatics champion Beverly "Bevo" Howard (1914–1971) flew in and out of Meyer's field, as did Leighton Holden Collins (1902–1995) and his son Richard Collins (1933–), publisher and editor, respectively, of *Air Facts*, a pilot's magazine.

Jim Meyer shared:

> *"Bevo" Howard was an FBO* [fixed base operator] *of Hawthorne Aviation in Charleston, South Carolina, where he lived. He was killed in an air show in Greenville, North Carolina.*

Garland O. Goodwin wrote:

> *Howard's Bücker Jungmeister came to the United States aboard the zeppelin* Hindenburg. *When its demo pilot destroyed the plane during a low inverted pass, aerobatic champion Mike Murphy purchased the remains, rebuilt the plane and used it with success during his air-show career. Bevo purchased the plane in 1946 after having won several World Aerobatic Championships in his clipped-wing Cub. He replaced the original, cranky 165-horsepower Siemens radial with a 185-horsepower Warner Scarab and flew the plane in hundreds of air shows and competitions until his untimely death in 1971, when the engine failed during a low pass. Mechanics at Bevo's Hawthorne Aviation rebuilt the airplane to non-flying status, and it may be seen today in the new Smithsonian Udvar-Hazy Center at the Dulles Airport, appropriately displayed inverted.*
>
> *I have never seen anyone fly a show as beautifully choreographed as Beverly Howard's. I saw him twice in as many years (at a Dayton Air Show and at Kitty Hawk), and for me the climax was not the inverted ribbon pickup, but rather the rolling 360-degree turns. I have never seen anyone else do that with the timing and precision of Mr. Howard. His roll rate was constant, turn rate constant, and the wings came level at each ninety degrees of turn. Now that is real aerobatics! But would anyone who has not tried to do a low roll in a Cub or a Luscombe appreciate that?*
>
> *Beverly Howard owned contract schools that trained some 10,000 pilots for the Air Corps in World War II and later for the Air Force. Howard held six first-place championships for precision aerobatic flying. He collected top fees for his flying in air shows, but he flew at least as many free for charities. Fellow air-show pilot Frank Price said of Howard, "He never failed to help anyone he came in contact with, always giving of his experience and knowledge to help new people coming into the sport of aerobatic flying," making him one of the most respected and beloved men ever to climb into a cockpit.*

Oscar Meyer with a flight student and an Aeronca. *Courtesy of James Andrews "Jim" Meyer.*

In June 1944, a carelessly thrown cigarette ignited a gasoline spill in Meyer's workshop, exploding into an inferno that incinerated five of his planes, most of his office equipment and two hangars. With only four planes remaining, Meyer continued to operate while rebuilding his facility.

Meyer and his crew serviced planes from all over the Southeast, refabricating wings, installing engines, overhauling engines and even building planes from scratch. With his charter service, Meyer transported businessmen throughout the Southeast. He also flew ambulance, once transporting a patient to San Angelo, Texas. And according to Beale Fletcher, Meyer frequently flew simply for his own enjoyment, "sightseeing in the sky, alone."

Since the early 1950s, Meyer and his pilots flew power line patrols for Carolina Power and Light Company and the Nantahala Power and Light Company—cruising at low speeds about thirty feet above the lines, looking for breaks. Oscar also flew fire patrols for the U.S. Forest Service.

Home Life

Oscar A. Meyer Jr. first married Doris Simmons and second, Amyrillis Knight (1916–2004), the mother of his two children, Amy Meyer Orr Stokes (1942–) and James Andrews "Jim" Meyer. Jim lives in Raleigh and Amy in Georgia. "Amy married Steve Orr from Hendersonville," Jim said. "He became a navy pilot flying F4s. With my dad's connections he was able to get Steve a job flying 727s with Eastern. Amy remarried years ago to a fine gentleman, Bill Stokes."

The Meyers lived on Druid Hills Avenue starting in 1943 and moved in 1955 to Lyndale Road in the Appledore subdivision—former estate of John Frampton Maybank. They later retired to Sanibel Island, Florida.

OSCAR'S FLEDGLINGS

Meyer's students included John Elmer Laughter (1914–1971), John Laughter Jr. (1943–), James Sidney Edney (1919–1999), Charles Beale Fletcher (1914–1994), Guy E. Dixon Jr., Barbara Boone Kitchens Lewis (1941–), Evelyn

Oscar Meyer at his airport with a flight student and a Navion. *Courtesy of James Andrews "Jim" Meyer.*

Oscar Meyer with a flight student in a Stearman. *Courtesy of James Andrews "Jim" Meyer.*

(Mrs. T.H.) Barker of Brevard, Garland O. Goodwin of Tryon, Jody Barber of Hendersonville and World War II air force bomber pilot Jesse Ingram Ledbetter (1922–2015) of Arden and Asheville. Some of these students went on to careers as military and commercial airline pilots.

James Sidney "Jack" Edney later served as commanding officer in the Maintenance and Supply Group at Bryan Air Force Base, Texas, and at Barstow Air Base in Winter Haven, Florida. He was made air attaché in Dublin, Ireland, and served in World War II, Korea and Vietnam. Edney was a World War II squadron commander (375th Bombardment Squadron, Fourteenth Air Force).

Meyer's childhood friend Grant Zickgraf went on to operate the Macon County Airport at Franklin, North Carolina.

Guy Dixon landed a career as senior captain with Eastern Airlines. He earned his commercial pilot's license and instructor's rating at Meyer's, and during World War II, he instructed Army Air Corps cadets at Meyer's field.

Garland O. Goodwin, a private pilot and aeronautical engineer, retired in 1988 after a forty-year career. Goodwin owned several airplanes over the years after having trained with Oscar Meyer in an Aeronca 7AC Champ and soloing in 1946. He started his career with Convair San Diego in 1956, working on the 880 and 990 jet transports as well as the F-106 and the canceled North American F-108. He later worked for Chance Vought and added the "direct-lift flaps" to the F8 Crusader for the French navy. When the company became LTV Aerospace, he got his name on the A-7 Corsair and Boeing 747 and the canceled SST. Then, in some twenty years as a contractor to NASA Langley, he got to play with the space shuttle, several satellites and helicopter rotor design, and finally, he put vortex flaps on the F-106.

Garland O. Goodwin. *Photo by the author.*

Guy Dixon

Guy Edwin Dixon Jr., aviator, inventor and entrepreneur, was born to Dr. Guy E. Dixon (1877–1952) and Nora Alexander Dixon (1882–1927) of Hendersonville. As a teenager, Guy Jr. developed a love of flying. Before he was sixteen years old, he built the first airplane he ever flew. He soloed at age sixteen and worked at Meyer Flying Service in Hendersonville. At age nineteen, he became the youngest flight instructor for the U.S. Army Air Corps and while stationed in Sikeston, Missouri, met Adagene Bowman (1917–2011), to whom he was married for seventy years.

In 1942, Guy and Adagene moved to Miami, where they built a home and raised their family. Guy became a pilot for Eastern Airlines, flying under contract for the Army Air Corps Military Transport Division to

Eastern Air Lines plane. *Courtesy of Krista Phillips Hare.*

South America and Africa during World War II and continuing as a captain for Eastern for twenty-five years. He started his flying career with open-cockpit planes and ended it flying the Boeing 727 Whisperjet.

Many years before retiring from Eastern, Dixon started the business that became his second career. He invented and patented the first folding doors to utilize full-height flexible hinges and, in 1953, founded Panelfold Inc. in Miami. Additional inventions relating to folding doors, accordion partitions and operable walls led to hundreds of worldwide patents and trademarks and the manufacture of Panelfold products in sixty countries.

In 1971, Dixon's company received the presidential E-Award and in 1986 the E-Star Award for Panelfold's excellence in exporting. President Ronald Reagan (1911–2004) presented the latter award to Dixon in the Rose Garden at the White House. The company passed to second and third generations of the Dixon family. Over the years, Panelfold has provided employment for tens of thousands of residents in South Florida and elsewhere.

In 1984, Guy and Adagene built their oceanfront dream home at the Ocean Reef Club in the Florida Keys, where they lived until they moved to Miami Lakes in 2006.

Jim Meyer shared:

> *Guy at one time worked for Dad* [Oscar A. Meyer Jr.], *who taught him to fly. I remember Dad telling me Guy was one of the smartest students he ever had because he soloed an airplane in three hours. In contrast, I soloed in five hours from Dad's chief instructor, Jim Brooks. Therefore, Guy was twice as smart! That was really proven in Guy's career. Guy was a pilot for Eastern and in his spare time invented the folding door. On the side, he started manufacturing the doors. The business became so large that Guy and his sons opened huge manufacturing plants in Brazil.*
>
> *Guy and his wife built a super-nice home called "Ocean Reef" in Key Largo, Florida, in the late 1960s. Just the landscaping cost close to a half million dollars, according to my dad. When my parents lived on Sanibel Island, they would visit the Dixons quite often at their super pad.*

John Laughter Jr., a former U.S. Navy pilot, made aviation his career, later flying for Southern Airways, having been hired as a pilot in 1973. Southern merged with North Central to form Republic, and Northwest bought Republic. Laughter retired from Northwest in 2003 at age sixty. Northwest and Delta later merged. Laughter's eldest son works for Delta.

One of Oscar A. Meyer's students, Evelyn Barker (1921–1961)—wife of Brevard city clerk Thurburn Howard Barker (1908–1989)—was the first woman in Brevard to solo, after only eight hours of flight instruction.

Barbara Boone Kitchens Lewis, the "First Lady of Georgia Aviation," lives south of Atlanta, Georgia. In March 2015, she wrote about her experiences with Oscar A. Meyer Jr.:

> *I soloed at age sixteen in Black Mountain at Nichols Flying Service. I grew up at Black Mountain and was around that airport from age twelve until they sold the property to Billy Graham for his radio station tower. Oscar Meyer used to fly to the Black Mountain Airport to do business with Red*

John Laughter. *Courtesy of John Laughter.*

Nichols [William Charles "Red" Nichols (1916–1988)]. *That was the first time I met him. He was flying a Ryan Navion aircraft and I believe he later sold it to Red who in turn sold it to "Simmie" Cross* [Simeon Roane Cross (1907–1952)] *at Marion, North Carolina. Mr. Cross owned Cross Mills. I remember that so well because Red checked Simmie out in the Navion and about six months later Simmie flew over to Christ School with his daughter* [Elizabeth Iverson Cross (1938–1952)] *and her friends* [Robert Eugene Lambeth (1936–1952) and William

Jay "Billy" Wilkerson Jr. (1936–1952)]. *On their flight back to Marion they ran into bad weather between Black Mountain and Old Fort and crashed, with no survivors. This was in 1952.*

I soloed on January 26, 1957—the day after my sixteenth birthday—and flew a Piper Cub over to Oscar's at Hendersonville in July. Oscar checked me out in a Super Cub N7071H. I loved the Super Cub and rented it a couple of times later in 1957. I flew another of his Super Cubs, a N7455H, several times up through 1960. I flew over to Hendersonville many times as a teenager when I could save enough money to rent the Super Cub.

I was just a kid and flying was my life. Oscar had the best airport! I loved it because there was so much activity, all kinds of planes, glider towing and so forth. The airport was always crowded with local people and children. Oscar stayed busy instructing and giving rides in the Navion. He always had a couple of Navions there. It might have been a favorite. I got to ride with him a couple of times when he had a seat available.

I ran into Oscar at a fly-in or North Carolina Aviation event years later. I flew into Hendersonville Airport through the years, mostly for business.[54] *Last time I saw Oscar, I believe, was in Oshkosh at the National Fly-In, but it might have been at Rockford, Illinois, before they moved the event to Oshkosh.*

It seemed, in those days, general aviation was booming everywhere—a lot of instructing and flying going on. Maybe the GI Bill was helping with that.

I flew a little clipped-wing Cub back then from the time I soloed, so I was around all the little airports in those days. I loved to go to Carrier Field at West Asheville on the French Broad River. A funny old fellow who was a dentist ran the airport. His name was Doc Owen. His favorite airplane was a vintage twin-tailed Bellanca. There was Emma Airport too. Not as active. I used to fly over to the old A&H [Asheville-Hendersonville] *Airport in my no-radio Cub and they would give me the light signal to clear me to land. I knew Paul McMurray and* [Ortez Devoe] *"Lacy" Griffin* [Jr.] *for many years until they passed away. They were at the current Asheville Regional Airport.*

In partnership with Thurman Baird, an attorney in Asheville, we built a Corbin Baby Ace in the basement of the Commerce Building in downtown Asheville. They did a write-up on the front page of the Asheville paper.

Those were some of my best years growing up in western North Carolina and I have fond memories of those wonderful people who made a difference in my life.

I bought that little clipped-wing Cub and flew for over thirty-five years. I have owned a Super Cub for many years and fly it regularly.

Barbara Boone Kitchens Lewis at the controls. *Courtesy of Barbara Lewis and Theresa Mitchell.*

A news article confirmed Barbara Lewis's recollections of the crash at Old Fort:

> *4 Marion People Killed in Crash of Private Plane*
>
> *Asheville, N.C., Nov. 3 (AP)—A Marion industrialist, his daughter who is a national champion horsewoman, and two preparatory school students were killed near here today in the crash of a single-engine private plane. The dead were identified by McDowell County Coroner S.J. Westmoreland as Simeon Roane Cross, 45, president of the Cross Cotton Mills Co., in Marion; his daughter, Elizabeth Cross, 12 or 13, recent winner of a national trophy as a junior horseback rider awarded in memory of a man killed in a plane crash; Robert Eugene Lambeth, 15, son of Mr. and Mrs. R.E. Lambeth, Sr., of Marion; and Billy Wilkerson, 15, son of Mr. and Mrs. William J. Wilkerson of Marion. Westmoreland said Cross was flying young Lambeth and Wilkerson from Marion to Black Mountain so the two youths could return to their studies at Christ School near Asheville. The crash occurred in a ruggedly mountainous section of McDowell County near the Buncombe County line and near a new super-highway from Ridgecrest to Old Fort. The plane burst into flames and started a forest fire. Floyd Huskins of Celo, a construction worker on the road project and one of the first to the scene, said he saw the plane flying along very low and that it suddenly dipped its nose and crashed. The forest*

fire raged over a fairly large area of the mountain, but appeared to be surrounded by fire breaks in the form of work roads built for the highway project. Mrs. Bob Hyatt of Old Fort said she heard a plane shortly before the crash occurred between 4:30 and 5 p.m. She said it passed over Old Fort at a low altitude and was apparently having engine trouble. Lt. W.S. Hunt, executive officer of Troop E of the Highway Patrol, said he thought Cross might have been trying to reach one of the level spots created by huge earthmovers for the new highway. Hunt said the plane apparently stalled just before reaching a level spot, struck a tree, and plummeted down. The Albert M. Jones Memorial Trophy for junior horseback riders was presented to Miss Cross in ceremonies at the Fulton-Dekalb Shrine horse show in Atlanta last year. The trophy is a memorial established by Mr. and Mrs. Albert M. Jones of Knoxville, Tenn., for their son who was fatally injured in a plane crash.

—Florence Morning News, *South Carolina, November 4, 1952*

Remembrances from another of Oscar Meyer's flight students, John Laughter Jr., also of Georgia, follow:

Oscar Meyer taught my dad, John [Elmer] *Laughter* [1914–1971], *to fly in 1953. Later that year, my mom, Caroline* [Andreasen Laughter (1917–1980)], *overcame her apprehension about flying and soloed—the first female licensed pilot in the area, in 1953. That meant we spent our Sunday afternoons at the airport. At ten years old, I spent a lot of time sitting in the Boeing Stearman dusters in the back hangar. My plan was to be a fighter pilot someday so the dusters provided just the right setting for my imagination to go flying. Many years later, having been a navy fighter pilot and an airline pilot, I had the chance to buy a restored 1938 Stearman PT-13, which I found in Missouri. On first glance through the logbooks, I saw that Oscar had signed off the inspections on this airplane in 1954. That was a sign to me, and it cinched the deal. I had to have that airplane and paid the asking price. So, thirty years later, I got to buy the same airplane I had flown as a boy.*

One of my first cross-country flights in my Stearman was to take it back to Hendersonville, to the old sod. Oscar had retired and moved to Florida by then so imagine my surprise when I shut down and saw Oscar, who was back for a visit, walking down the field to greet me. We had a fine afternoon together.

Oscar was the "Great One" when it came to flying an airplane. He could do things with an airplane that couldn't be done by others. Beyond

Carroll Leroy "Chip" Lamb. *Courtesy of Chip Lamb.*

> *that he was the most savvy mountain pilot ever and shared his knowledge with others. He made a good living running a small airport. All aspects of the business showed a little profit from five-dollar sightseeing rides around Jump Off Rock to five-cent Cokes from the dispenser. The tradition at Meyer's was that when a student soloed they had to buy Cokes for everyone. Most airports cut off the students' shirttails, but I think Oscar saw a better profit from his Coke tradition.*
>
> *Fifty-some years ago Oscar turned me loose, alone and unassisted, in an Aeronca Champ. Nearly every year on the anniversary of that solo I fly around the pattern in a friend's Aeronca, just about sunset, and recall Oscar and that wonderful day. As I flew my three takeoffs and landings Oscar made his traditional walk down the length of the field, keeping an eye on his new pilot. The lessons he taught have served me very well.*
>
> *So I ended my career right where I started—flying little airplanes from grass runways.*

Chip Lamb (1954–), a decorated combat veteran with missions over Iraq, is a certified Level 1 (Unrestricted) demonstration pilot and acts as the Trojan Phlyers air show coordinator and scheduler.[55] After eight years of flying fighters during three overseas tours of duty, Lamb left active air force duty in 1985 to fly F-16s with the Texas Air National Guard at Kelly Air Force Base, the same year joining the commercial rank of pilot for American Airlines, after which he flew for twenty-three years on international routes. After thirty years in the military (twenty-three of them flying fighters), he retired as a colonel in the U.S. Air Force Reserve in 2007. Lamb holds FAA Certified Flight Instructor, Instrument and Multi-Engine Instructor ratings. About Meyer Flying Service he recalled:

> *My flying career started at the Hendersonville Airport, where both my father* [Carroll Leroy Lamb Sr. (1919–2002)] *and I learned to fly. As a young boy, my father lived on Shepherd Street next to the airport and in 1936, as a seventeen-year old, he started taking flying lessons from Oscar Meyer. He obtained his private pilot's certificate and continued flying at the airport for thirty years. He worked part time at the airport on weekends to make extra money for flying time. On those work weekends I would tag along and spend my afternoons walking among the airplanes and watching them fly.*
>
> *As a child, I always enjoyed watching Oscar Meyer perform aerobatics in his Super Cub on the occasion of the airport's annual open house. I also enjoyed the spectacle of Johnny Laughter over-flying Hendersonville in a navy fighter and climbing high into the sky in afterburner. So I think it was only natural that I too would want to fly, and I wanted to fly jet fighters.*
>
> *My father and I were both involved in the Civil Air Patrol, he as a senior member and I as a cadet. The CAP unit was based at Oscar's airport and it offered me a way to learn about the United States Air Force and to fly. Just as my father had, I started my flying lessons as a seventeen-year old, with my turn in 1971. The CAP offered me an opportunity to attend the USAF Academy where I received a commission in the air force and an assignment to fly fighters. It was a dream realized!*
>
> *I ended up spending thirty years in the military—twenty-three of them flying fighters (F4/F16). I also spent twenty-three years flying for American Airlines where, in 1987, I had an opportunity to fly with Jim Kilpatrick, who lived in Hendersonville and who then owned the airport. Small world!*
>
> *I am now retired from the military and from the airlines, but I still fly aerobatics at air shows and continue my association with my "home" airport as a life member of the Western North Carolina Air Museum.*

Testimonials

Oscar purchased a Taylor E-2 Cub, actually the second Cub ever built, with a thirty-seven-horsepower engine in it, and it was in bad need of repair. We worked and rebuilt and recovered and repainted this Cub, and I began to get regular flight instruction from Oscar in the Cub. I soloed on September 21, 1936, I believe shortly after my sixteenth birthday. The time that I had was a total of three hours and two minutes actually in the air and was spread out over the preceding year.

I took a number of courses in high school that helped me in my flying. I was good at math and physics and the science courses, and I took shop and drafting and geography and meteorology. This was a bit surprising for this time; but we had a professor by the name of "Uncle" Tommy Valentine [Thomas Wood Valentine (1866–1937), Australian born]. *He had a goatee, smoked a corncob pipe, was the local weatherman and taught in the high schools. He was most helpful in giving me a good basic understanding of weather and weather forecasting. This came in handy later in my flying career.*

—Guy E. Dixon Jr.

No one knew just when Oscar would solo a student. His way was to get out of the airplane at the far end of the runway and tell the student to take it around alone. In the office, all eyes were on the airplane at the far end of the field to see if Oscar would get out. When he did the atmosphere in the office became intense. Oscar would then walk the length of the field while the student flew.

On Sunday afternoons, Oscar would sometimes, without announcing his intentions, saunter out to the Super Cub, crank it up and take off across the field—up over the bushes on the dike running the length of the runway and into an acrobatic routine that included everything you would see at an air show. If there were any wind blowing he would slow the airplane into the wind and just "hover" over the airport. I guess he did this to get the spectators sitting in their cars in the parking lot to buy airplane rides. I think he did it also just for the hell of it.

Oscar could build, fix, sell, instruct in and fly anything with wings. He taught to fly a power-off approach from abeam the landing spot. This requires piloting acumen. Most of all, it prepares you for a successful landing in the event of engine failure. Oscar taught to always have a field in mind in case the engine quit. I have that in the back of my mind all the time I'm flying—having an awareness of what's below me and if I have sufficient altitude. It paid off once in the Stearman. Today, flight instructors teach powered approaches in light airplanes. That's the way you land jets. I think it is very wrong to be in a position where you are on final, the engine quits and you can't make the runway.

—John Laughter Jr.

SHOWMAN

Aerobatics is almost as old as flight itself.
—Garland O. Goodwin

One of the most popular of all the Flying Circus acts was one called the "Flying Old Woman." Oscar Meyer dressed like an old mountain woman and wearing a big, old-fashioned bonnet, would run to Haskell A. Deaton [1917–1983] *as he emceed the show and express a desire to ride in an airplane. Haskell, microphone in his hand, would try to talk the "old lady" into going on back to the grandstand until the show was over. At this point, a plane would taxi up, and the pilot would get out to speak to Haskell. Oscar (the old lady) would jump into this plane and accidentally push the throttle and the plane would begin to taxi down the field. Haskell and several assistants would give chase, Haskell shouting all along into the microphone, "Stop that old lady! She can't fly! Stop her!"*

The plane would zigzag down the field, leap into the air, fly straight up for a few feet, then into a nosedive…straighten out, then hit the ground on both wheels like a rubber ball and bounce several feet straight into the air. Meanwhile, Haskell continued to shout into the microphone, trying to tell the "old lady" how to land the plane. The plane would fly sidewise, climbing all the while, then suddenly pop into a barrel roll in the other direction, then come in to land…nose up…tail down.

"Old woman, your tail is dragging…get it up!" Haskell would shout.

The tail of the plane would shoot up…the nose lower. Then Oscar would land the plane on one wheel, step from the cockpit and run back to the grandstand. Thousands laughed themselves silly at such antics.

—Charles Beale Fletcher

North Carolina's Only Miss America

Maria Beale Fletcher (1942–) was Miss America in 1962—the only Miss America North Carolina has ever produced. Fletcher was born to actor/dancer/aviator Charles Beale Fletcher (1914–1994) and Margaret Byers Don Gatley "Peggy" Fletcher (1915–1998), founders of the Fletcher School of Dance and the Land of the Sky Civic Ballet. Maria; her brother, Walter; and her sisters, Margaret and Bonnie, were great-grandchildren of Dr. George Washington Fletcher.

From Asheville, North Carolina, Maria was a graduate of A.C. Reynolds High School. She worked as a Radio City Music Hall Rockette prior to winning the Miss America crown. She also won the Miss America Preliminary Swimsuit Competition, and her overseas tour included visits to thirty-one army hospitals and servicemen's clubs. During the late 1960s, Fletcher served as cohost of the *Noon Show* on the Nashville television station WSM.

When asked to recall an embarrassing moment she could share, Fletcher recalled wearing her Miss America gown, complete with hoop, on the Miss America Float in the Orange Bowl Parade. Unbeknownst to her, the gown caught fire. A Good Samaritan jumped aboard and extinguished the blaze, saving both Fletcher and her gown—all before she realized she was on fire.

In his earlier years, Oscar Meyer would fly over crowds with his buddy Grant Zickgraf swinging by his hands from a rope attached to the wheels of Meyer's Bird biplane.

> *In those days it seems Grant was always hanging from something. When we were young teenagers he used to hang from the biplane glider while I pulled him with my motorcycle. He'd wear roller skates to get started, then jump into the air, and hanging from the glider he'd hop, skip and jump about, maybe soaring up to ten or fifteen feet.*
>
> —*Oscar A. Meyer Jr.*

In another of Meyer's stunts, he forced his plane to weave and swerve, dragged a wing and then took off just as he ran out of airstrip. Once airborne, he would let loose a roll of toilet paper, and as it unfurled, he gracefully maneuvered the ship until its propeller had shredded all of the tissue into thin ribbons. He named this performance the "Drunk Flying Act."

Meyer was known to land a lightweight plane on frozen Highland Lake at Flat Rock and throw out a rope—tied to the tail—to skaters eager to be towed at full rudder. According to William "Wick" Andrews, "Oscar was just a splendid flyer."

SQUADRON TRAINING

The Western North Carolina Squadron, as it was known then, was established under the leadership of Jack Rogers (1918–1984) in early 1942. Sometime between February 1942 and February 1945, command passed to Captain Oscar A. Meyer Jr., and in February 1945, the division was renamed the Asheville Squadron and placed under command of First Lieutenant Edward L. Clasz (1906–1963). At the same time, the Macon County Squadron was formed under the command of Captain Meyer. During that time, the squadron participated in various activities such as the missing aircraft search, cadet training and forest fire spotting. CPT (civilian pilot training) students studied at Brevard College and learned to fly at Meyer's field in a Culver Dart and other planes.

Before World War II, the federal government granted approval to Meyer to teach flying as part of the CPT program. Tommy Stocks, a childhood friend, assisted and also served as commander of the Western North Carolina Squadron of the Civil Air Patrol (CAP) wing with the rank of major from 1943 to 1944. The wing included Franklin, Canton, Asheville and Hendersonville. "Here is an outlet for the adventurous spirit of youth," Meyer said. Meyer and Stocks trained several of the men who flew America's fighters and bombers that helped win the war with Japan. Jody Barber also commanded Henderson County's CAP flights.

CAP lieutenant colonel Milton Prince Arnette (1908–1993), a student of Meyer's, served as a squadron commander of Henderson County CAP. Arnette was injured in a crash while flying a search to find a downed airplane in May 1978. Jim Meyer reminisced:

> *Prince Arnette worked part-time on Sunday flying passengers for Dad. Dad thought the world of him and he did an outstanding job for him. If I remember correctly, Prince worked for the Boyd car dealership.*

J.D. King [Joseph Daniel "Joe" King (1921–1985) of King Hardware in Hendersonville] *assisted Dad in training young men for basic pilot training for World War II. Dad thought so much of J.D. that he would allow him to fly his new Aeroncas from the factory to Hendersonville. Back then they called it "ferrying aircraft." When I became a pilot it was always fun to fly in a Navion with Dad and J.D. because they always had the best of times flying together.*

Crop Dusting

After the war Oscar purchased Stearmans just to obtain the gasoline from them. Then he would sell them for crop dusters. Crop-dusting pilots used Meyer Flying Service for fuel and service. Some of those flyers included Oscar Case, a pioneer in aerial crop dusting in the southeastern United States. Case owned and operated Case Farm Service on Sugarloaf Road. He had a crop dusting operation stationed at Dad's airport. At that time, the "dust" was DDT and in a form that looked like flour. I mean toxic as hell. My dad did not like the smell or mess it made at the airport but the dusters purchased gas and aircraft maintenance from him. After all, the color of money is green.

Oscar Case was a terrible businessman and his outgo exceeded the income. My way-too-generous dad allowed him to back up in gasoline bills for over six months. Since Case could not pay his bills, Dad took three of his Stearmans to help cover the debts. Back then Stearmans were a dime a dozen and since the dusters dropped the stock 220-horsepower Pratt and Whitney engines in favor of 450-horsepower radial engines—to carry heavier loads—the resale was terrible. Oscar Case went out of business and left the area.

Along came Perry [Walter] *Jones* [1919–1984] *and he went into the dusting business. We liked him because he would pay his bills. Perry was as wild as a March hare. He raced stockcars in Asheville on Saturday nights. He would come to the airport the next day to do some dusting and be missing a few more teeth. He smoked like crazy and seemed to thrive on the DDT. I used to see Perry fly over the field inverted in the 450-horsepower Stearman wide open until the engine would almost quit. The Stearman did not have an inverted engine system—the reason for wanting to quit. We all liked Perry because he was so full of life. He later started a crop-dusting business in Homestead, Florida, and did really well.*

One of the dust bag boys, John Duncan, who loaded the Stearmans, almost lost his life breathing the DDT. I remember them carrying him to hospital in the back of a truck. From then on, he started using a respirator when loading the hopper in the Stearman. John later became a FAA tower controller at the Asheville airport.

I remember taking used aircraft engine oil and putting it on the parking lot to keep the dust down and on the dirt roads also. No EPA at that time or Oscar's airport would have been shut down.

—*Jim Meyer*

Oscar Burrell Case (1913–1998) flew a crop duster for twenty-eight years. As an avocation, he wrote gospel songs.

Others in the crop-dusting field included Ernest Horace "Ernie" Marshall (1924–1999) and George Bascombe Marshall (1916–1970). George Marshall's son Clyde David "Dave" Marshall (1942–1966) crashed his plane and died near Battle Creek Road in Horse Shoe on August 22, 1966. David was named for George's sibling, who also died young.

He was dusting a tiny squash patch and probably stalled, or the engine quit, after a pass and sharp pull over trees—although some rumored that moonshiners might have shot him down. Do you know Battle Creek Road? It's next to the railroad tracks at Horse Shoe. Wanders up the creek and dead ends after a mile or two. Anyway, there was a fire and lots of melted aluminum—plus the body. I remember going up there. Pretty gruesome.

—*John Laughter Jr.*

OSCAR MEYER'S LATER YEARS

My father had a lot of fun in his working years because he enjoyed his work and never had a boss—other than maybe my mom. In 1968 [recorded January 1969] *Oscar sold his airport to Bob Winkler, one of his former students. You should have seen the smirk on Oscar's face! He was retiring at fifty-seven years old and would be a free man. Mom and Dad purchased a Winnebago and started traveling around the United States before building a house on Sanibel Island, Florida. Those days were the happiest I had ever seen them.*

—*Jim Meyer*

Oscar Meyer was said by many to have been kind, gentle and patient. "Generous to a fault," said his son, Jim, "he extended months of credit to customers for fuel and service." According to Jim, his dad was a most forgiving man, who gave folks "way too much rope." He was generous with his time and patient with his students. He chose his words methodically and was never known to be rude or to disparage anyone.

With more than ten thousand flying hours in fixed-wing aircraft under his belt, Oscar sold his airport and retired to Sanibel Island full time. Thirty-seven years had passed since he flew an OX-5-powered Bird from his own airport. He later owned Waco, Cubs, Stearmans, Navions and Cessnas. He was a Cessna dealer and even in retirement he took on work as an aircraft broker. "Super Cubs and Navions were Dad's favorite aircraft," his son, Jim, said.

> *I liked to fly my Citabria to visit my parents at their winter home on Sanibel Island. From Charlotte to Sanibel, I normally never obtained an altitude of higher than five hundred AGL* [above ground level] *feet. I really liked to sightsee at low altitudes and sometimes crop dusters would fly up alongside and wave at me. Since I performed my own maintenance of the aircraft, I had a lot of faith in the bird to not quit on me. I'd land on Sanibel and walk to my parents' house. Real estate became expensive on the island and they built houses on the landing strip. After that I would buzz my parents' house—to get their attention, letting them know I'd arrived. Dad would drive over to Page Field at Fort Myers and pick me up. This was in the days before cellphones so we used a different communications method. Later on, I wised up and used my two-meter handheld amateur radio through a phone patch to call them while in flight. Same principle used by cellphones today.*

Oscar Meyer sold his airport to Robert Overbeck "Bob" Winkler Jr. (1918–1985), who renamed the enterprise Winkler Aviation and continued serving private planes. Winkler Field boasted a 3,200-foot paved runway. The Winklers lived in Flat Rock.

Today, the field is known as the Hendersonville Airport (K0A7) Aerolina Inc., owned by John Michael Fadok (1954–) since 1999. The runway length spans 3,075 feet, and the width is 40 feet of asphalt with 40 feet of grass on the western side. Johnson Field lies adjacent to the property, owned and developed separately by Elmo Leland Johnson Jr. (1935–) and includes the Western North Carolina Air Museum. The museum, accessed from Gilbert Street, is a private, tax-exempt organization dedicated to preserving and promoting the flying heritage of the western North Carolina mountains

Bob Winkler (left) and Oscar Meyer. *Courtesy of James Andrews "Jim" Meyer.*

region. Johnson's father, Ira Elmo "I.E." Johnson (1901–1983)—a Hendersonville city commissioner, chamber of commerce president, member of the planning and zoning board and manager of Hendersonville's F.W. Woolworth store—kept three Stearmans at Oscar's field.

Before Fadok owned Oscar's field, James Frazier "Jimmy" Kilpatrick (1946–) purchased the airfield and sold it in 1983 to David Storm Cowan (1939–), CFI, who now resides in the state of Washington. Captain Kilpatrick, who soloed at Meyer Flying Service (under Jim Brooks), was a pilot with American Airlines after having served active duty flying F-100 fighters during the Vietnam War in the U.S. Air Force. Kilpatrick flew 257 missions from 1970 to 1971 and earned Distinguished Flying crosses and numerous other medals. He piloted jets to Tokyo and London for American Airlines. When Kilpatrick owned the airfield, he offered charter flights and flight instruction and owned a Cessna dealership. He currently owns and flies a Van's Aircraft RV7 homebuilt and a Russian Yak-52.

Oscar A. Meyer Jr. died in 1998. His pallbearers were Hugh Randall, Frank Bell, Leonard Schroeder, Roy Duncan, Ken Stubbs and Ted

Elmo Leland Johnson Jr. with his 1946 Piper Cub J3C-65, the last plane flown by Oscar Meyer. *Photo by the author.*

Jimmy Kilpatrick with his Yakovlev Yak-52 "warbird" (Soviet primary trainer aircraft). *Courtesy of James F. Kilpatrick.*

Lewis—all fellow pilots and motorcycle riders. Elmo Leland Johnson, in his Piper J-3 Cub, was one of thirteen pilots to fly over Meyer's grave. In December 2003, the Wright Brothers National Memorial at Kill Devil Hills recognized Oscar A. Meyer Jr. as a pioneer of aviation.

Like aviation pioneer Glenn Curtiss and several other pilots, Oscar Meyer Jr. had a passion for motorcycling.

> *He took me for my first motorcycle ride. A few years before his death in 1998, I gave him his last earthly ride on my motorcycle. Life does go full circle.*
>
> —*Jim Meyer*

> *On a bright, cold morning in January, when the skies are blue and mountains capped in white, you may see a tiny plane flying in the sky, banking and curving like a graceful swan, bright wings glistening in the sun. It could be Oscar handling the joystick with a delicacy and precision of movement that spells artistry in any man's language. He's probably flying around up there just for the fun of it... looking things over.*
>
> —*Charles Beale Fletcher*

North Carolina Aviation Timeline

1880	Robert Henderson Roper of Washington County is the first American to jump from a balloon with his homemade parachute.
1880–1881	Dr. Daniel Asbury of Anson County builds a steam-driven airplane in Mecklenburg County.
1902	Jacob Aaron Hill of Forsyth County builds a dirigible.

December 17, 1903	Orville and Wilbur Wright conduct the first powered, heavier-than-air flights from Kill Devil Hills.
1907	William Luther Paul of Carteret County claims to fly his *Bumblebee* (helicopter) four to five feet into the air.
1911	James S. Spainhour of Lenoir builds a monoplane.
June 21, 1913	Georgia Ann "Tiny" Thompson Broadwick of Granville County is the first woman to jump from an airplane.
1915	Forrest Wysong of Guilford County builds an airplane on the campus of present-day NCSU.
1918	Hubert DeVault McLean of Gibsonville, Guilford County, opens an airfield—North Carolina's oldest.
1919	Carr E. Booker of Wake County builds his *Hummingbird*, a sixteen-foot-long biplane with a Harley-Davidson engine.
October 1919	Belvin Maynard of Sampson County wins the Double Transcontinental Aerial Derby.
1924	Viola Gentry of Rockingham County is first woman in the state to learn how to fly an airplane.
1932	Oscar A. Meyer Jr. opens Meyer Flying Service in Hendersonville.
1933	Asheville-Hendersonville Airport opens.
1940	Tom Davis establishes Piedmont Aviation, Inc.
1948	Tom Davis founds Piedmont Airlines in Winston-Salem, and Piedmont dispatches its first flight from Wilmington, North Carolina, to Cincinnati, Ohio, on February 20.

1961	Asheville Regional Airport opens.
July 19, 1967	Piedmont Flight 22 crashes in Hendersonville–North Carolina's worst aviation disaster to date.
1969	Warren Wheeler starts Wheeler Flying Service in Raleigh, becoming the first African American to establish and run a commercial air carrier.

An advertisement in the Mullin-Kille & Times News 1969 *Hendersonvillle City Directory* stated:

> *Air Service: Hendersonville is served with passenger, express, freight and air mail service by United, Delta and Piedmont with 25 flights daily. Direct service is available to 35 major cities with connections on all major airlines to any part of the United States and to foreign countries. The Civil Aeronautics Administration has a control tower and 24-hour weather and communication station located at Hendersonville's airport. The airport is located 11 miles north of Hendersonville, connected by a paved highway.*

ASHEVILLE-HENDERSONVILLE AIRPORT

Shown as early as 1936 on a U.S. Geological Survey (USGS) topographical map, the Asheville-Hendersonville Airport was depicted as a single unpaved north–south runway, labeled "Airport," with a few small buildings on its southwest sector. The location was north of the intersection of Mills Gap Road and L.A. White Drive in Cane Creek, Hoopers Creek Township, in north-central Henderson County—the original municipal airport for the town of Asheville, located southeast of the city. The earliest reference to the Asheville-Hendersonville Airport, in the Airport Directory Company's 1933 *Airports Directory*, described Asheville-Hendersonville Airport as a fifty-acre field, having two runways in an L shape, measuring 3,100 feet north–south and 1,200 feet east–west. A hangar was said to have "Asheville Airport" painted on its roof.

Oscar Meyer's first solo flight in his homebuilt monoplane. *Courtesy of James Andrews "Jim" Meyer.*

Skyline Airways letterhead, Asheville-Hendersonville Airport. *Courtesy of Sindy Drake Hamilton.*

Asheville-Hendersonville gained its second runway at some point between 1936 and 1937, as the directory described it as having two silt-loam runways, with the longest being a 3,100-foot north–south strip. Mark Lafayette Reed (1902–1944), a wing commander of the Civil Air Patrol, managed the Asheville-Hendersonville Airport before World War II. A prominent Asheville businessman and accomplished aviator, Reed died from injuries in a plane crash.

The first airmail letter was delivered to Hendersonville on September 11, 1924—from California to Washington by plane and from Washington to Hendersonville by train. The first commercial and passenger service by air came to Hendersonville on October 12, 1937, when Eastern Airlines delivered the first shipment of airmail (four thousand pieces) to the Asheville-Hendersonville Airport. The outbound flight carried outgoing mail. The envelopes, stamped with "franking" insignia honoring the historic flight, read: "First All North Carolina Air Mail Flights—Oct. 11–16, 1937."

Henderson County native Susan Flack Summerville (1955–), a collector of all things historical pertaining to the county, owns pieces of mail from the historic drop. One piece was a letter mailed by Summerville's grandmother Flo Flack to her parents, Mr. and Mrs. A.G. Williams, in Washington, D.C.

The 1940 U.S. *Airport Directory* described the Asheville-Hendersonville Airport as having two runways: a 2,200-foot east–west paved strip and a 3,200-foot north–south turf strip. In May 1941, the 14M Regional Aeronautical Chart designated it as a "commercial or municipal airport."

The airport added a third runway at some point between 1940 and 1942, as the 1942 USGS topographical map depicted the field as having three runways. The April 1944 *U.S. Army/Navy Directory of Airfields* described the Asheville-Hendersonville Airport as having four thousand feet of hard-surface runway and indicated that both the army and navy conducted flight operations from the field.

As stated by Hillis "Al" Cunliffe (1947–):

> *Commercial airline service at the Asheville-Hendersonville Airport began after World War II, provided by Delta, Capital and Piedmont airlines. Asheville was one of the en-route stops on Piedmont's inaugural service from Wilmington, North Carolina, to Cincinnati, Ohio.*

Hendersonville's first airmail, 1937. *Courtesy of Susan Flack Summerville.*

Cunliffe asserted that the Asheville-Hendersonville Airport had some use in the testing of ejection seats. The Stencel Aeronautical Research Corporation, which produced aircraft ejection seats, operated a plant "located about two miles from the Asheville Airport on the main access road from Route 25." Cunliffe's father, Hillis Wilmont Cunliffe (1911–1984), worked for the Stencel organization from the day it opened in 1958 until his retirement in 1982. Cunliffe added that his father was

> *one of the original dozen or so people employed by the company's founder, Fred B. Stencel* [1909–1988]. *He was hired because of his background as an A&P mechanic and master parachute rigger. He maintained the three different aircraft the company operated to support their research and prototype department. Stencel's airplanes were kept at the Asheville Regional Airport.*

Al Cunliffe was born in Rocky Mount, North Carolina, and worked at the Asheville Regional Airport for Asheville Flying Service as a line-boy (1964 to 1967). He entered the air force in March 1967 and served on active duty for more than twenty-three years, retiring as a senior master sergeant in August 1990. He is a licensed commercial pilot and certified flight instructor but did not fly with the military. Piedmont Aviation later bought Asheville Flying Service.

Piedmont Airlines

As a youth, Tom Davis (1918–1999) flew for Camel City Flying Service of Winston-Salem. With Davis at the helm, Piedmont Aviation Inc. grew out of Camel in 1940. Davis created the Piedmont Airlines division of Piedmont Aviation as a small local service carrier in 1948.

In 1961, Richard A. Henson (1910–2002) formed Henson Aviation. The carrier's first scheduled flight departed from Hagerstown, Maryland, and landed at Washington National Airport in 1962. Piedmont Airlines Inc. absorbed and rebranded Maryland-based Henson as the Piedmont Regional Airline in 1983. (Hagerstown Regional Airport was renamed Richard A. Henson Field.) USAir Group (US Airways) began negotiating to buy Piedmont in 1987 and by 1989 had absorbed Davis's interests. The Piedmont name was resurrected in 1993 and US Airways (founded in 1937) merged Allegheny Airlines (founded in 1939) into Piedmont in 2004.

The 1960 *Jeppesen Airway Manual* depicted the Asheville-Hendersonville Airport as having three paved runways, with the longest at 4,079 feet—Runway 4/22—as well as a taxiway leading to a ramp on the east side of the field, around which were clustered several small buildings and a tower.

In January 1961, the new Asheville airport (today's Asheville Regional Airport) was opened three miles to the west of the old one. The new airport featured a much longer runway, which would be more compatible with modern airline flights. The Asheville-Hendersonville Airport was closed at some point between 1961 and 1963, as it was labeled "abandoned airport" on the May 1963 *Charlotte Sectional Chart*. The 1965 USGS topographical map labeled the old field as "Asheville-Hendersonville Airport (abandoned)." According to Al Cunliffe, "The old airport was used as a drag strip for several years, then became the Cane Creek [Fletcher] Industrial Park." Industrial buildings eventually covered most of the runways.

A piece in the *Western Carolina Tribune* dated March 10, 1972, under the headline "Old Airport Property Sale Approved," stated:

> *The sale of the 287½ acre old Asheville-Hendersonville Airport property was approved by the commissioners of the three governments owning the property—City of Asheville, City of Hendersonville and Henderson County—following special meetings.*

A follow-up article, dated May 12, 1972, stated:

> *Total sale price to Harlee-Quattlebaum is $161,287.50. Asheville will receive approximately $85,000, 52.2 percent of the proceeds, and Henderson County $61,000 of the money. The rest or 10 percent will go to the City of Hendersonville. All three owned portions of the old airport. The sale was made with a restriction for industrial development only for 10 years so the old airport will become an industrial complex. Henderson County will benefit exclusively from additional ad valorem taxes from the park since it lies in Henderson County.*

A patch of tarmac at the Fletcher Business Park, former site of the Asheville-Hendersonville Airport. *Photo by the author.*

The Fletcher Business Park occupies the site of the former Asheville-Hendersonville Airport. As of 2016, businesses in the park have included Asheville Thermoform Plastics, BorgWarner Thermal Systems, Steelcase, Eaton Corporation, Diamond Brand Manufacturing, Meritor Automotive Inc., the Country Malt Group, Tercon Logistics and Wilsonart International. Traces of tarmac from the old runways may still be seen in sections of the park.

Since 2004, the *Airport Facility Directory* has listed the Cane Creek Airport (4NC6) as a private airfield consisting of a 2,680-foot turf runway. The owner was listed as L.A. White with seven aircraft listed as being based at the field, including five single-engine planes and two gliders. Quonset hut–style buildings served as hangars.[56]

Federal Aviation Administration

1926	Air Commerce Act passed.
1927	Pilot and aircraft safety regulations established.
1938	To ensure a federal focus on aviation safety, President Franklin D. Roosevelt signs the Civil Aeronautics Act. This legislation establishes the independent Civil Aeronautics Authority (CAA) with a three-member Air Safety Board to conduct accident investigations and recommend means of preventing accidents. The legislation also expands the government's role in civil aviation by empowering the CAA to regulate airline fares and determine routes served by individual carriers. The Civil Aeronautics Act transfers federal civil aviation responsibilities from the Commerce Department to the Civil Aeronautics Authority, a newly formed, independent agency.
1940	President Roosevelt splits the Civil Aeronautics Authority into two agencies: the CAA (Civil Aeronautics Administration) and CAB (Civil Aeronautics Board). The offshoot of the original CAA retains responsibility for ATC, airman and aircraft certification, safety enforcement and airway development. CAB responsibilities include safety rulemaking, accident investigation and economic regulation of the airlines.

1958	Federal Aviation Act is passed, created under the name "Federal Aviation Agency," adopting its current name (Federal Aviation Administration) in 1966 when it becomes part of the U.S. Department of Transportation. National Aeronautics & Space Administration (NASA) formed.
1967	A new U.S. Department of Transportation (DOT) combines major federal responsibilities for air and surface transport. The Federal Aviation Agency's name had changed to the Federal Aviation Administration in 1966 as it became the largest of several agencies. The FAA administrator would no longer report directly to the president but would instead report to the secretary of transportation. At the same time, a new National Transportation Safety Board takes over the Civil Aeronautics Board's role of investigating and determining causes of transportation accidents and making recommendations to the secretary of transportation. CAB merges into DOT with its responsibilities limited to the regulation of commercial airline routes and fares.
1968	FAA establishes aircraft noise standards.
1978	Airline Deregulation Act phases out CAB's economic regulation of airlines.
1979	FAA directed to define noise pollution contours.

Regional Fields

Small public and private airports in the region include Six Oaks (NC67) at Asheville; Cane Creek (4NC6) at Fletcher; Hendersonville (K0A7), W.N.C. Air Museum (8NC9) and Bearwallow Farm (0NC1) at Hendersonville; Fox Haven Plantation (58NC) and Rutherford County/Marchman (KFQD) at Rutherfordton; Brevard (NC16) and Transylvania County airports (K22W/3NR3) at Brevard; Jackson County (K24A) at Sylva; Macon County (K1A5) at Franklin; Western Carolina Regional (KPHP) at Andrews; Avery County/Morrison Field (7A8) at Spruce Pine; and Shiflet Field (9A9) at Marion.

ASHEVILLE REGIONAL AIRPORT

Ranked fourth largest in North Carolina, the Asheville Regional Airport (AVL) shares its provenance with Henderson County. A major economic engine in western North Carolina, AVL continues to grow, bringing new commercial and general aviation services to the region.

Seeking an airport in 1925, the Asheville Chamber of Commerce appointed an aviation committee to research the feasibility of development. The committee identified land between Asheville and Hendersonville, leased it and in 1928 airport development began. In 1936, the cities of Asheville and Hendersonville and Henderson County together purchased the 122 acres and unpaved runways in exchange for land and cash totaling a value of $31,000. Wartime brought runway improvements by 1944. The U.S. Army Corps of Engineers operated the airport from 1943 to 1947, providing air transportation for their communications and weather headquarters. During this time, federal funding was acquired to build a trio of four-thousand-foot paved runways, a control tower and a fire station.

By 1954, members of the Asheville Chamber of Commerce and others proposed an airport on eight hundred acres on the Biltmore Estate's west side, and a fight ensued. Bonds were defeated, and the proposal was voted down two to one in 1955. A similar proposal had been made as early as 1948.[57]

Because of expansion limitations due to the proximity of mountain ranges surrounding the campus, leaders in Asheville planned a new location and airport in 1957. As a measure to grow the airport to accommodate larger crafts used in commercial air travel, a bond issue authorizing the City of Asheville to expend up to $1.2 million was passed.

By January 15, 1961, the new $2.2 million Asheville Regional Airport was approved to operate daytime and nighttime commercial flights. The airport

Asheville Regional Airport. *Courtesy of the Greater Asheville Regional Airport Authority.*

consisted of 740 acres, a 25,060-square-foot terminal building and a 6,500-foot runway, and it was operated by the City of Asheville. The terminal building opened on June 7, 1961, allowing the airport to join the ranks of fully operational commercial airports.

In 1962, an instrument landing system was installed, providing the added safety measure of an "invisible highway" to the airport runway. A piece in the *Western Carolina Tribune* dated February 25, 1972, stated that work had begun on the installation of radar at the Asheville Airport:

> *The radar installation will enable controllers in the airport tower to "read" aircraft 30 miles away from the port. The site for the radar tower has been cleared. Laying of cable to the site is to start this month with the radar tower construction to begin in May. Completion of the $1.3 million project is scheduled for May 1973. The radar was ordered by the FAA after the July 19, 1967 air crash* [of Piedmont Flight 22] *at Hendersonville, that took 82 lives.*

In 1978, a runway extension project commenced with federal funding of $2 million for the project. In 1979, the Department of Public Safety building was added to the campus to house a growing staff of police and fire rescue professionals whose jobs were to provide a safe and orderly environment for the traveling public, visitors and airport employees. In 1980, operational management of the airport shifted from the City of Asheville to a newly created Asheville Regional Airport Authority, governed by an independent board made up of appointees by the Buncombe County Commission and Asheville City Council. The runway extension project was completed, improving safety and allowing larger aircraft access to AVL on the 8,001-foot strip. The baggage-claim facility was tripled in size, and a new gate area doubled capacity for growing passenger numbers.

By 1981, the Asheville Regional Airport was first in the nation to offer in-house travel agency services to passengers. In 1986, a state-of-the-art wind shear detection system was installed to improve safety. A $20 million airport expansion and renovation project began in 1987. The major expansion project was completed in 1992, resulting in expansion of the ticket lobby, baggage claim area and administrative office space. A second-level boarding area and jetways were constructed, as well as an atrium to the existing lobby. The ground-level boarding areas were expanded and renovated. These changes boosted AVL to the fourth-largest airport in the state. An airport welcome center opened in 1994. By 1998, a loop road was added to the campus to better manage growing passenger traffic. A new ten-thousand-square-foot passenger lounge opened in

2003—three times larger than the previous space, and wireless Internet access was added.

In 2006, the airport added a new apron and ramp area next to the terminal, which enabled the parking of up to thirteen aircraft at one time. This year also saw remaining non-renovated areas of the airport getting facelifts, including the ticket lobby and Great Hall with waiting areas, and a new maintenance facility was constructed. HonorAir made its premiere flight departing from Asheville Regional Airport in 2006. HonorAir, the national Rotary Club program that hosts World War II veterans on free trips to Washington, D.C., to experience the World War II Memorial, was launched in Hendersonville, North Carolina, by Jeff Miller (1954–).

In 2008, new boarding ramps were installed, and a rental car facility was constructed to accommodate up to five rental car companies. In the same year, the authority board appointed its first Henderson County member. A guest services center, an additional baggage carousel, rental car desks, offices and security enhancements were added in 2009. Under the American Recovery and Reinvestment Act of 2009, the FAA awarded AVL with $7.5 million in economic recovery funds to be used for terminal improvements.

In 2010, AVL saw its largest number of passengers in history, due in large part to the growth of air service, amenities and the strong regional support of the area's residents. In addition, the newly expanded gate holding area was opened with two-story-high ceilings, floor-to-ceiling windows overlooking the runway, new jetways and an expanded security checkpoint area.

On June 28, 2012, the North Carolina legislature voted to change the structure of the board to a state-sanctioned independent airport authority with more regional representation and governance. The Greater Asheville Regional Airport Authority (GARAA) was then the sole governing body for the airport. The GARAA consists of two appointments by the Asheville City Council, two appointments by the Buncombe County Commission, two appointments by the Henderson County Commission and one regional at-large appointment by the six board members.

In 2014, the Greater Asheville Regional Airport Authority broke ground on Project SOAR—which will result in a complete redevelopment of the airfield. This $75 million, five-year project was the most significant development project undertaken by the airport since it was originally built and opened in 1961.[58]

Afterword

The advent of mass transportation unlocked the wilds of mountainous western North Carolina. Explorers, hunters, settlers, missionaries and farsighted capitalists moved tenaciously to conquer this final frontier of the Old North State, carving a network of road and rail beds through virginal woodlands and intermittently treacherous terrain, along natural passes and over waterways and ridge tops. Surveyors and road builders, with the aid of convict laborers, opened this natural milieu to settlement, industry and agriculture, destination resorts, state and national forests and campgrounds, retirement communities and thriving towns and cities. Having forever shed its former status of isolation, the region has come to boast top-producing orchards, floriculture, wineries and breweries and world-class golf courses and master-planned communities in the midst of accessible natural resources, protected forests and four seasons of color and clime.

Researching this subject harked me back to a boyhood fascination with all things mechanical, when favorite playthings included Tonka trucks and Lionel train sets, model racecars, homemade airplanes and baking soda–powered boats in the bathtub. Adding the finishing touches to this manuscript I take away a newfound appreciation and respect for the genius of invention and the vision and tenacity of our forebears who enhanced this wonderland we call western North Carolina.

Notes

1. Later the Spartanburg & Asheville and Asheville & Spartanburg—lines of the Richmond & Danville Railroad—reorganized as Southern Railway Company by 1895.
2. French Broad Baptist Church, constituted 1791.
3. Some have written that Joseph Marion Rice (1761–1850) shot the last American bison east of the Mississippi River above Bull Creek, a tributary of the Swannanoa River.
4. Approximately 14,000 people count among the registered members of the Eastern Band of Cherokee Indians. Nearly 300,000 people are enrolled in the Cherokee Nation, with approximately 190,000 of them living within the state of Oklahoma.
5. In 1791, Blount chose James White's Fort, near the confluence of the Holston and French Broad Rivers, as the territory's new capital. He dubbed the capital "Knoxville" after his superior, U.S. secretary of war Henry Knox (1750–1806). In 1790, Blount negotiated the Treaty of Holston with Cherokee leader Kunoskeskie (aka John Watts, circa 1720–1792) and other chiefs, defining a border, resolving land claims south of the French Broad River and obtaining permission for a permanent road between the territory's eastern settlements and the settlements of Cumberland. Secretary Knox proclaimed the treaty in 1791 and President Thomas Jefferson (1743–1826) signed the proclamation on November 11 at Philadelphia.
6. Three major branches of the Great Philadelphia Wagon Road: the Great Valley Road, Upper Road and Fall Line Road.
7. Gleaned from the writings of John Preston Arthur, Mann Batson, Edmund Cody Burnett, Wilma Dykeman, Forster Alexander Sondley and Wilbur G. Zeigler, with further genealogical research for dates and the correct spellings of names.

8. Dr. and Mrs. Luke Dorland founded the Dorland Institute in 1887. The Presbyterian Church U.S.A. took over the school in 1893. It became the Dorland-Bell Institute in 1918. The school closed and moved to Asheville in 1942 as part of Warren Wilson College.
9. Thomas Jefferson Lee (1809–1873) owned Sherrill's Tavern for a brief time and renamed it Cold Spring.
10. Some sources state 1828 as the year of completion of the Buncombe Turnpike.
11. The Piedmont Air-Line System: Richmond & Danville; North Carolina Railroad; Northwestern North Carolina Railroad; Charlotte, Columbia & Augusta Railroad; Atlantic & Charlotte Air-Line Railway and the Columbia & Greenville and its branches.
12. The restored *Hattie Butner* resides in the Clemmons Village Hall.
13. Chaple was a shoemaker in New York before removing to Transylvania County and then Hendersonville.
14. Milas Monroe Shepherd (1867–1929).
15. Lloyd "Tommy" Thompson (1925–2014).
16. Hardwick's obituary read in part, "The veteran railroader began his career as a railroad man in Montgomery where he was born 63 years ago. After working as a telegraph operator in this city he accepted the position of general passenger agent of the Richmond-Danville road, 20 years ago. When this road was absorbed by the Southern the office of passenger traffic manager was created expressly for Mr. Hardwick. It was the first position of the kind."
17. The Flat Rock station stood at East Flat Rock on Depot Road (today's Blue Ridge Road).
18. Convict camps at Saluda included one at Horse Shoe Curve and another at Big Fall Creek.
19. The depot was called Flat Rock but located in East Flat Rock.
20. The Biltmore station was originally called "Bilton" and "Best Station."
21. A former Standard Oil station from the 1930s, later Tosh's Whistle Stop Café and the Gypsy Blue restaurant and currently a realty office.
22. The last run was on December 5, and the books were closed on December 8, 1968.
23. The National Railroad Passenger Corporation doing business as "Amtrak."
24. Established by individual owners of railroads, gauges ran the gamut from two feet or less and four feet, ten inches to broad gauges between five feet and six feet. Narrow gauge measured between two feet and three feet, six inches. Southern railroads generally employed a broad gauge of five feet. Lines of competing railroads rarely met, even in cases where they ran through the same town. Such variance proved troublesome in linking railroads, either requiring an interchange of equipment or, in many cases, difficulty in achieving connections. A trend from 1880 to 1890 moved toward a nationwide standard gauge of four feet, nine inches.
25. Tanner was a private going into the service and a private mustering out, in accordance with the Soldiers and Sailors Database. He served the Confederacy in Company G, Fifth Regiment, South Carolina Troops.

26. Because of construction challenges, the CC&O was known as the costliest railroad in America.
27. According to Frank L. FitzSimons, Anderson Street was originally named Depot Street. The road is currently called Seventh Avenue East. A 1912 Sanborn Fire Insurance Map shows it as "Seventh Avenue East."
28. Charles A. Carlson was convicted of defrauding Dr. Fuller "out of about $45,000," according to reports in the *French Broad Hustler*. The December 17, 1914 issue of the *Western Carolina Democrat* reported that Sheriff Jackson Cleophus Drake (1867–1948) had traveled to New Jersey to "take charge of Carlson."
29. William Hoyt Bangs (1877–1944), born in Illinois; died in Hendersonville, North Carolina.
30. The map shows the spelling "Hights."
31. Moland-Drysdale Corporation bought the Fletcher brickworks in 1943.
32. Richard Martin Pryor (1854–1951).
33. James Dyer Justice (1787–1857), county commissioner and sales agent and supervisor of the Speculation Lands of the county, is also credited for road surveys.
34. The Blue Ridge Mall was built on the site of the former Blue Ridge School for Boys.
35. Since the circa 1900 iron bridge was installed, it has been known as Gorman's Bridge.
36. Concerning "Bridge Funds" in the Henderson County Pleas & Quarter Sessions, June 1848, "Ordered by Court that John McClain be allowed the Sum of five Dollars for Services Rendered as Commissioner of McClain's Bridge from the year 1846 to the present date and for removing obstructions from Said Bridge." McClain had been a member of the Bridge Committee since September 1845 together with fellow commissioners James Spann and David Shuford. By March 1846, William Brittain and John Woodfin had been added to the committee, and Shuford and McClain had dropped off. Contemporary maps cite McClain's Bridge with the spelling "McLean."
37. According to Zeeveld, the girders (too deep to ship flat via rail) were shipped vertically for the reason that, laid flat, their width would have exceeded the allowable rail-load width restrictions.
38. Bridge Survey & Hydraulic Design Report, NCDOT, 1997.
39. The 1921 *Miller's Directory* lists Glover T. Orr's Auto Livery at 226 North Main Street: "Baggage Transfer."
40. The *Hustler* misspelled the surname as "Fenegan."
41. James B. Brookshire's tombstone bears the inscription, "1875–1930." His World War I draft card registration, North Carolina death certificate, North Carolina death indices and family trees list his birth year as "1874."
42. Grafonola: A crank-driven, internal-horn record player produced by the Columbia Graphophone Company beginning in 1907.
43. Phaeton: A sporty open carriage popular in the late eighteenth and early nineteenth centuries, drawn by one or two horses and featuring a minimal body lightly sprung atop four oversized wheels. With the advent of the automobile, the term was adapted to open touring cars known as "phaetons."

44. In 1905, Sylvanus F. Bowser (1854–1938) of Indiana invented a pump for gasoline and called it a "filling station," the first of its kind.

45. The Skyland Hosiery Company opened in 1906 in East Flat Rock. In 1925, Frank L. Chipman (1866–1930) and Vivian Clifford Burrowes (1883–1944) took over operations as the Chipman-Burrowes Hosiery Mills Company. In 1933, the company merged with LaCrosse Hosiery Company of LaCrosse, Wisconsin, and changed its name to Chipman-LaCrosse Hosiery Mills Inc. The company moved part of its operation into two floors of the old Joines Motor Company building on East Allen Street in Hendersonville in 1936. The business, which employed more than five hundred persons, closed in 1968.

46. Henderson County Technical Institute changed its name to Blue Ridge Technical Institute, Blue Ridge Technical College and in 1987 to Blue Ridge Community College. The institution currently boasts two campuses: one located at Flat Rock, Henderson County, and the other at Brevard, Transylvania County.

47. Construction of I-40 began soon after the 1956 Interstate Highway Bill passed. The route from Salisbury through Asheville followed the course of the old Western Turnpike.

48. Williams was mayor of Hendersonville.

49. Annual Report of the Chief of Engineers, U.S. Army Corps (USACE), 1875, p. 817.

50. Ibid., 1876, 718.

51. Ibid. 1878, 525.

52. William Dalton McAdoo (1878–1947) of Greensboro, North Carolina, and St. Petersburg, Florida, was a land speculator in Henderson County in the early 1900s. At one time, McAdoo owned the historic Chanteloup estate.

53. A&E denotes "Airplane & Engine" and refers to an aircraft maintenance technician's license. Since 1952, this designation has been called A&P ("Airplane & Power plant").

54. Lewis towed advertising banners with her Super Cub.

55. Trojan Phlyers Inc. is a group of aviation professionals dedicated to preserving the rich history of the North American Aviation Company's T28 Trojan. The group is based out of Mid-Way Regional (KJWY), just south of downtown Dallas and southeast of downtown Fort Worth.

56. Sources include Paul Freeman, "Abandoned & Little-Known Airfields," www.airfields-freeman.com and newspaper archives.

57. Covington, "The Airport Fight," chap. 7 in *Lady on the Hill*, 125–135.

58. Greater Asheville Regional Airport Authority, Public Relations & Air Service Development and newspaper archives.

Bibliography

Adair, James. *The History of the American Indians*. London, England: Edward and Charles Dilly, 1775.

Alexander, Edwin P. *Iron Horses: American Locomotives 1829–1900*. New York: Bonanza Books, 1941.

Arthur, John Preston. *Western North Carolina: A History (from 1730 to 1913)*. The Edward Buncombe Chapter of the Daughters of the American Revolution of Asheville, NC/Raleigh, NC: Edwards & Broughton Printing Company, 1914.

Bailey, Louise Howe, and Jody Barber. *Hendersonville and Henderson County: A Pictorial History*. Norfolk, VA: Donning Company Publishers, 1995.

Batson, Mann. *Early Travel and Accommodations Along the Roads of the Upper Part of Greenville County, South Carolina, and Surrounding Areas*. Taylors, SC: Faith Printing Co., 1995.

———. *The State Road: Poinsett Bridges and Culverts*. N.p.: Self-published, 2003.

Blackmun, Ora. *Western North Carolina: Its Mountains and Its People to 1880*. Boone, NC: Appalachian Consortium Press, 1977.

Brunk, Robert S., ed. *May We All Remember Well: A Journal of the History and Culture of Western North Carolina*. Vols. 1–2. Asheville, NC: Robert S. Brunk Auction Services Inc., 1997, 2001.

Burnett, Edmund Cody. "Hog Raising and Hog Droving in the Region of the French Broad River." *Agricultural History* 20 (April 1946): 86–103.

Chapman, Alicia. "The Buncombe Turnpike and Its Impact on Western North Carolina's Drovers and Economy." Asheville: University of North Carolina–Asheville Press, 2009.

Covington, Howard E., Jr. *Lady on the Hill: How Biltmore Estate Became an American Icon*. Hoboken, NJ: John Wiley & Sons, Inc., 2006.

Cox, Reverend Carl. "Solomon Jones the Road Builder." Easley, SC: Self-published; compiled by Carlene Sears Phelps, 1963.

Dixon, Guy Edwin Jr. "Oscar Meyer." Unpublished paper. Key Largo, FL, 1999.
Duncan, Barbara R., and Brett H. Riggs. *Cherokee Heritage Trails Guidebook*. Chapel Hill: University of North Carolina Press, 2003.
Dykeman, Wilma. *The French Broad*. New York: Rinehart & Company Inc., 1955.
Edney, Kermit. *Where Fitz Left Off*. Alexander, NC: WorldComm, 1979.
FitzSimons, Frank L., Sr. *From the Banks of the Oklawaha*. 3 vols. Hendersonville, NC: Golden Glow Publishing Co., 1976–79.
Fletcher, Charles Beale. "Oscar Meyer." Unpublished paper. Fletcher, NC, circa 1980.
Fossett, Mildred B. *History of McDowell County*. Durham, NC: Seeman Printery, 1976.
Gilbert, John, and Grady Jefferys. *Crossties Over Saluda*. Raleigh, NC: Crossties Press, 1971.
———. *Crossties Through Carolina*. Raleigh, NC: Crossties Press, 1969.
Goodwin, Garland O. *A Boy in the Amen Corner*. Spartanburg, SC: Reprint Company, Publishers, 1999.
Henderson County Genealogical and Historical Society. *Henderson County, North Carolina Cemeteries*. Spartanburg, SC: Reprint Company, Publishers, 1995.
Huger, Arthur Middleton [Hugh Deveron]. *The Hills of Ottaray*. Burnsville, NC: V.L. Edwards, 1916.
Miller's Hendersonville, N.C. City Directories. Asheville, NC: Miller Press, Inc., 1915–65.
Morgan, Robert. *Boone: A Biography*. Chapel Hill, NC: Algonquin Books of Chapel Hill, 2007.
New South Associates. "Poinsett Bridge: A Historic Context and Archaeological Survey, Greenville County, South Carolina." Stone Mountain, GA, 2004.
Parramore, Thomas C. *First to Fly: North Carolina and the Beginnings of Aviation*. Chapel Hill: University of North Carolina Press, 2002.
Passenger Department Office. *Illustrated Guidebook of the Western North Carolina Railroad*. Philadelphia: Allen, Lane and Scott, 1882.
Plemmons, Jan C. *Ticket to Toxaway*. Jacksonville, FL: Drummond Press, self-published, 2004.
Polk County Historical Association Inc. *Polk County, North Carolina, Cemeteries*. Spartanburg, SC: Reprint Company, Publishers, 2006.
———. *Polk County, North Carolina, History*. Spartanburg, SC: Reprint Company, Publishers, 2002.
Poole, Cary Franklin. *A History of Railroading in Western North Carolina*. Johnson City, TN: Overmountain Press, 1995.
Powell, William S., and Michael Hill. *The North Carolina Gazetteer*. Chapel Hill: University of North Carolina Press, 2010.
Ray, Lenoir. *Postmarks: A History of Henderson County, North Carolina, 1787–1968*. Chicago: Adams Press, 1970.
Reid, Christian [Frances Christine Fisher Tiernan]. *The Land of the Sky: Adventures in Mountain Byways*. New York: D. Appleton and Company, 1876.
Rhodes, Raymond R., and Virginia W. Thompson, eds. *Minutes of the Henderson County, North Carolina Court of Pleas and Quarter Sessions: 1839–1849*. Vol. 1. Spartanburg, SC: Reprint Company, Publishers, 2010.

Sondley, Forster Alexander. *A History of Buncombe County, North Carolina*. Vols. 1 and 2. Asheville, NC: Advocate Print, 1930. Reprint, 1977.

Taylor, George Rogers, and Irene D. Neu. *The American Railroad Network: 1861–1890*. Chicago: University of Illinois Press, 2003.

Terrell, Bob. *Historic Asheville*. Alexander, NC: WorldComm, 1997.

U.S. Department of the Interior, National Park Service. National Register of Historic Places Continuation Sheets. "Carolina Cadillac Company Building, Guilford County, NC." 2014.

———. "Poinsett Bridge: A Historic Context and Archaeological Survey, Greenville County, South Carolina." Stone Mountain, GA, 2004.

Waldman, Carl. *Atlas of the North American Indians*. Rev. ed. New York: Checkmark Books, 1985.

White, Emmett. *Revolutionary War Soldiers of Western North Carolina*. Vol. 2. Greenville, SC: Southern Historical Press, 1998.

Wood, Dorothy (Kelly) MacDowell. *Gleanings from the* French Broad Hustler, *Hendersonville, North Carolina*. 4 vols. Hendersonville, NC: Self-published, 1991–96.

Zeigler, Wilbur G., and Ben S. Grosscup. *The Heart of the Alleghanies* or *Western North Carolina*. Raleigh, NC: Alfred Williams & Co., 1883.

WEB RESOURCES

airfactsjournal.com
airfields-freeman.com
ancestry.com
archives.chicagotribune.com
archives.ncdcr.gov
cherokee.org
chroniclingamerica.com
cmhpf.org
courtrecordfinder.com
exhibits.archives.ncdcr.gov
fairviewtowncrier.com
flyavl.com
genealogytrails.com
genforum.genealogy.com
hendersonheritage.com
highcountryhost.com
history.com
hpo.ncdcr.gov
landofsky.org
laurelparkcivicassociation.org
learnnc.org
legacy.com
living-in-the-past.com
ncpedia.org

newrivernotes.com
news.google.com
obgcs.com
pilotonline.com
railga.com
srha.net
thealbanyjournal.com
virtualblueridge.com
wikipedia.org
wikitree.org
wncmagazine.com

Index

A

D

G

H

L

M

P

Q

R

Y

Z

About the Author

Terry Ruscin on the Blue Ridge Parkway. *Photo by Charles A. Herrmann.*

Terry Ruscin, author, columnist, photographer, researcher and retired advertising executive, is a member of the Henderson County Genealogical and Historical Society Inc., Historic Flat Rock Inc. and DRAC (Design Review Advisory Committee, which oversees the city's historic districts for the Hendersonville Historic Preservation Commission), as well as a commissioner with HRC (Henderson County Historic Resources Commission). Ruscin has served on the boards of the Henderson County Heritage Museum and the California Missions Foundation.

Ruscin wrote the books *Glimpses of Henderson County, North Carolina*; *Hidden History of Henderson County, North Carolina*; *Hendersonville & Flat Rock: An Intimate Tour*; *Mission Memoirs* (a Benjamin Franklin Award winner in 2000); *Dining & Whining*; and the travelogues *Los Duendes: A Nostalgic Journey through Spain* and *Taste for Travel* (about England, France and Italy). Ruscin and Louise H. Bailey's son Joseph Bailey Jr. finished Louise's tenth book, *Historic Henderson County: Tales from Along the Ridges*, published posthumously in 2010. Ruscin has also collaborated on other books on history and travel and writes the monthly newspaper column "Beyond the Banks" for the *Hendersonville Times-News*.

A graduate of Wayne State University in Detroit, Ruscin owned and served as creative director for Ruscin Advertising Inc. in San Diego, California, before retiring to Hendersonville, North Carolina, in 2004. In addition to research and writing, he enjoys photographing architecture and the wonders of nature in western North Carolina.